CHRISTIAN NATIONALISM AND THE
BIRTH OF THE WAR ON DRUGS

Christian Nationalism and the Birth of the War on Drugs

Andrew Monteith

NEW YORK UNIVERSITY PRESS

New York

NEW YORK UNIVERSITY PRESS
New York
www.nyupress.org

© 2023 by New York University
All rights reserved

Please contact the Library of Congress for Cataloging-in-Publication data.
ISBN: 9781479817917 (hardback)
ISBN: 9781479817924 (paperback)
ISBN: 9781479817993 (library ebook)
ISBN: 9781479817931 (consumer ebook)

New York University Press books are printed on acid-free paper, and their binding materials are chosen for strength and durability. We strive to use environmentally responsible suppliers and materials to the greatest extent possible in publishing our books.

Manufactured in the United States of America

10 9 8 7 6 5 4 3 2 1

Also available as an ebook

CONTENTS

Introduction

*Protestant Moralities, Substance Use,
and the Millennial Kingdom*

Los Angeles (1923)

On July 21, 1923, Aimee Semple McPherson and the women of the Angelus Temple marched through the streets of Los Angeles dressed in white capes and wearing helmets with scripture written on them, singing along to "Onward, Christian Soldiers" as marching bands accompanied their peregrinations. McPherson was a big name in both Los Angeles and the wider United States, a Christian celebrity from the Foursquare wing of Pentecostalism. That Saturday in 1923 she led the Angelus Temple's "crusaders" into battle: As the *Los Angeles Times* put it, the march was the opening to a "Narcotics War."[1] Although the *Times* may have claimed that this was the first salvo, it was hardly such—the term "Drug War" and other variations, such as the War on Drugs, had already been in play for more than a decade, and the very earliest stages of the war itself had begun at least a century before Sister Aimee took to the streets. Reflecting afterward on the environment of the march—the white battle gear, the power of the music—the Angelus Temple's own periodical explained that "it seemed for a few moments as though the millennium had come."[2]

When the marchers finally reached the Los Angeles Coliseum where the antinarcotic rally was being held, McPherson got her chance to address the full crowd of concerned Angelenos, including many who were not part of her church. She decried narcotics as an evil that had infiltrated America and denounced them as a force allied with Satan. She described how "little broken wisps of humanity" wasted away in Chinatown, their skin full of infected needle wounds and their minds ruined, and how she wept for them. Although she identified Chinese immigrants as the epicenter of narcotic infection (a common trope for the day), drugs were a menace that plagued the nation and trapped all Americans who turned to it out of "despondency," "sickness," and a chasing after "the gay life." In Pentecostal fashion, she proclaimed the power of The Lion of Judah (an idiom for Jesus) to break the chains of addiction and to bring healing to those sick with the habit. Although McPherson considered the war itself to be one front in a larger battle between God and Satan, she also thought that Christians had an obligation to participate in it, too. It was their somber duty; Foursquare Gospelers concerned themselves not just with loyalty to scripture, but loyalty to the United States as well.[3] She passionately told her listeners that "we owe it to God. We owe it to our country. We owe it to our forefathers of the Mayflower. We owe it to the children yet unborn." Sister Aimee was optimistic about where that duty could take them, claiming that since "the state and church join hands," the United States would soon witness God annihilating drug addiction in America, just as he had defeated alcohol.

McPherson was not alone in positioning Christians as warriors arrayed against drugs, nor in fact was she the chief instigator. The march and the rally were both planned by the Christian activist Richmond Pearson Hobson, a man whom McPherson compared to "a modern St. George" in her speech, a man who worked to slay the narcotic dragon and to whom she explicitly pledged full Angelus Temple support. Hobson wasn't Pentecostal, though. Nor was the rally itself a Pentecostal event. Hobson was devoutly Protestant and that Protestantism informed his antidrug activities. Yet in contrast to McPherson, he often kept his Christianity to himself. When he had been a Prohibitionist, Hobson wore Jesus on his sleeve. Yet his years in Prohibitionism taught him that a little bit of interreligious diplomacy could go a long way, and by 1923 he had reframed his rationales for opposing substance use. By no means had he deserted Christianity, he had only concluded that he could more effectively accomplish God's work by using more inclusive approaches.

McPherson was one of many speakers that Hobson arranged that day, and his choices were designed to demonstrate that the Drug War wasn't just for Protestants, it was for everybody. Hobson invited prominent Catholics to speak at the rally under the auspices of the International Narcotic Education Association, his non-profit organization. The bishop of Los Angeles, Joseph Cantwell, and the archbishop of San Francisco,

Edward Hanna, both accepted his invitation. Edgar Magnin, the rabbi of Wilshire Boulevard Temple, also spoke at the rally. California Representative Walter Lineberger, California Senator Samuel Shortridge, and a state senator who spoke on behalf of the governor's office had also shown up, as had the Boy Scouts of America and coteries from both the US Army and Navy.[4] This combination of attendees was a powerful symbol for the time, communicating a diverse America whose citizens were capable of working together under an aegis of secular liberty to stare down a dangerous foe.

Hobson's strategy worked: People saw his mission not as a Christian project but as a universal cause. The *Los Angeles Times* reproduced his argument, claiming that

> The campaign has been indorsed by leaders in every walk of life in the United States, and public-spirited citizens are most enthusiastic as to the possibilities of the move, realizing that the boys and girls of this and future generations will be virtually immune from narcotic addiction through the activities of the International Narcotic Education Association's campaign.[5]

This kind of universalism was exactly what Hobson wanted. On the one hand, Aimee Semple McPherson enunciated a Pentecostal variation on a much older, more generally Protestant theme: Substance use was antithetical to Christianity; it was a blight on America and a particular danger to certain races; and it was something that Christians should oppose and rectify through assorted methods, including the use of state power. *The Bridal Call*'s reference to "the millennium" (a perfect, utopian Kingdom of God that many Protestants expect to reign on earth at the end of time) also invoked a concept fundamentally important for Protestant reform movements of the nineteenth and early twentieth centuries. While her specific take on the End of Days was a little different from the one championed by earlier generations of American Protestant reformers, McPherson's argument still represented the heart of a long-standing, established approach: Substance use was a problem that required Protestant solutions. Hobson didn't want to erase or segregate that religious position from the greater Drug War, he merely wanted to ally it with other arguments in the interest of pragmatism.

Hobson's arrangement of Protestants, Catholics, and Jews together on an antinarcotic stage indicated that the cause was "non-sectarian"—opposing drugs wasn't a Protestant thing, it was an everyone thing. To borrow a contemporary colloquialism, Hobson read the room. He operated in a 1920s cultural milieu where people were beginning to think more often of the United States as "Judeo-Christian" rather than as a white, Anglo-Saxon Protestant nation.[6] The presence of legislators further indicated that this was not just a religious event. A century prior, the United States had few drug laws anywhere, but by 1923 Hobson was able to plausibly present drug control as a self-evidently governmental concern. Adding Boy Scouts to the parade emphasized a kind of wholesomeness to the cause and it reminded people that children were one of the vulnerable populations whom reformers wished to spare from addiction. Finally, the addition of military personnel to the parade showed that this was, in fact, a literal War on Drugs. Hobson (who was himself a famous veteran) consistently placed military officers at the forefront of his antidrug efforts. His goal was to show that while Christians would and should remain an important and primary force in the battle, the War on Drugs was all-encompassing and needed every force of American culture down in its trenches.

The Purpose of This Book

The Drug War developed from the confluence of multiple cultural forces, but this book argues that Protestant Christianity was a critically important contributor to its genesis. One part of the Drug War's origins can be found in the Christian Temperance movement. In the nineteenth century, transdenominational Protestantism held a profoundly hegemonic grip on American culture. (By "transdenominational" I mean the positions that many or all Protestants agreed to or found acceptable; I find this term more accurate than terms like "non-denominational" or "non-sectarian," which can falsely imply religious neutrality.) Christian Temperance was an explicitly Protestant movement in the nineteenth century that first sought to persuade people to either quit drinking or to at least only drink in moderation. This eventually evolved into Prohibition, which sought to abolish drinking by law. Because their arguments against intoxication were deeply indebted to transdenominational concepts of morality, many Protestants accepted that law represented one valid method for controlling alcohol. From its earliest days as an organized movement, Christian Temperance reformers also identified other substances like opium and tobacco as dangerous elements that people should avoid. These Protestant reformers drew few to no distinctions between the substances. We today might identify Christian Temperance and the Drug War as different things, but Christian Temperance activists did not: They wished to abolish *all* illicit substance use.

Yet to stop with that answer alone would represent the early Drug War too flatly. This book argues that Christian Temperance and the early War on Drugs were unified projects, but it also argues that Protestant postmillennialist eschatology shaped many of the moral norms that engendered a War on Drugs. (The term "eschatology" refers to doctrines or explanations about how history will end.) Sister Aimee held to a premillennialist eschatology, which is likely to be familiar to more readers today since it is now the most common eschatology for conservative American Christians. Premillennialism is the eschatology of *Left Behind*—as time runs down, the world will devolve into evil and chaos and the Antichrist will oppress Christians until Armageddon. When things cannot become any worse, Jesus returns to set everything aright. He defeats the Antichrist and then inaugurates a realm known as "the Millennial Kingdom," which is a perfect society that he will rule for 1,000 years. (The "pre-" of "premillennialism" is that Jesus returns *before* the Millennial Kingdom can be established.) Postmillennialism is quite optimistic in contrast. Postmillennialists think the world is getting better—everything is slowly building up into the Kingdom of God. Instead of all things declining into darkness, we are collectively heading toward a point when human society will embrace biblical morality fully, an era when sorrow, disease, sin, and poverty will be defeated. Only when this utopia has been established will Jesus return to rule it. (It's "post-" because Jesus arrives *after* the Kingdom is established.) Postmillennialism dominated Protestant thought in the nineteenth century, not just as a point of doctrine but as an ethos that generated its own moral obligations and expectations, including those that shaped the Drug War.

Postmillennialism was complemented by the notion that Americans could craft themselves into a biologically better race. If postmillennialism is a model of history in which human society is gradually approaching a perfect utopia, then all areas of human life are fair game for improvement. Influential scientists shaped a narrative about human heredity in which ancestry mattered for people's intelligence, fitness, moral ability, and general wellness. They also proposed that the modern world had produced conditions that threatened to destroy biological integrity (degeneracy) and suggested that humans should take control of their own evolution by ensuring that the fittest specimens reproduced, while the "defective" people were removed from the gene pool (eugenics). There is nothing about this position that *requires* Christianity, but many American Christians accepted its premises as legitimate science and incorporated it into their theology. For postmillennialists it was entirely plausible that human heredity would improve as the world advanced toward the Kingdom, yet drugs threatened this improvement. Although most eugenicists saw addiction as the symptom of an already defective mind, some experts thought drugs themselves could cause degeneracy. Regardless of which position they took, they ended up at the same place, which is that substance use was a serious problem for biological progress.

This book makes the case that religion—and especially American Protestantism—played an important role in generating the early Drug War. It would be quite reasonable for someone to ask why they had never heard this before if religion was really so central to the story. It's a good question. The first answer is that few people realize that the United States even had a War on Drugs this early; even senior scholars sometimes wrongly claim that Richard Nixon invented it. Nobody can convey religion's importance for something that they didn't realize existed. However, there is also a more complicated answer which has to do with what scholars have emphasized instead.

Few scholars have written about the earliest era of the Drug War, but those who have usually center upon other aspects. The most common approach is to read the early Drug War as a product of racism. Scholars who focus on race as a contributing factor (or sometimes as the *only* contributing factor) are observing a real and important element. At times, early proponents of the Drug War were so overwhelmingly racist about it that it can be hard to see anything else at work. Media emphasized Black, Latin, and Asian folks as both causing and especially suffering from drug addiction, and professional criminologists as well as police powers (including the Federal Bureau of Narcotics under Harry Anslinger) accepted this racial explanation when identifying drug use as a danger to America.[7] Scholars who position racism as a cause for the Drug War are right to do so. The early War on Drugs was unquestionably, emphatically, and disastrously racist; any history of the Drug War that ignores race is uncredible. Yet race cannot be separated from religion in the American context (or perhaps any context), and so these racist maneuvers were often religious at the same time, an important aspect of the Drug War that has been largely overlooked.

Other scholars sometimes emphasize the colonialist elements of the Drug War. Again, they're right to do so, and it is worth noting that colonialism is quite closely related to race. Other scholars are also right when they argue that drug prohibition didn't emerge solely from American sources but argue that other colonial powers and China were crafters too. This book doesn't refute that internationalism, but it does argue that Protestantism—and especially American Protestantism—was uniquely influential in the way antidrug colonialism played out.

Some scholars have focused more upon the legal frameworks for drug control, drugs' relationship to commerce, or the foreign diplomacy involved in garnering international cooperation. Once again many of these studies do good work, yet they usually miss religion. It's not that these scholars are unaware of religion's role in the story (well, some of them are), but rather that they give it only passing notice. Religion gets reduced to a note that so-and-so held deeply evangelical convictions or that a missionary organization promoted some specific antinarcotic policy, but religion is almost never treated as its own influential force. When scholars do identify religion as significant in its own right, it tends to be in the form of a journal article that focuses on some hyperspecific facet (an article about one particular activist, drug policy, etc.). This elision in the scholarship is a shortcoming. The reason someone might not have heard about religion's core place in the early Drug War is because scholars have ignored it to focus on other components.

Religion crafted the global War on Drugs, but religion's position is also quite complex. We aren't looking at race *and* colonialism *and* religion as forces that created the Drug War, for these categories bleed into one another, constitute one another—they are inseparable. The idea that race represented real biological differences which accounted for a hierarchy of superior and inferior peoples lends itself easily to colonialism. But racial thinking was also deeply embedded in religious thought, and religion shaped how racialized power structures developed. Religion was also intractably part of colonialism. Colonialism evolved from crusader law and religion maintained a prominent location in its self-explanatory logic. It is sometimes analytically helpful and cognitively more manageable to think about these three areas as separate things, and scholars have done useful work with these artificial partitions. As unwieldy as it is though, the reality is that race, colonialism, and religion are hopelessly entangled.

This book brings religion to the forefront of the early Drug War and in particular it locates American Protestants as central players in its creation. They did not act alone—this was a global project and they had support from many other quarters (especially other Protestants in the UK). However, the ideology that gave logic to global drug prohibition developed out of explicitly Protestant concerns about civilization and culture. It emphasized virtues commensurate with transdenominational Protestantism and decried vices that particularly clashed with US Protestant moralities. Christian activists drove much of the fervor at home and missionaries championed drug reforms from abroad, and those parties worked together. These Christians were critically important for the creation of an international Drug War, and it is possible that it would never have developed without them.

The story of the early Drug War is difficult to tell because it has so many moving parts. Most of the data for this book came from archival sources, emerging from dusty and sometimes mislabeled folders. Its pieces often overlap chronologically and are so interrelated that it confounds efforts to order them. An additional challenge is that the early War on Drugs developed in a culture whose norms were not identical to those of the United States today. Nineteenth-century racism was often structured and expressed differently from twenty-first-century racism. While Christians today still care about what American government looks like their rationale and approaches are usually different from those of their forebears. The United States still engages in international reform projects but often speaks of "development" and "human rights" rather than "civilizing" foreign peoples.[8] To look back at the American past is to look back into another culture, which means that making sense of it requires some translation.

In order to explain how the Drug War came into existence—and why religion matters for the story—one must first grapple with some foundational concepts. The most important of these is morality, which is not so clear-cut of a term as it might seem. This book also argues that postmillennialist eschatology and colonialism were important features too; these therefore need definition as well. These concepts all relate to one another in the context of the Drug War, and by interrogating them we can get a better understanding of how Protestant antidrug activists viewed their world. In some ways, this book is a story about morality as much as it is an explanation for the Drug War.

Defining Morality

"Morality" is one of those terms that often gets used as though the meaning were self-evident. Often, contemporary religious studies scholars elide defining "morality," even when the term makes up a central part of their argument or book title. This silence is problematic: Not everyone means the same thing when they use the word, and the term itself has implied different meanings in different eras. For some people, "morality" has been reliant upon religious concerns, and for others it conveys a secular concept. At times "morality" has implied a transcendent, rules-true-for-everyone universalism, yet in other contexts it has meant a contingent, ongoing discussion of consensual expectations. There's no consensus on it.

Any definition of "morality" is contingent upon the speaker, and so I make no pretense to have a permanent, unassailable version that will work for all times and places. Like "religion," though, one must start somewhere if there is to be any productive conversation about it. This book most closely follows a version of "morality" borrowed from Margaret Urban Walker in which "morality" is best understood as those behaviors, emotions, actions, or ways of being for which someone is accountable to others. In her 1998 book *Moral Understandings: A Feminist Study in Ethics*, Walker argues that morality is "fundamentally interpersonal" and that it "consists in a family of practices that show what is valued by making people accountable to each other for it."[9] She also argues that these "practices of responsibility" are not evenly distributed; the expectations placed on people differ based on their social location, gender, privilege, ability, or various other criteria. Additionally, morality is pluriform: Different social groups or subcultures may hold different moral expectations, and while these may sometimes overlap, they can also come into conflict when expectations clash about who has responsibilities to whom, and what it is that they are specifically responsible for.[10] Walker's position, then, is that morality is fundamentally about what we owe one another and that this system of expectations and responsibilities is embedded within and contingent upon the specific social world that we inhabit. Few of the historical actors in this book expressed "morality" in Walker's language but her explanation does a good job of describing their concerns nonetheless. It also offers scholars a useful interpretive framework that demands no claims to what is *really moral*, but instead allows us to track what our subjects *consider to be moral*.

Morality is not just about the other, it is also about the self. Judith Butler notes, "there is no morality without an 'I'" but that the self "cannot be understood apart from its social conditions." Selves do not emerge *ex nihilo* but rather develop from within a preexisting world, with "subject's self-crafting . . . always [taking] place in relation to an imposed set of norms."[11] Those cultural norms people are socialized into become central to "self-recognition" and moral formation.[12] In other words, people's self-understanding cannot be detached from the kind of moral responsibilities that their varied social worlds demand of them. Acceptance and standing in social worlds are often contingent on how well one lives up to these responsibilities, with some responsibilities mattering more than others. Thus, morality is not just about accounting for oneself to *others*, it is also about accounting for oneself to oneself, encompassing at least part (if not all) of what is sometimes called "conscience." Morality cannot just be reduced to a discourse or formal code, then; it should also be understood as a lived practice. It is experiential. Moral behavior involves self-governance, but one's ability to perform that morality partially shapes (and is shaped by) whether one can self-recognize as a worthwhile and likeable person.

Morality and Substance Use

While law is self-evidently important for the early Drug War it is not its sum whole.[13] If Christian Temperance and the War on Drugs began as the same thing, neither started primarily as an effort to legislate behavior but rather as a way to impel people toward self-selected antidrug lifestyles (at least insofar as white consumers were concerned—colonized populations were another matter). In an 1836 address to the Young Men's Temperance Society of Lowell, Massachusetts, Dr. Elisha Bartlett explained that alcohol, tea, coffee, tobacco, and opium all violated "the laws of temperance" and thereby posed a threat to democracy, morality, and physical well-being.[14]

> It is every man's duty, a duty as clearly recognized by his reason and his conscience, if these are honest and enlightened . . . to train and manage and use the body which his Creator has given him, as to promote and secure its most *perfect development*, its *freest action* and its *longest life*. We have no moral right to disregard this duty, excepting at the call and under the sanctions of still higher and more imperative obligations.[15]

Bartlett felt that while distilled liquors might be damnable enough to warrant governmental legislation, temperance societies' real purpose was to convince, educate, and admonish individuals to voluntarily live without substance use. God may have called on humans to "subdue" the evil of intemperance, but that conquering of sin was premised on moral willpower rather than police force. Morality has been a consistent and primary feature of antidrug worlds since the earliest days of temperance, and policeable law is thus only one piece of a greater emphasis.

At the same time, the Drug War has typically been conceptualized and understood as a juridical matter. Law is of course consequential and often functions as an epistemological rationale for today's mass incarceration of substance users.[16] Certainly any explanation of the Drug War demands a consideration of law. It is helpful, however, to push beyond formal, codified law by considering the moral building blocks that serve as its necessary prerequisites. A *solely* legal focus can quickly reduce human belonging, meaning, and worthiness only to how one is punished by the state. Yet, if Michel Foucault was right about power being diffused throughout society, sometimes institutionalized and sometimes not, then understanding the Drug War requires consideration of the moral expectations and the "geographies of responsibility" (Walker's term) of substance use, too.[17] In other words, the War on Drugs is just as much about social discipline, self-policing, and moral canvassing as it is about jurisprudence.

The moralization of substance use—the idea that people are responsible to themselves or others for what psychoactive compounds they consume, and that they are duty-bound to use substances properly—is a cultural phenomenon rather than a transhistorical truth. As historian Joseph Spillane notes, drugs are "both a social construction and a legal fiction, useful for regulatory purposes but hardly helpful for sorting out distinctive substances."[18] The category itself is more or less a dumping ground for a wide range of disparate compounds that people have decided are in some way bad. To be clear, there are legitimate medical reasons why someone should not smoke heroin or snort cocaine. Even so, the category "drugs" has very flexible boundaries rather than a natural taxonomy, and the transfiguration of substance users into "fiends" is not itself the automatic result of health concerns. Furthermore, what counts as "drugs" remains flexible. For instance, attitudes toward cannabis have shifted back and forth over time, and some substances that people opposed as moral problems a century ago would be surprising to people today. Relatively few Americans would now argue that tea constitutes a moral threat, yet caffeine represented a commonplace concern during the early Drug War.

The antidrug world we inhabit today evolved out of Christian Temperance, a movement that treated alcohol consumption as profoundly immoral behavior. The explanations they offered for why drinking was bad—and for why people were accountable for it—were largely identical to how they thought about other kinds of substance use. For the earliest temperance activists, alcohol was often the most widespread form of substance abuse, but Bartlett was not unique in classifying other substances alongside it. As we shall see, temperance activists considered substance use a threat to public morals, safety, economies, families, salvation, and progress toward attaining the Kingdom of God. Although there is nothing about antidrug morality that requires Christianity per se, in the American context Protestantism represented an especially important channel of moral norms and formation. Whether or not the Drug War remains "Protestant" today is an open question, but this book contends that it most definitely began that way.

Religion, Protestantism, and Postmillennialism

Nineteenth-century and early twentieth-century Americans typically thought of morality as universal; while individuals' or societies' *understanding* of morality might differ, there were behaviors and attitudes that were truly moral and that transcended human idiosyncrasies. For Protestants, morality was usually also considered a particular kind of revealed truth, often one that could be discerned from the careful reading of scripture. They also operated hegemonically in nineteenth- and early twentieth-century white American culture, setting the terms of politics, education, law, gender, social norms, labor, and science.[19] The Drug War has often been treated as a self-evidently secular project, but I follow Anthony Petro in their assertion that morality is Janus-faced, frequently translating religious norms into purportedly secular ones.[20] That principle is germane to the early Drug War's formation. In this period, Protestants saw each other taking similar moral positions across denominational lines, and, in their language, this feature made such normative positions "nonsectarian." If Methodists, Baptists, Presbyterians, and Lutherans could all agree that the King James Bible was an acceptable textbook for public schools, then including it as part of a curriculum did not violate the principles of non-establishment so far as they understood its contours.[21] Because they saw morality as a kind of universal truth, and because they frequently considered themselves to have worked out some consensus about what humans knew for sure was true of God's moral expectations, they frequently saw their transsectarian religious norms as non-problematic truths that all people should embrace.

If "morality" is a flexible term that evades easy definition, so too is "religion." On one hand, many of this book's subjects considered "religion" something important, identifiable, and clearly demarcated from other spheres of human activity. Often they thought of "religion" as something that "civilized" white people had mastered but that "savage" races had yet to properly taste. "Religion" for them was drawn from a Christian (and usually Protestant) model: It was what one believed, often with a contemplative focus and an interest in doctrine, particularly doctrine drawn from sacred texts. It was inclusion within a bounded "sect" or "denomination." It was about interacting with or venerating a god or gods. It was ritual, most often rituals that symbolized something, rather than the efficacious rituals they more commonly labeled as "magic" or "superstition."[22] It might, in the language of William James, include "feelings," although Protestants sometimes disagreed about whether or not emotional religion was good.[23] Religion was something that some people had but others did not, and it was a category in which societies could make progress, moving from inferior religions to better ones over time.

It is important to recognize that this is often the sort of thing that this book's subjects had in mind when they referred to "religion." That approach is a historical construction, however, and not what I myself mean when I use the term more generally. I am sympathetic to scholarly approaches that leave the term loose, flexible, and non-essentialist. For one, to track "religion" as a matter of denominational loyalty or formal creeds is to both privilege a very particular model of "religion" as well as to grossly oversimplify how religion works. Religionists don't live in ideological vacuums, they interact with their cultures and often draw upon diverse methods for living meaningful lives.[24] When considering historical actors whose whole lives might lay before a researcher, fragmented and reduced into whatever bits of paper archives chose to preserve, it becomes evident that people change their minds or modes of living as they get older. Describing their "religion" at age 20 may be very different than what they show at age 50. Like all people, they're also sometimes just inconsistent. It's not meaningless to say so-and-so was Jewish or Catholic or Methodist, but these are sweeping generalities that only give us a starting point. "Religion" as I understand it cannot be separated from other spheres of human activity. To rely on this denominational or creedal model to understand "religion" is a bit like trying to navigate Montreal using a road atlas of Canada.

When it comes to individuals, I am most interested in "religion" insofar as it involves questions of meaning (particularly what gives people a sense of "fullness," to borrow language from Charles Taylor), social and cosmic belonging, self-recognition, and epistemology.[25] I'm also quite interested in it as a mode of social structure—how it is that religion conditions socialization, shapes communities, or augments institutional power. This requires a little bit of cognitive juggling—some historical actors in this book might have considered their own religiosity to be only privately held beliefs or practices that were segregable from other parts of their world, but the more capacious approach I've employed is quite different from that. What people privately believed about eschatology, for instance, had great influence over what meanings they ascribed to culture, nations, law, economics, and so on. Furthermore, it's also the case that religious moralities frequently escaped their origins, expanding beyond whatever original boundaries they emerged from. (When Catharine Albanese introduced the term "public Protestantism" into the religious studies vocabulary, this is partly what she had in mind.)[26] In the American context, Protestant hegemony translated contingent moralities into supposedly universal norms.[27] This is one reason why maintaining a rigid definition of "religion" is unworkable for a book like this. I never argue that the Drug War was "religious" in the sense that some wandering Methodist preacher stitched it together from scriptural inferences and hymnals, but rather I argue that its religiosity lies much more in that "public Protestantism" where collective ideas about what people owe to each other, themselves, and God slips into aspirationally secular attitudes about what substance use means.

One of the most important areas where this public Protestantism shaped American attitudes toward substance use is that of postmillennialist eschatology. Nineteenth-century American Protestants were mostly postmillennialist, with premillennialism only gaining any serious ground after the Civil War.[28] This is critical for understanding how the Drug War developed, and it ties together some otherwise disparate concepts. In Christian Bibles, Revelation describes Jesus as ruling over a kingdom on earth that lasts for 1,000 years ("the Millennium"), but the details about when and how that kingdom emerges are fuzzy. Postmillennialism draws on concepts like the parable of the mustard seed (Matthew 13) in which the Kingdom starts out small and grows bigger and bigger, or the parable of the leaven (Luke 13) in which the Kingdom is compared to a little yeast eventually working its way through the entirety of the bread dough. Because postmillennialism presents a model of history in which the Kingdom is already in motion and continually growing, it permits Christians to place themselves in the story in important ways. Postmillennialists often approached the Kingdom's advance as requiring human intervention, particularly voluntary intervention and reforms driven by conscientious Protestants.[29] American Protestants typically embraced this view in the nineteenth century, considering their social reforms and scientific advancements to be part and parcel of the Kingdom's growth. There's also a theodicean element to postmillennialism, which is that evil exists simply because it has not been conquered yet. Much of the Kingdom's progress comes in the form of Christians recognizing imperfections and working to correct them—in a sense, overcoming evil.

Such approaches allowed postmillennialists to see *all* reforms and civilizational advancements as sacred progress. In 1899, for example, the New York-based Episcopalian magazine *The Spirit of Missions* argued that missionaries and Anglo-American culture would produce conditions amenable to global Protestantism. The article highlights how intermingled religious optimism and secular culture were for many theological thinkers, as well as demonstrating how even minor cultural changes could be sacralized. The author wrote:

A century hence there will be, possibly, 700,000,000 and certainly 500,000,000 English-speaking people on the globe, all subject to Christian law, maintaining Christian civilization, and exhibiting a much higher standard of morals than is seen in either England or America to-day. The spirit of Christian law will pervade the statute books and courts of justice of all nations. Religious liberty will have become the unchallenged right of the whole human race. Railways will have penetrated to the most remote corners of the earth. The influence of the Protestant nations will be paramount everywhere, and every other public influence, whether religious or political, will be on the wane. The English language, already a potent factor in many mission fields, will have become the *lingua franca* of the world, and will assist wonderfully in perfecting the later stages of the missionary enterprise. In such an age, with a world so revolutionized, and with all the terms of the problem so changed, the final conversion of all nations will no longer seem a far-off vision of a few enthusiasts.[30]

Some readers today might be surprised that railways and globalized English were considered important steps toward the Kingdom. Some Protestants thought English was among the most civilized languages, though, a position that social scientists sometimes supported. The locomotive had allowed quicker transport of goods and passengers, radically changing many people's quality of life. Railways and language choice might seem "secular" today, but for postmillennialist missiologists the conversion of nations and secular progress were mutually constitutive— the secular was spiritual.

If the Millennial Kingdom advances through human cooperation, this means that a great deal of cultural activity—anything that can be compellingly labeled as "progress"—becomes sacred. In its later iterations this postmillennial ideal was deeply embedded in the concept of the "Social Gospel," which drew on multiple strands of American Protestantism to advocate for widespread social transformation, first at home and then globally. This particular style of postmillennialism was most active in the late nineteenth and early twentieth centuries. Social Gospelers valued personal salvations, but they considered the aggregate to be more important than the individual.[31] They also emphasized a need to "Christianize" the United States as an important first step toward global salvation. Much of this took shape as political reform movements, which taken together do not map easily onto contemporary US politics. A Social Gospeler was just as likely to advocate for labor unions and a living wage as they were for prohibition. These reforms, though, shared a core element: a desire to bring human culture into alignment with their expectations of what a utopian Kingdom of God should look like.

American Protestants often combined postmillennialism with a form of Christian nationalism, and many of them considered the end of slave labor as validating this. God's hand had been at work in the Revolution, and progress in science, technology, industry, government, and other areas of cultural life demonstrated that the United States was a chosen nation.[32] Many pro-slavery Christians maintained that position after the Civil War, but abolitionists often saw God's hand at work in the Northern victory, which they took as evidence that God was guiding American history.[33] Abolitionism also came to serve as a model to substance use prohibitionists, who considered addiction a kind of slavery. Especially after the Civil War, many postmillennialists believed that God was transforming the United States into a paragon of Christian virtue and that America would lead the entire world toward the Millennial Kingdom. The expansion and preservation of individual freedom was often treated as a hallmark of progress.

Morality played an indispensable role in shaping postmillennial reforms and ideals, and indeed, postmillennialism cultivated its own sets of moral expectations. First, American Protestants understood themselves to be bound by Christian duty to aid those who needed it. To help others was a moral act and to refuse was a betrayal of kin and country. Since Christians were also accountable to God, they needed to be able to defend their behavior to him at some point in the future. Sitting on the sidelines as the Kingdom advanced was unacceptable. Second, other people's behavior was often something that postmillennialists wished to align with Kingdom values. New hospitals and agricultural science might be one type of progress, but the eradication of sin was another. Bringing their wayward neighbors out of saloons and sex work meant that those people would now live more moral lives, too. The former prostitute and the newly minted teetotaler would soon be able to look their neighbors in the face as redeemed citizens and then in turn help liberate others. Third, advancing the Kingdom was a shared project, not an individual one. Others' sin affected the community and nation, not just the individual sinner. Furthermore, in an extension of the first point, Christians had a duty to help those impacted by the consequences of others' sins. This moral duty was most often expressed as a responsibility to children in particular, who needed protection from such dangers as pornography, fights, gambling, movies, and substance use.[34] Fourth, in the American context, postmillennialism usually involved the translation of white Protestant nationalism into a putatively secular set of goals to which all races should aspire, a particularly salient position for understanding US colonialism.[35] In short, postmillennialists saw themselves as morally bound to advance the Kingdom; as responsible for helping others abandon their sin; and as responsible for protecting the vulnerable from predatory social evils, both domestically and abroad.

However, while Protestants openly avowed their religious rationale for reform in the early years, by the early twentieth century they had gradually begun backing away from explicitly religious language. There were multiple reasons for this, including shifting attitudes toward religious tolerance, but an important one was pragmatism. The Kingdom of God was an unstoppable force that would keep rolling as long as God wished it to do so. Christians had a duty to cooperate with God's plans, but this didn't necessarily mean they had to announce their thinking when they did. Protestants could ban drinking while announcing it as a Christian crusade, or they could ban drinking while staying mum about religion altogether. In both cases the end result would be the same: an end to legal alcohol abuse. It was just as much an advance of the Kingdom if they remained silent as it would be if they shouted their religious reasons from the rooftops. By the twentieth century, immigration had altered the American religious landscape and many Protestants had simultaneously grown aware of non-Protestants' discomfort about some of their arguments, which is most noticeable in the changing language of health textbooks and in antidrug lobbying efforts. Between the later nineteenth century and World War II, American attitudes toward pluralism also shifted toward a less confessional model of belonging.[36] Concurrently, many reformers repackaged their positions in more universalist language. Reform rationales didn't change but the wording did, and some believed that by removing sectarian language they had legitimately turned their reforms into neutral, secular projects.

This book takes the position that morality is culturally constructed, yet most of the historical actors in this book (including the confessional Christians) would have argued that morality was a universal truth. Universalists in places such as Britain or the United States frequently enshrined their own cultural norms as true morality, but as hegemonic as Protestantism was in Britain and the United States, this naturally meant that the universal reflected the Protestant.[37] The Protestant-cum-secular norms segued into explanations of what counted as "civilization," a moral translation that undergirded what they called "the Civilizing Mission."[38] White American colonists frequently saw themselves as liberators duty-bound to rescue racial others from their own backwardness, taking great pains to align foreign cultures with the colonizers' utopian fantasies for them. Substance use would prove to be a major concern for colonizers, and the instinct to protect colonized populations from their supposed cultural infantilism encouraged the first international drug regulations.

Colonialism and the Civilizing Mission

Colonialism formed the world we live in today and indeed still persists in global projects that are now called by other names. Colonialism has a long genealogy; as a formal institution it reached its peak in the early twentieth century, but it evolved out of a process going back at least to the Crusades. The colonial period most germane to this study is that of the nineteenth and early twentieth centuries. Although colonial logics frequently drew upon earlier ideology and formats, colonialists' self-understandings in the nineteenth and twentieth centuries were somewhat different from those of the conquistadores or the Tadoussac fur trappers. By the nineteenth century many Europeans were theorizing colonialism as a benevolent cultural project that required their supervision, a theme Americans embraced as well.[39]

Nineteenth-century American colonialists predicated their colonialism upon the civilizing mission. By the late eighteenth century, French philosophers had developed an interpretive framework that separated all societies into categories of "savage," "barbarian," or "civilized." In this view, societies advanced through different stages of civilization, evolving out of savagery into barbarianism, and then eventually acceding to civilized status.[40] In the French context, *la mission civilisatrice* emphasized how the developed cultural standards of the French elite could benefit *les sauvages* if they were to offer them a hand with governance and cultural reform. This interpretation presented colonialism as a selfless mission to help other people become more like their colonizers.

As a general rule Americans shied away from thinking of themselves as "colonizers," even while the United States engaged in most of the same kinds of colonialism as Europeans. Americans often identified themselves with a tradition of republican government that was anti-monarchy and anti-conquest. Looking back from the twenty-first century that position may seem incongruous with a century of Indian Wars, annexations, slavery, the settler colonialism in Liberia, Manifest Destiny, the overthrow of the Hawaiian Kingdom, the acquisition of an insular empire, and the Latin American filibusters. Although some Americans did indeed recognize US interventions as colonialism, the dominant narrative read differently. With the Indian Wars, for instance, one common interpretation was that the United States had acquired its western territory through legal purchases and/or the voluntary submission of its denizens to US sovereignty. US courts recognized American Indians as having the legal right to *occupy* certain territory, but in most cases it also recognized sovereignty over land as vested with the American government and not the tribes. As such, if federal powers wanted to displace Indians and repurpose their land, this was not "colonialism" to most white Americans, it was the United States exercising legal rights over its own possessions. With annexations such as Puerto Rico, the popular interpretation was that the United States had rescued them from tyrannical Spanish rule.[41] Americans often interpreted US colonialism as projects of liberation, generosity, or self-management.

Many Americans adopted the French *mission civilisatrice* as their own prerogative, and in the US context, the civilizing mission took on a decidedly evangelical tone. The French version posited Catholicism as a civilizing influence, but Americans overwhelmingly jettisoned the Catholic part of this (a religion that they quite frequently identified as intrinsically tyrannical and antidemocratic) and replaced it with Protestantism. Missionaries frequently served as the first front of American colonial projects. There was already a long history of American Protestants working to convert American Indians to Christianity before the French gave new language to the civilizing mission, but as Euro-American thinkers began theorizing culture with new idioms, much of that discourse made its way into missiology. This often generated partnerships between missionaries and American institutions of government. For example, in the early nineteenth century the American Board of Commissioners for Foreign Missions explicitly prioritized civilizing Indians, teaching them English, and converting them to Christianity. Federal authorities recognized this as a potential strategy for subduing Indians and therefore supported the ABCFM's efforts to build plantations and schools in the Mississippi Valley; missionaries believed that by teaching them English and Euro-American models for manual labor, they could begin the long process of civilization.[42] That wasn't an outlier. Missionaries were involved in the erasure of Native Hawaiian sovereignty, the management of Indian reservations, invasive interventions into Puerto Rican life and law, and the maintenance of racialized slave labor in the United States.

Recognizing this relationship between American Protestantism and the civilizing mission is necessary for understanding the early Drug War; controlling colonial substance use was one part of a larger moral project. Christians often felt they were responsible for treating their neighbors well (an explicitly biblical charge) and with transforming the world in ways that make it better. The Bible describes some specific moral actions (feeding the hungry, looking after widows, etc.), but overall what it means to "love your neighbor as yourself" remains undefined. Inaction is also an action—failure to do anything can be immoral if your neighbor needs help. American Protestants considered themselves accountable to God, to each other, and to the United States to participate in activities that benefited and improved others' well-being. The civilizing mission also rested on the premise that some societies are better or more advanced than others, treating certain contingencies of culture (such as approaches to government, customs, styles of thought, labor practices, language, legal systems, land management, kinship, and religion) as qualities that can be ranked. Oftentimes (and probably always) civilizers constructed morality as a tiered accomplishment. For instance, the Anglican Frances Power Cobbe explained that savages had little moral understanding, yet the next stage of social evolution brought forward reverence for just gods, and the third stage—the civilized stage—was when religion included "Moral Sense" of "considerable development."[43] When Europeans and Americans considered the full array of what made a culture "civilized," it invariably placed European cultures at the apex of civilizational advancement with indigenous cultures at the bottom. This notion of "civilizing savage races" helped cement American colonialism as a palatable practice.[44] American Protestants also frequently felt that the civilizing mission would help propel global Christianity, and so such missions ultimately fit comfortably into a postmillennialist worldview.

Sometimes people characterize projects like colonialism as "using" Christianity to "rationalize" or "justify" particular actions. The implication here is that Christianity was really just a cover for an avaricious project since real Christians would never have done such things. There are sometimes situations where Christianity can be mere performance, but we should be careful about assuming that religion is disingenuous just because someone gets something out of it. Sometimes genuine religion produces effects that we ourselves might find morally reprehensible. "Religion" doesn't always fit what we consider to be "good," and to assume that religionists who do unsavory things are really just faking or finessing religion in pursuit of baser goals is to assume that religion is by nature benevolent.[45] It doesn't have to be benevolent, though, and religionists sometimes make unfortunate choices. The racism, ableism, and cultural genocide embedded in nineteenth- and early twentieth-century American Protestantism was often quite sincere.

Science served as a regime of truth for many nineteenth-century Christians. (A "regime of truth" is a term borrowed from philosopher Michel Foucault, who argued that people approach particular modes of understanding, such as psychiatry, as holding authoritative knowledge. "Truth" is not necessarily fact but rather those positions that people *accept* as factual or authoritative.)[46] Race science constituted a major portion of the civilizing mission. For those who accepted the framework of that civilizing mission *and* that of postmillennialism, the only moral action available was to participate in helping savage races advance toward civilized status. This is largely how white American Protestants felt about racial others—to ignore the uncivilized or undercivilized was to ignore the neighbor in need of help. Erasing indigenous cultures through colonialist interventions was for many a Christian act.

Christianity, Race Science, and Substance Use

Although today it is overwhelmingly rejected as pseudoscience, race science was considered legitimate for most of the nineteenth and some of the twentieth century. Race science is more or less the notion that humanity is divided into races, which are biologically distinct from one another and which have their own hereditary traits. There is nothing about this idea that requires a god, but neither is it intrinsically oppositional to Christianity (indeed, some scholars have argued that Christianity produced it).[47] Race scientists made a wide array of claims, but important for this book is that they took racial differences that they assumed were real, studied those differences, and then represented their findings as objective neutral truth.

The incorporation of race science into Protestant agendas was consequential for the Drug War. For one, it complicated the civilizing mission. Civilizational hierarchies elevated European and American cultures to the pinnacle position of what was achievable, and in the American and British contexts it lionized the "Anglo-Saxon" race in particular.[48] Race scientists argued that some races were naturally prone to uncivilized behavior or that they experienced serious psychological difficulties when forced to live within a civilized world.[49] Race science produced narratives about various races that were imagined to be scientific fact: Africans were impulsive and smaller brained; Finns were more cowardly than Mongols; Africans and American Indians were hypersexual and prone to perversity.[50] If nature had created Europeans to be superior, it was unclear to reformers how much progress they could expect from these "child races."[51] Writing from a Roman Catholic context, the French race scientist Arthur de Gobineau claimed that even "the most degraded savages" were capable of some religious understanding, which made them different from beasts, but he cautioned that "the fact that certain Tahitians have helped repair a whaler does not make their nation capable of civilization."[52] For most Christian civilizers the claims of race science engendered new questions about moral capacity.

Even for those who accepted the premise that lesser races could advance and become civilized, substance use proved to be an especially menacing challenge. Civilization and self-government were tied to Enlightenment styles of "reason" and "rationality," which were themselves ideological constructs.[53] Reason and rationality represent a kind of normative consciousness: They are a style of being that deemphasizes the significance of "irrational" religions (meaning here religions that incorporate material objects too much or that accept animist frameworks), and that highlight structured, argumentative epistemologies over other ways of knowing.[54] Reason and rationality also elevate cognition over emotion—emotions are something to be tamed. Nineteenth- and early twentieth-century experts were often conversant with philosophy as its own regime of truth, and although they often disagreed about specifics, a slate of important philosophers (René Descartes, Immanuel Kant, Jean-Jacques Rousseau, the Common Sense Realists, etc.) more or less accepted the premise that morality was universal and knowable. Because the mind was the seat of reason, and because substance use altered cognitive performance, their extrapolations held that substance use diminished and adulterated human capacities for moral knowledge.

Many (if not most) Protestants in this era also considered cognition the site of salvation. Protestants' emphasis on belief—sometimes to the exclusion of all other categories—renders the mind especially significant spiritual terrain, for it is by believing that one becomes saved. (Staunch predestinarians might frame this differently, suggesting that salvation occurs outside of human choice and that the transformation of the mind is the result of salvation, not the salvific catalyst itself.) Some even considered that insanity could block people from understanding the gospel and thereby shut them out of salvation.[55] Nineteenth-century Protestants frequently treated the mind as a sacred location for God's work on earth.

Substance use became a religious problem in this context. Because many people considered opium use inherently immoral, addicts were often shut out of church attendance (and thereby separated from the gospel), a situation missionaries in China found troubling.[56] Furthermore, substance users' inability to think clearly—and thereby recognize and respond to Christian knowledge properly—meant that addicts were predisposed to reject salvation. One British Protestant expressed exasperation in 1840 that "every individual who is once enslaved by the use of Opium, is *morally* and *physically* incapacitated from giving any attention to the voice of Christian instruction!"[57] Missionaries also sometimes saw substance use as having idolatrous potential. In 1925, a Presbyterian journal decried that many Indians considered peyote to be "the Way, the Truth, and the Life," and thereby "in their blindness they are hurled into the abyss of darkness and despair."[58] Substances were considered potential or guaranteed barriers to Christian conversion, thought, and practice.

By the later nineteenth century, American Protestants had grown up in an environment shaped by Christian Temperance and abolitionism. They were socialized into a world where they were accountable to each other and to God for helping the Kingdom creep forward. They also grew up accepting that some cultures were better than others and that they had an obligation to help weaker cultures improve. Failure to do good was something for which they would be held accountable. Various scientific regimes of truth identified substance use as catastrophically bad, voicing narratives about drugs driving people into chronic madness, degeneracy, and unrestrained immorality. Beyond just its colonialist implications, race science also evolved into the eugenics movement, which sought to perfect whiteness. Addicts represented a kind of biological failure that should be wiped from the gene pool, thus the critiques Christians had of colonial others blended into concerns about future Americans' capacity for moral civilization. When Aimee Semple McPherson passionately proclaimed that Christians had a duty to God, their nation, the Mayflower, and future generations to wage war against drugs, she was giving language to a position her audience already knew and knew deeply, for even their parents had grown up with this moral understanding.

Chapter Plan

All of this context is a starting point for the story of the Drug War and hopefully clarifies why religion is so relevant for this history. The overarching argument of this book is that Protestant Christianity, particularly in its American iterations, helped to germinate the Drug War. There are different facets to this story, and I have tried my best to organize it in a way that puts the most foundational elements first.

Chapter 1, "Christian Temperance, Millennial Progress, and the Immorality of Addiction," argues that Christian Temperance/Prohibition was really just one side of the War on Drugs rather than something separate. It was explicitly tied to Protestant concerns about society and morality. From the earliest days of the movement, Temperance and Prohibition activists frequently identified alcohol as one category of substance abuse. Medical discourse about alcohol also presented it as a substance that produced insanity and destroyed the body. Many treated alcoholism as a kind of literal slavery, often comparing it to slave labor and identifying substance slavery as the worse condition. Christian Temperance also established many of the patterns and approaches that would characterize the wider Drug War, particularly when it came to arguments about how drinking threatened to destroy society and why legislation was necessary. Furthermore, the Millennial Kingdom would be a place of sobriety; excising substances like beverage alcohol was an important eschatological goal.

Chapter 2, "Sin, Addiction, and Biomorality," explains how addiction theory developed in the nineteenth century as well as how biomorality played a critical role in the development of the Drug War. European authors like Thomas De Quincey and Jacques-Joseph Moreau helped to generate consensuses that certain substances like opium or hashish produced madness. Phrenology helped cement the idea that morality was vested in neurobiology and could be damaged or destroyed through substance use. This chapter also introduces degeneracy theory, a scientific theory that biological species as well as human civilizations could degenerate as well as evolve. Under this theory substance use becomes a threat to stability and heredity. People who used substances—especially addicts—undermined not just their own well-being, but that of their entire community. Objections to substance use also drew on Christian narratives about the body being a sacrosanct object, and which if defiled through substance abuse created an offense to God.

Chapter 3, "Degeneracy, Eugenics, and the Great American Race," explains how the American eugenics movement took degeneracy theory and biomoral models and translated them into a sociocultural and legal movement. By tying individuals' "fitness" to the collective well-being of "the American Race," eugenicists transformed private health into a moral obligation. Although not all eugenicists were Christians, many were, and the underlying assumptions about what a eugenic utopia would look like emphasized Protestantism even when the eugenicists themselves rejected Christianity. Morality, rational religion, productive labor, physical and mental fitness, and progress were all framed as eugenic goals, whereas substance use threatened them. In contrast, addiction was not only degenerative, it was frequently portrayed as a symptom of degeneracy already at work before the addict ever took their first dose. Because eugenics is fundamentally about planning "progress," it overlapped conceptually with postmillennialism. This was particularly true for Christian eugenicists, who positioned the Kingdom as a place for the fit and called for sterilization of the unfit.

Chapter 4, "US Colonialism and Substance Use Prohibition," explains how American authorities worked to control substance use for American Indians and Native Hawaiians. Colonial power structures are complex: Some among the colonized cooperate with colonizers or champion their goals, whereas others resist and subvert the colonialists. Peyote control represents a pronounced version of this dynamic. The complex matrix of relationships between tribal factions, states, missionary groups, and the Bureau of Indian Affairs engendered a motley patchwork of regulations. Because peyote produces visionary experiences, some treated it as a Pan-Indian religious technology, yet to many tribes in the twentieth century this was a new, suspicious substance. Missionaries and BIA agents were vocal critics of peyote as a retrogressive substance that impeded Christian conversion and the civilizing mission; these represent anti-peyotists' two most significant objections. This chapter also argues that while federal or international drug reforms are important, they aren't the whole story. Peyote prohibition played out on a much smaller stage, sometimes with the decisions of only one or two people producing widespread disruptions to its use.

Chapter 5, "Protestants, Colonialism, and International Drug Reform," traces how missionaries helped generate international drug policy. Charles Henry Brent, the Episcopalian missionary bishop to the Philippines, was especially important. Brent was a colonial postmillennialist who saw opium use as a challenge to civilizing lesser races, a position that many missionaries—especially those in the Far East—had been arguing for the better part of a century. He was also well-connected and secured Teddy Roosevelt's help in convening an international conference to promote global drug control. Under Brent's leadership, this conference and the ones that followed created the legal framework for international drug regulations. The League of Nations inherited oversight of drug control after World War I, cooperating with missionaries toward a shared goal of global abolition. They also cemented the savage/barbarian/civilized framework in formal policy with the mandates system, monitoring substance use in these colonial contexts. This chapter also highlights how explicitly Protestant language began to shift toward secular idioms.

Chapter 6, "The Products of a Moral Panic," argues that moral panics contributed to the generation of a Drug War. Stuart Hall characterized moral panics as being about respectable people denouncing dangerous others as a problem, and this fits the shape of the early Drug War quite well.[59] Popular media and celebrities emphasized the dangers that addicts' immorality posed to the United States. Missionaries and activists may have shaped the ideological framework for many antidrug positions, but when the voting public took aim at narcotics it offered an impetus for tighter controls. Richmond Pearson Hobson, a Spanish-

American War hero, Alabama congressman, and Christian Prohibitionist, was particularly adept at this work. After the prohibition of alcohol in 1920, Hobson turned his attentions to narcotics. He took many of the strategies developed by previous reformers (including the use of religiously neutral language) and successfully applied them to narcotic regulation. Hobson and other activists also framed drug addiction as a foreign threat to the United States, one in which sinister cabals of anti-American peddlers sought to weaken Americans through deliberate addiction. This approach helped to create conditions ripe for new legislation and for educational reform. Using the "Scientific Temperance" model, Hobson introduced a narcotic education program into schools across the United States.

In the end I argue that the global War on Drugs developed hand-in-hand with American Protestantism and does not make sense without it. If this part of the story has largely gone untold before now, that is because its other aspects seemed more important to previous historians. It is also because those who shaped the Drug War in the early twentieth century wanted to place a comfortable distance between religion and legal reform. As American attitudes to the separation of church and state evolved, the strategies for moral legislation changed as well. Their strategy worked. Americans today have grown up in a society where it seems self-evident that governments should regulate substance use, even if people disagree about which specific substances merit control. The immorality of substance use also remains part of our Drug War, a moral position that today requires no explicitly religious overlay. That's not how it began, though. This book tells the story of how religion cultivated, curated, and created many of the Drug War's most enduring elements.

1

Christian Temperance, Millennial Progress, and the Immorality of Addiction

Cincinnati (1874)

On May 16, 1874, the Cincinnati police arrested 38-year-old Abby Leavitt and 42 members of her women's temperance prayer group. Leavitt and her followers had chosen to defy orders to vacate the sidewalk outside of a saloon, where they conducted open-air religious services in an attempt to reach sinners. Leavitt and her friends were convinced that alcohol was undermining American society and God's wishes for the nation. By May 16 they had enacted their temperance ritual many times over: Select a saloon, arrive at the saloon, request to hold religious services inside, and if denied entry, pray and sing on the street outside. Sometimes saloons permitted them to enter, but in this instance, the saloonkeeper A. Bothmund did not. Police officers who had been present at the planning meeting urged the women not to march down to the saloon, yet the sense of security their prayers produced led them to disregard that advice. The police who met them at the saloon permitted them to finish singing "Rock of Ages" and perform a brief prayer before they were all arrested by one Captain Churchhill. Arresting all 43 of them had been their own suggestion.[1]

Abby Leavitt's goals and rationale were typical of the Christian Temperance Movement. She did not view this as a mere political statement, but rather relished her arrest as evidence that she was doing God's work. Christian Temperance reformers saw alcohol as an obstacle to Christian progress at best, but far more commonly they saw it at its worst: an actively evil substance that poisoned the bodies and eternal souls of drinkers. It should be unsurprising that many temperance reformers saw drinkers as a type of heathen and therefore a mission field. (Indeed, Leavitt was the head of her church's foreign missions program long before she began agitating for temperance.) In its earliest years, the Christian Temperance Movement sought to encourage drinkers to moderate or abstain, only occasionally seeking to change behavior through law. By the later part of the nineteenth century, Prohibitionist sentiments were overtaking temperance as an ethos, insisting that law might be the best means available to combat substance abuse.

Such notions underscore the salience of postmillennialist Protestantism for substance abuse campaigns. Temperance dominated the nineteenth century's substance abuse discourse, but that was because reformers considered alcohol to be a more serious, pervasive problem than opium or tobacco addiction. There were far more alcoholics than opium habitués and far more cultural acceptance of drinking than of opiates. Alcohol also had a much longer cultural legacy. (As historian Timothy Hickman pithily phrased it, "The Romans drank wine, [but] Christians could scarcely imagine Jesus inviting his disciples over for a shot of morphine.")[2] To that end, temperance activists focused on alcohol even though tobacco and narcotics sat alongside it as a concern at least as early as the 1830s. Anti-alcohol activism built and routinized the strategies and ideals that were later applied to a robust antidrug movement.

Temperance activists denounced alcohol through a variety of ways, but during the nineteenth century, Protestantism was an explicit part of many (if not most) criticisms. Christian Temperance was international in scope, with American and British reformers in close conversation with one another. Both British and American temperance activists viewed personal sobriety as a starting point, but society-wide sobriety was the ultimate goal. Indeed, English tea parties were invented for this reason—temperance reformers in the 1830s held mass gatherings in industrial towns, where sweets, tea, and coffee were served as "antidotes to spirits," with the goal of convincing the British middle class that wholesome beverages were a better choice than alcohol.[3] Tea parties may have been a little less popular in the United States, but American reformers encouraged sermons, print culture, and education as means for disseminating anti-alcohol positions to mass society. It was not enough for one to be sober individually—the whole world needed to embrace it.

The Christian Part of Christian Temperance

To speak of Christian Temperance is to speak of a long and diverse movement. Some Christians saw the world as a damnable place, with alcohol being one sin among many that Christians must avoid.[4] Some believed the world was progressing toward a bright and glorious future, with alcohol prohibition marking one more potential achievement for Christendom. Many made no explicit claims about how banning drink might fit within a larger schema but instead based their claims on how alcohol violated Christian morality. Even though Protestants dominated the Temperance Movement, Roman Catholics also participated in significant numbers. The movement spanned roughly 150 years, with late eighteenth-century reformers creating the first organizations and Prohibitionists representing an evolved form of it in the nineteenth and early twentieth centuries.[5]

Temperance reformers believed alcohol was bad for a number of reasons. In his 1829 sermon, Baptist preacher Ebenezer Nelson outlined many of the most enduring complaints among hardline teetotalers. For Nelson, scriptural interpretation was the primary source for complaint—his reading of 1 Corinthians 6:10 and 6:19 held that drunkards cannot be saved and that they desecrate their bodies, which are the "Temple of the Holy Ghost" for true Christians.[6] One may be wedded to lusts (in which he includes alcohol) or they may be wed to Christ, but they cannot be wed to both. Beyond this, though, Nelson argued that even moderate drinking is un-Christian, using what might be called a "stumbling block" argument. In 1 Corinthians 8:13, Paul declares he will eat no meat so long as it tempts someone else into sin. Nelson used this premise to argue that the moderate drinker tempts the immoderate drinker through his example. Furthermore, the moderate drinker is incapable of rebuking others for their vices; Nelson argued that blasphemers will not take moderate drinkers seriously since they themselves sin by drinking. Nelson also claimed that medical doctors repudiated alcohol since it harms both body and mind. His sermon recounts the tale of a Londoner who died from alcohol poisoning, and, when dissected, the ventricles of his brain were found to be soaked with gin, concentrated enough to be smelled, tasted, and set afire.[7] Finally, Nelson tasked his audience with joining and supporting the work of temperance societies and argued that these societies must above all publish.

> Give the people knowledge on this subject, and your temperance societies
> will increase. The venders of liquid poison will join you, this part of their
> merchandise will diminish, and will feel that a rum-buying community
> is undesirable, and that on the whole their loss is gain.[8]

Nelson's take on alcohol was fairly common for nineteenth-century appraisals—drunkenness was a grave sin; moderate drinking was a stumbling block to others; alcohol damaged the body, mind, and spirit; and the job of temperance organizations was to inculcate society with a kind of saving knowledge that was both mundane and eternal.

Postmillennialism contributed significantly to temperance goals. Postmillennialists interpreted the Bible as indicating a glorious future Kingdom of God arriving on earth, yet in contrast to premillennialists, they saw the march toward this Kingdom as both gradual and synchronous with human progress. They thought of this partly in terms of revivals and spiritual conversions and partly in terms of civilizational advances, such as the abolition of slavery and oppression.[9] Postmillennialism cannot be underestimated when it comes to interpreting nineteenth- and early twentieth-century reform movements—in fact, one could reasonably say that postmillennialism was responsible for them in the first place. For postmillennialists, Jesus will not return until the Kingdom has already commenced, which means it is therefore up to Christians to reshape society into that Kingdom. Additionally, if one accepts the premise that biblical predictions of the Kingdom are certain and immutable, then this necessarily means that society is moving forward toward it, with the world getting better, healthier, and nobler. That which is antithetical to God is passing away, and that which is of him grows fuller. This more or less sacralizes human progress. If alcohol is un-Christian—a common position for temperance advocates—then it must go, for by remaining it hinders the Kingdom.

Many temperance authors identified the Kingdom of God as a goal, both explicitly and implicitly. In 1837, Professor Edward Hitchcock of Amherst College published *An Argument for Early Temperance; Addressed to the Youth of the United States*, in which he claimed that "the golden age of temperance" required not just abandoning alcohol, but also "those powerful narcotic substances, tobacco and opium."[10] Such substances led to economic impairment, moral bankruptcy, and impeded the Kingdom. Hitchcock estimated that 1.76 billion gallons of alcohol had been consumed in the United States since 1790, resulting not only in $50 million less profit each year, but also 25 million bushels of grain redirected annually from the food supply to alcohol production. Hitchcock claimed that if the waste from alcohol, tobacco, and opiates were corrected, the money could be redeployed for better purposes; specifically, he argued that it could pay for 16,000 miles of railroad; a canal from the Gulf of Mexico to the Pacific; 800,000 male students in public schools; or "a missionary for every 2000 souls in the unevangelized parts of the earth."[11] Hitchcock claimed that substance use caused madness and death, as well as a "powerful excitement" antithetical to "the simple and noiseless pleasures of home," and that it plays "havock [sic] with the moral and religious principles of the country."[12] He decried "the work of desolation made perfect," which he explained meant Sabbath breaking, blasphemy, effeminacy, theft, fraud, and murder.[13] In closing his piece, Hitchcock lamented drunkards' eternal damnation, but also offered a hopeful note: "The intelligent youth of our land, who have no such habits or prejudices strongly fixed, will yield to the united voice of Philosophy, of Self-interest, of their Country, and of Christianity." These youth will embrace total abstinence. "What a noble example for the World! and how soon would Millennial Temperance reign in all the earth, and Millennial Happiness follow in the train!"[14]

Hitchcock's argument was paradigmatic for temperance and antidrug ideology that emerged over the next century. Hitchcock worked with a dualist model of good and evil, in which virtue lies on one side (total abstinence from alcohol) and evil on the other (death, crime, avoidable poverty, blasphemy, damnation, vulgarity, and more than a few passages about deviant gender performance). He also explicitly tied the abolition of drinking to progress: economic (railroads, canals, and an increased GDP), education, public morality, salvation (both personal and missional), and in the end, to the progress of the Millennial Kingdom itself.

Taken together, Nelson and Hitchcock represent an early "no punches pulled" model for substance use moral norms, which more or less goes something like this: Vice and virtue cannot cohabitate within a single person. The vicious person not only damns themself, but taints society as a whole. Alcohol production and consumption also violate Christian principles for labor, diminishing industriousness and wasting resources upon a frivolous and self-damaging pleasure. Alcohol decays personal morality, permitting other vices to consume a person—assorted lusts, vulgarities, and blasphemies. It wrecks the body. Because society is the collective whole of individuals, and because that whole must be honored and protected over and above any one individual, it is the Christian's duty to stay sober and teach others to do the same.

Interpreting Alcohol and Narcotics as Slavery

Nelson and Hitchcock offered important conceptual frameworks typical of temperance literature, but nineteenth-century temperance activists emphasized another equally important theme: slavery. It's tempting to think of this as metaphor, but there's no indication that reformers thought of slavery only as an analogy—in fact, they seem to deploy the term quite literally. This is less surprising if one considers addiction phenomena in conjunction with the fact that medical models of alcoholism were only just emerging during the latter half of the nineteenth century.[15] Set aside for a moment contemporary interpretations of alcoholism as a neurological syndrome and instead imagine a time when psychology and psychiatry do not yet even fully exist as disciplines. One cannot turn to them to explain addiction. If we can place ourselves in such a setting, then we are left with some hard-to-interpret behavior: alcoholics trek to the local saloon to spend all of their money on booze, often despairing of their own behavior and yet finding themselves unable to stop. Without cognitive science, alcoholics would appear to be driven to their self-defeating behavior by some other force. This puzzled people. Some observers considered alcoholism to be a question of personal will: Since some men and women were able to handle drinking in moderation and others were not, it might be the case that drunkards were simply morally lazy. Yet another interpretation is that alcohol possessed the capacity to literally enslave. Few (if any) theorized the nature or mechanisms of this enslavement, but the position was both commonplace and enduring. Slavery dominated nineteenth-century interpretations of substance use and remained a potent line of thought into the twentieth: Those who ingest alcohol or opium gamble with their freedom in very literal and consequential ways.

By equating substance use with slavery, reformers grafted an abolitionist political motif onto alcohol. However, it was an abolitionism that even former slaveholders would eventually favor—the South participated partially in the Temperance Movement in antebellum days and more fully in the postwar years, but the association of Christian Temperance with Northern abolitionism made many Southerners wary of the movement.[16] According to many abolitionists, slave labor had been the worst national sin in the United States' short history: a violation of Enlightenment principles, Christian blasphemy, and a disgusting injustice heaped upon millions of blameless men, women, and children. To say alcohol was also enslaving was to place it in the worst possible light. Even for white Americans who favored slaveholding, the thought of oneself or one's family being enslaved would have been horrifying, too. By rendering alcoholism a problem that individual willpower was ineffective to control, temperance activists marked it as an issue requiring government intervention: If individuals literally could not restrain themselves from drinking, then it was up to society to save them.[17] If morality is essentially about what we owe one another, then the sober free had a duty to rescue enslaved drunkards. Additionally, it was also commonplace for many Americans to interpret divine providence as responsible for slavery's end.[18] To identify addiction as a genuine and real variety of slavery was a way of identifying it as uniquely un-Christian, as well as identifying it as a moral crisis demanding strong legal regulation.

Slavery was not merely a descriptor for the relationship between alcoholics and their alcohol, but also indicated a particular quality of life. As a savvy speaker and president of the Woman's Christian Temperance Union (WCTU), Frances Willard was easily the most celebrated reformer of the movement—a statue of her remains in the US Capitol to this day. In one of her many writings she included a short morality tale about an alcoholic, whom she describes as "a slave to the rum-shop down the corner." Willard didn't focus solely on the fact that he cannot quit drinking, for she also claims that his love and his money go to the barkeep's family rather than the man's own. The saloonkeeper's wife has nice clothes and a carriage to take her places and his daughter has white shoes and a white dress. The alcoholic's wife wears faded calico and must walk wherever she goes, and his daughter—though fairer than the barkeep's—dons rags. The drunkard's shack pales when compared to the brick home of the rum seller while sometimes his own family goes hungry. After a temperance reformer directly confronts the alcoholic, he quickly comes to terms with it: "You speak the truth, madam—I am a slave." His admonisher does not ask him to sign a temperance pledge since as a slave he is incapable of honoring it. In the end, he must reject the devil and pray to Jesus Christ for his deliverance. According to Willard's story, God chose to hear his sinner's prayer, and the man was freed from his condition with his material wealth and familial happiness restored to their full measure.[19] The moral of the story is twofold: First, alcohol is literal slavery, both in obedience to drink as well as the attendant poverty of slavery where wealth gets siphoned off to the slavemaster, and second, only Jesus can free the enslaved from their demons.

When temperance ideologues compared alcohol slavery to slave labor, they frequently concluded that alcohol slavery was graver and far more serious. At an 1871 meeting for Massachusetts teetotalers, for instance, E. S. Tobey (who was also president of the American Missionary Society) posited this, arguing:

> It is but recently that this nation was elevated to a height of grandeur never before attained, when it struck the fetters from four millions of its people. To-day, a bondage more awful in its consequences, self-imposed though it be, holds millions as slaves of appetite and custom, who are sapping the very foundations of the social fabric.[20]

Tobey's sentiment was remarkably common. Although for many today it may be hard to consider alcoholism a worse condition than permanent race-based slavery, that attitude was quite normal for the Christian Temperance Movement. This may have been due partly to white speakers' ignorance of what slave life was like, but more than that it reflects the prioritization of interiority and mind over body. As far as reformers were concerned, slave labor can break the body, steal wealth, and force people to live lives of pain and squalor, which is indeed horrible. But addiction does all that *and more*, in that it gradually decays the mind, conscience, and possibly damns the soul to eternal misery. For most nineteenth-century Protestants, the mind was the most sacred space available—it is where salvation manifests, it is where belief occurs, and it is where truth resides. To damage the mind is to violate the holiest part of humanity.

Alcohol, Madness, and Crime

Christian Temperance also championed the position that alcohol engendered insanity. This premise can be found across many theological approaches, and indeed, medical texts as well—it is hard to say which field originated the notion. One of the earliest American advocates for alcohol reform, Dr. Benjamin Rush, left an indelible mark on the early Temperance Movement. Rush saw alcoholism as a contractible "disease of the will," whose symptoms included madness and weakened (or even ruined) morality.[21] Rush's concerns represent an early interest in alcoholic insanity, which was to become a major trope within Gilded Age approaches to alcoholism. Alcohol theorists who succeeded Rush found themselves fascinated by the phenomenon of delirium tremens, the Latin term for a bad case of what today is called "withdrawal." Nineteenth-century medicine fixated upon delirium tremens, whose symptoms include paranoia, anxiety, shaking, and hallucinations. Temperance literature frequently referenced this phenomenon, and it represented a serious concern for reformers. However, their discussions of madness were often broader and not fully about medicine. These discussions often cited medical symptoms as part of their anti-alcohol rationale but madness was more often identified by immoral behavior.

Proto-madness theories were already in circulation in the early nineteenth century. In 1826 for instance, one of Lyman Beecher's sermons included a series of symptoms resembling later accounts of alcohol insanity. Beecher suggested that alcohol "steeped [the liver] in fire," which led to acid, indigestion, organ damage, "filling the stomach with air and the head with fumes and the soul with darkness and terror." Furthermore, intemperance is identifiable by "irritability, petulance, and violent anger," and "the slightest touch causes painful vibrations and irritations, which defy self-government." Additionally, "the temper becomes like a flash of powder, or ungovernable and violent as the helm driven hither and thither by ragging winds and mountain waves." The intemperate lose their ability to be religious as well, with the "religious affectations" dissolving "until conscience has lost its power, or survives only with vulture scream to flap the wing and terrify the soul."[22] Beecher did not *explicitly* link drunkenness to madness, but rather linked it to the components of what later reformers would identify as insanity's symptomology. The inebriate he describes is haunted by "darkness and terror," prone to wild and uncontrollable mood swings, and saddled with a dying conscience.

Later sources were more explicit about alcohol insanity, linking it verbatim to immorality and crime. *The House I Live In* (1887), a schoolbook used in the later nineteenth century, explained that "alcoholic drinks are one of the chief causes of insanity," which is "the worst fate that can befall anyone," and that "alcoholic drinks tend to cause men to commit crime."[23] This was not an isolated sentiment, but rather typical for the era. Breakfast magnate and health reformer Dr. J. H. Kellogg argued that for the drunkard, "sin does not seem so sinful, crime so criminal, nor dishonor so dishonorable."[24] Temperance advocates commonly understood alcohol to be a gateway to insanity, as well as immorality, since damaged minds were considered prone to deviance. In turn, that immorality led to its close cousin: crime. As Reverend George Tugwell of the United Kingdom put it, "there is scarcely one convicted criminal whose downward career has not been hastened and completed by the habit of overdrinking."[25]

Victorian-era medicine reproduced this same discourse about alcoholic insanity and its relationship to crime. By 1909, Dr. Charles L. Dana was able to open a medical article by saying, "The case against alcohol as a cause of insanity is of the kind which really has only one side. I have no need to make an argument to prove that alcohol is a cause of insanity."[26] Alcohol madness was so commonly accepted among medics that Dana felt no need to even present a case for it. In 1889, Dr. R. J. Kinkead of Galway, Ireland, wrote similarly, treating alcohol's causal link with insanity as a given—what Kinkead felt needed redress was the murkiness of British law on the matter. "The responsibility of the insane, and more especially as regards those who are insane from the action of alcohol, [the law] is singularly uncertain."[27] Kinkaid's concern was that those deemed insane are not always legally culpable for their transgressions, and therefore determining alcohol's legal status when it came to crimes committed while insane required clarification. Medical discourse sometimes reproduced explicitly Christian themes (such as sin), and almost uniformly treated immorality as a predictable outcome of alcoholic insanity, yet it omitted any specifically religious references just as often. In other words, medical experts in the nineteenth and early twentieth centuries gradually came to accept the premise that alcohol was a causal agent for insanity and that insanity encompassed not only phenomena like hallucinations and paranoia, but also immorality and criminality.

Michel Foucault wrote that "the asylum is a religious domain without religion, a domain of pure morality, of ethical uniformity."[28] What I take him to mean is that behind the scientific veneer of modern medical asylums lay a religious code of right/wrong behavior, a code that had been naturalized in the terms "sane" and "insane," but which had as much to do with religion as with medicine. When treating madness this way, alcoholic insanity partly fits this bill. In one sense, contemporary medicine would suggest that addiction is a real cognitive disorder that exists wholly independent of any cultural or historical context, as well as suggest that withdrawal symptoms are predictable and replicable. In that sense, part of what nineteenth-century reformers called "alcohol insanity" indeed addressed something medical. On the other hand, by also identifying "immorality" as "alcohol insanity," they exemplified Foucault's claims about how "insanity" can be "a religious domain without religion." The kinds of behaviors that temperance marked as immoral—wasteful spending, wantonness, fraternizing with the wrong people, and general sinfulness—are culturally interpreted phenomena rather than self-evident matters of sanity.

Many authors didn't separate sanity from religious frameworks. Some did. Foucault's reading of asylums syncs well with "Scientific Temperance," which was one part of the Christian Temperance Movement that sought to rely on epistemologies of medicine and reason rather than theology, and which was first created by the WCTU. Scientific Temperance was, as one historian has put it, "the quest for authoritative truth amid competing expert claims."[29] In the 1880s, Scientific Temperance developed partly in response to critiques that Christian Temperance was sectarian and alarmist and partly in concert with evolving social views about medical authority. As medical science gained new levels of credibility, reformers sought to make greater use of its claims. The WCTU responded to criticisms of sectarianism by seeking new channels of persuasion—it was a move to secularize religious arguments that was reproduced in other temperance spheres as well.[30]

With a vaguely positivist ethos undergirding it, Scientific Temperance sought to denounce alcohol on solely scientific and medical principles. This was less about abandoning religion as a line of argument and more about overcoming sectarian objections—if science could demonstrate authoritative truths about alcohol's despicability, the argument would transcend disagreements about whether or not the Bible actually condemned drinking.[31] Scientific Temperance also emphasized education, with a premiere focus on textbooks and legal mandates for instruction.[32] In short, Scientific Temperance sought religiously neutral language and arguments for banning alcohol in an effort to gain new ground with non-Protestant audiences.

Scientific Temperance made use of several rationales that were typically presented as medical truths. The first was that alcohol causes criminal madness. The second was that—as the eminent biologist and American eugenicist David Starr Jordan put it—"alcohol has been demonstrated to be a poison."[33] In this line of argument, drinking alcohol was exactly the same thing as drinking toxic waste, and while some people did drink poison, it was too problematic an activity to count as a "personal right." Scientific Temperance also argued that even the moderate use of alcohol leads to disease: By weakening tissue and impeding proper nutrition, alcohol facilitates infection and viral invasion.[34] Such illnesses represent a threat not only to individual health, but to public health as well—the drunkard thus became a contagion. Finally, in the parlance of the times, alcohol led to degeneracy. Scientific Temperance applied this in three ways: (1) alcohol leads to sterility and infirmity (physiological degeneracy); (2) alcohol leads to birth defects in offspring (hereditary degeneracy); and (3) it leads to mental degeneracy, which included not just weakened intelligence but also morality.[35] Scientific Temperance used this style of argumentation to emphasize physiological and moral reasons for prohibiting alcohol which did not rely on Protestantism as a prerequisite position.

Illness and toxicity became particularly prominent themes in later Prohibitionist discourse. As one proponent put it,

Alcohol not only reduces the efficiency of a nation, but life insurance experience has shown that the death-rate among steady drinkers supposed to be temperate—even within the bounds of so-called moderation—is nearly double that among average people. Drink may lead you into trouble, possibly a miserable death. Why deliberately expose yourself to this sort of machine-gun fire?[36]

Such a sentiment demonstrates both a trust in statistics as well as an argument that drinking damages health badly enough that merely on self-preservation terms, one ought to abandon it. The author furthermore suggests that this kind of deficiency diminishes national productivity as well. Significantly, though, this underscores the moral link between personal health and national integrity that preoccupied so many reformers.

Alcohol, Industry, and Waste

In line with Scientific Temperance rhetoric, reformers also emphasized industry and commerce as spheres that alcohol damaged. Although this was usually presented as a secular concern in later years, one should consider the relationship Protestantism has had with industriousness. Max Weber's now-classic *Protestant Work Ethic* argues that "wasted time" and failure to be productive have intimate ties to Protestant ethics.[37] Failure to work and/or a proclivity to indulgence both reflect disdain for God. Labor-as-sacrament remained a widely held value. In 1937 and in "Muscular Christianity" fashion, the popular magazine *Liberty* expressed disdain for images of an "effeminate" Jesus, arguing that he in fact had a rugged body and spent six times longer working as a carpenter than he did preaching. The article claims that Jesus worked partly to take care of his mother, but even more so "to dignify for all time the divine life of Labor."[38] One ought not to take the secularity of economic objections at face value; even if reformers sometimes understood themselves to be making a non-religious argument, their understanding of secular labor was premised upon Protestant ethical norms. Furthermore, because productivity was so central to Protestant moral norms, any emphasis on alcohol's deleterious effects upon productivity would have been interpreted by Protestant readers through such a lens.

Nineteenth- and early twentieth-century presentations of labor-as-virtue often invoked this Muscular Christian rationale for hard work (although of course Weber traced antecedent American morals of productivity as far back as the Puritans).[39] To say that Protestants considered productivity to be a moral requirement is not to suggest that Protestants were simply serving as economic handmaidens to capitalist forces and industrialization; all the evidence suggests that their treatment of labor as virtuous was genuine and not contrived by some economic puppet master. But because productivity is often taken to be a self-evidently secular goal, the quietly religious underpinnings to productivity sometimes get overlooked. In the case of Christian Temperance, criticisms of alcohol's drain on industriousness might superficially appear to be merely a secular tie-in or perhaps a convenient excuse for anti-alcohol ideological goals. However, temperance advocates who presented underproduction as a reason to avoid alcohol were often still working in a religious register.

Concern for wasted resources and money began in the earliest days of Christian Temperance and peppered activists' arguments throughout the nineteenth century. By the twentieth century, "waste" increased as an enunciated concern even as Prohibitionists began to discuss "sin" less often.[40] Yet this only measures the language used to represent the problem, not the morality that undergirded it. What people say in public isn't necessarily identical to private ideals. We have already seen this modeled with Scientific Temperance—shifting attitudes toward religion in the public sphere produced new forms of discourse that emphasized religiously neutral explanations. Additionally, for many Christians— and certainly for many if not most of those Protestants involved in Prohibition—waste *is* sin. Individual wastefulness was treated as a moral failing at the personal level, but it was also an affront to the American people as a collective. Those who took such a view were in essence evaluating drinkers' moral obligations to the nation—moral obligations derived from religious ideals—and determining that alcohol posed a problem. Industriousness was a moral code that allowed for people to object to drinking on either religious or secular grounds simultaneously.

Personal poverty was a consistent and negative theme within temperance literature. The notion that drinking led to destitution did not emerge from nothing. During the nineteenth century there were indeed some individuals who drank themselves into the poorhouse. Temperance activists took such cases and made them central components of anti-alcohol discourse, a discourse that transcended historically contextual events (such as when a specific individual drank away their money) and transformed those into an enduring interpretive lens for the larger world (drinking leads to destitution). In other words, it's not the case that everyone who drank alcohol became impoverished, nor even that most people who drank encountered such troubles; however, because there were sufficient examples of the phenomenon, the "drinking = poverty" formula came to be a convincing and lasting standard.

The threat of personal poverty carried multiple meanings. One meaning is purely pragmatic—poverty inherently means a lowered capacity to buy material goods and services. There is also a politics of shame that goes along with poverty. As historian Douglas Carlson has explained, "fundamental to Temperance ideology was the Janus-faced conviction that individual moral and financial advancement proceeded from temperance, while drinking brought dissolution and ruin."[41] Carlson also explains that—at least for Southerners—impoverishment also meant the desecration of one's reputation before "friends and kin" in their "churches and communities."[42] Although Carlson was concerned primarily with temperance in the Deep South, the shame of alcohol-induced poverty arguably applied to Northerners as well. Additionally, Temperance literature throughout the nineteenth and early twentieth centuries produced the specter of a drunk husband and father, who first emptied the family savings for alcohol, and then, *if* he returned home, beat his wife and children.

The fictional depiction of alcoholic dereliction was perhaps most famously illustrated in *Ten Nights in a Bar-Room* (1854), a tale in which alcohol drives the characters mad, children die at the hands of drunk adults, people lose property and livelihood, Christians cease church attendance in pursuit of illegitimately gained wealth, gambling ensues, and drunk men murder their family members.[43] In a similar portrayal, a short vignette claiming to be "a true incident" appeared in an 1874 edition of *Advocate of Peace*, wherein an impoverished mother with child journey into a saloon to beg for money. When the barkeep asks what has driven her to enter such a disreputable place for women to be, she cries "whiskey!" and explains,

> I was once happy and surrounded by all the luxuries that wealth could procure, with a fond and indulgent husband. But in an evil hour he was tempted, and not possessing the will to resist that temptation, fell, and in one short year my dream of happiness was over, my home forever broken and desolated, and the kind husband and the wealth, once called mine, lost, lost, never to return, and all by the accursed wine cup.[44]

The maudlin language is meant to convey not a personal failing on the mother's part, but an affliction visited upon her by an alcoholic husband—the failing is his and he has betrayed his loved ones. The moral of the story is that alcoholic poverty is a despicable thing to do to your family; better to never start drinking than to risk robbing a mother and children of happiness forever.

In addition to personal poverty, reformers depicted drinking as a road to financial distress for employers, too. Writing of cognate concerns in British contexts, in 1882 the *North American Review* explained that the men of one ironworks spent every weekend drinking; the plant had to remain closed on Mondays because after their Sunday boozing they were in no shape to work. As a result, these men lost 260,000 days of wages annually and the ironworks forewent £30,000 of profit.[45] Some industries such as the railroads deliberately culled drinkers from their workforce, suspecting that drinkers led to more accidents, less productivity, and less profit.[46] Employers often asked workers about their drinking habits and many barred employees from drinking even when off-duty.[47] Such notions had a long pedigree; early American industrialist Samuel Slater (late eighteenth/early nineteenth century) commented that he never employed anyone who drank spirits, and that in New England drunkards generally could not find work.[48] This blackballing of drinkers occurred due to the widespread understanding that drinkers were less efficient and less competent workers, and that those who employed them invited accidents and profit loss.

Prohibition and temperance literature also emphasize the personal responsibility that individuals have to the nation, including economic responsibilities. Rarely do these texts explicitly argue that individuals owe their best work and their efficiency to their nation; instead, these texts discuss that principle as though it were already self-evident. One has a moral duty to perform industriously, and, given the lack of apologetics for the position it would appear to be an ideological constant (or as close to a constant as one should expect to get).

This collective ethos served to bridge matters of personal and private underperformance and poverty with the national economy. Every alcoholic who slacks at work or earns less than he could simultaneously deprives the nation. In 1882, the Quaker Prohibitionist Neal Dow claimed that liquor is in deadly hostility to every interest of nation, state, and society. It wastes the wealth of the country, undermines the virtue of the people, and is the source of a very large part of the poverty, degradation, insanity, and crime that curse the nation. It sends misery into hundreds of thousands of homes, which but for it would be prosperous, peaceful, and happy. The strength of a nation is in proportion to the intelligence, virtue, industry, and thrift of the people.[49]

In 1915, Richmond Hobson similarly claimed that alcohol decreased national efficiency by 21.5 percent, and that "liquor entails an economic burden upon the American people greater than the concurrent cost of maintaining all the war operations going on in the world."[50] The claim (which was likely an exaggeration) is stunning given the scope of worldwide war operations in 1915. These kind of claims were standard for anti-alcohol campaigners and dovetailed notions of personal responsibility to the nation. *The Mother's Book* (a 1919 guide for cultivating children's morality) framed it this way: "This sense of mutual responsibility is the basis of true citizenship and true patriotism . . . The man who believes that all men are brothers, and that *the nation is but the extension of the family*, is the ideal citizen" [emphasis added].[51]

What *The Mother's Book* calls "true citizenship and true patriotism" represents a significant element of American moral obligation during the Christian Temperance and Prohibition years; it is the claim that no man is an island and that duty therefore compels the devout to offer the nation their best. But implicit in this position is a claim that those who do *not* offer their best undermine the greater good. The preceding cases were all twentieth-century examples, but this trope appeared in nineteenth-century literature, too; generally speaking, many complained of the connection between the burden that drinking and poverty placed on society, and speaking specifically, Edward Hitchcock's objections represent much earlier cases of the same critique.[52] "Patriotism requires that the man who loves his country should shrink from no personal sacrifice," he wrote, following the sentiment with a detailed explanation of the financial and moral burden that drinking creates on a national scale. Hitchcock estimated that the United States lost $50 million due to inefficiency, plus an extra $12 million spent on alcoholic beverages.[53] (That would translate to billions of today's dollars.) The point here is that throughout the Christian Temperance and Prohibition eras, it was taken for granted that individuals were accountable to the national body as a whole; productivity was patriotic, and for many Christians, it was also a moral obligation. If alcohol damaged productivity, then it was a serious problem.

Temperance Politics

Let's return to Abby Leavitt and the events of May 16, 1874, for there is still more to the story. Prior to their street preaching, the husbands of some of the leading women—themselves all doctors or ministers claiming to represent a coterie of interdenominational clergymen—approached George W. C. Johnston, the Cincinnati mayor. They read him a resolution, in which they emphasized the Christianness of opposing the sale and consumption of liquor, and demanded that "peaceable Christian women"—"the wives and daughters of many of the best and most worthy citizens of Cincinnati"—be protected by the city government rather than hindered. They also accused the mayor and the police of "alarming violations of law and encroachment upon true Christian liberty."[54]

As it happens Mayor Johnston did not agree with their assessment. In his own proclamation he argued that Cincinnati laws required that streets and public spaces be kept open to traffic and free movement, and that while the women held the Christian "moral [high] ground," they were still required to follow those laws. Dozens of women kneeling in front of saloons to pray formed a barricade. The mayor further suggested that some of their actions were dangerous incitements to mob violence—by "trespassing upon the rights of others," they were provoking riots.[55] In other words, Temperance women might have godly intentions, but righteousness did not translate into legal immunity if they prevented other people from exercising their own right to move freely into a saloon.

The *Cincinnati Gazette* reported that after being released from jail, the women congregated in the Third Presbyterian Church for jubilant services. The Christian Temperance leaders who were present—those "best and most worthy citizens" of Cincinnati—sermonized their accounts of the day's events, contextualizing them in both religious and political terms. By this I mean that while some of their rhetoric focused on challenging the governmental and societal power structures of American democracy, other parts explicitly pointed to God and religiously derived morality as features of their cause. It would be a mistake to suggest that this means they were doing two separate things, for here the political and the religious cannot be disentangled from one another. Their political positions bled into their religious views, and their religious views guided their politics. Not only was this very typical for the Christian Temperance / Prohibitionist milieu, it is also a conceptual model that antidrug lobbyists later reproduced.

To be more specific, the Cincinnati activists portrayed their local politicians (and especially Mayor Johnston) as having gone to war against God. The first speaker, Mr. Rowland, compared Cincinnati's approach to liquor licensing to the Missouri Compromise, and suggested that the city government included the kind of people who would "repeal the Ten Commandments on a square vote." Rowland went on to say that while he wasn't xenophobic, three-fourths of all saloonkeepers were foreigners and he wanted no further immigrants arriving to sell liquor to Americans. The Baptist Reverend S. K. Leavitt (Abby's husband) argued that the Cincinnati government was "in league with hell" and that the solution was for Christian "citizens to assert their sovereignty." From a Presbyterian pulpit and to an interdenominational congregation, he called for Mayor Johnston's impeachment. The next speaker, the Methodist preacher Dr. Payne, echoed Leavitt's views, repeatedly calling the mayor a coward. A Dr. Fowler referred to the arrested women as "the immortal forty-three" and accused the city government of arresting them while freeing Barabbas, but he also went on to portray Temperance in cosmological terms. "The devil of slavery took five years to come out, but out he came. Now, the liquor devil is down and foaming, because he knows he will have to come out." The meeting concluded with some remarks from Abby Leavitt, a listing of the "martyrs" (the names of those who had been arrested for the cause), and the congregation singing what seems to have been a rather intense rendition of the doxology.[56] It was an extracurricular church service that blended political change with religious idealism.

It is a commonplace assumption in the United States today that religion and government ought to be separate, and, furthermore, that such separation is possible. Many in the Christian Temperance Movement would have found such ideas both preposterous and offensive. Jefferson's phrase "a wall of separation between church and state" would have made sense to them insofar as the government could not interfere with or obstruct religion, and that no specific, individual church could exert undue influence over the greater whole. But as far as they were concerned, transdenominational Christianity had every right to influence and shape government, and indeed moral agreement across denominational categories represented what healthy democracy was supposed to be.

The conversion strategies intrinsic to Protestant evangelicalism worked for Christian Temperance ideals, too. Individuals could be led to understand and accept the truth about alcohol, and once converted to sobriety, invited to join a likeminded group. These likeminded individuals could then continue the work of converting more drinkers into dry men and women, as well as agitate for political and legal change. Ohio as it happens birthed the two most influential anti-drink societies devoted to personal moral conversion and widescale legal reform: the WCTU in Cleveland (1874) and the Anti-Saloon League (ASL) in Oberlin (1895).[57] Although these organizations were wide-ranging in scope (especially the WCTU, which was the more important one), their primary purpose was political reform.

The WCTU's two most emphasized and significant legislative goals were first, the eradication—or at least the constriction—of alcohol sales, and the second was mandatory temperance education in schools. As we will see later, there are important parallels between temperance education and narcotic education. But the WCTU and A.S.L. served as central vehicles in the move from Temperance efforts (which mostly aimed for voluntary sobriety) to outright Prohibition (which sought to effect sobriety through law enforcement).

Frances Willard's leadership of the WCTU has much to do with the successful move from Temperance to Prohibition, and her religious outlook makes this move more understandable. First, Willard considered alcohol to be an enslaving substance. The inebriate could not free themselves from drink; their freedom came only through outside intervention from either God or his servants. If one considers alcohol to be such a dangerous slavemaster, it seems logical to suggest that people should not have access to it at all. Second, Willard saw alcohol as a threat to

Christendom. Speaking to audiences in England, Willard argued that "there are two serpents, intemperance and impurity, that have enclosed and are struggling with the infant Hercules of Christian Civilization," and implored that they "strike at both, for purity and total abstinence must go together."[58]

If one considers Willard's analogy, there is more to be said here, for the reference to Hercules suggests postmillennialist ideals. In Greek mythology, Hercules' jealous stepmother Hera dumps two venomous snakes into his crib as attempted infanticide, yet he is so strong that he crushes the snakes barehanded before they can harm him. Analogously, if Willard identified Christian civilization as something very young ("the infant Hercules"), this suggests not a premillennialist trajectory of civilizational decline, but rather a postmillennialist era where civilization is still growing up into maturity. The snakes of intemperance and moral impurity suggests something demonic, too—serpents that seek to kill Christian civilization before it can mature into adulthood have symbolic similarity to Pauline readings of the Eden snake.

Additionally, Willard's take is emblematic of what historian Suzanne M. Marilley has called the "feminism of fear." Marilley's argument is that Willard's "new and radical vision" about women's roles in society had less to do with "rights" and everything to do with "security." Marilley contends that Willard and the WCTU saw their mission as a "spiritual duty" to "celebrate and preserve creation," often using law as an instrument.[59] Marilley's argument is compelling, since the WCTU frequently presented both the home and the nation as endangered and themselves as warriors fighting to salvage dignity, sanctity, and sobriety. If "Christian civilization" meant the dawning of a postmillennialist utopia for Willard, then it was a utopia under threat and alcohol representing its fiercest enemy. Convincing other people that this was the case, then, paved the way for legal intervention.

As we will see, while some parts of the Drug War emulated the moral suasion strategies of Christian Temperance (especially education), it had much more in common with Prohibitionism. In 1920, the Volstead Act placed Prohibition in the US Constitution as the Eighteenth Amendment. If one accepts the premise that alcoholism is the same thing as slavery then law makes sense as a solution, especially in an American context. Abolitionists only managed to end slave labor through law and battle. Furthermore, if alcohol overrules drunkards' self-will and self-control, then no amount of persuasion can reach them—prohibiting alcohol is the only way to rescue them. Prohibitionists saw their work as a mission to save individuals from the predations of the alcohol industry and greedy saloonkeepers, and the United States itself from decay and demise.

Although Prohibition laws may have been nonsectarian, they were far from non-religious. Nor did many reformers want them to be. In 1911, the Anti-Saloon League reprinted an article from *The United Presbyterian*, which claimed that the church and the state "are both of God and both have to do with the great interests of men," arguing that Christian citizens must consider God's laws in relation to politics, and that they have a responsibility to see that morality "govern[s] us in all our relations."[60] Illinois Methodists articulated similar sentiments, arguing that the Church's job included "successfully attacking vices and social customs that have been safely entreated for ages," and tying this task to the fulfillment of an American covenant with God.[61] Episcopal Bishop Charles Henry Brent took a complementary approach, claiming that "a separation of Church and State, as in our own country, that separation does not mean divorce. . . . A great statesman must first be a great Christian."[62] After the Eighteenth Amendment was passed, Brent argued that it became a part of law as sacred as the Constitution itself, and "an integral part of the most sacred and binding obligation governing American citizenship . . . the man who disregards it is as disloyal a citizen as if he were a slave owner."[63] Wilbur Crafts, writing for the WCTU's *Union Signal*, argued that because the Supreme Court had declared government's primary objectives to be "public health and public morals," that Christians therefore had a duty to press for legal reform, arguing that "we can make morals by law precisely as we make health by law."[64] In context, Crafts explicitly identified Christianity as the basis for these morals, saying "the Supreme Court has left us no room to doubt" that Christian morals are what they meant. Thus, Prohibitionists' approach to law was frequently predicated on a blending of Protestant morality with transdenominational government.

Prohibitionists approached moral government both explicitly and implicitly. Some of their strategies were religious in very obvious ways, but other strategies were religious in ways that might not immediately register as "religion." Prayer meetings and days of fasting were common practices, for instance, and there's no hint of secularity with such activities. When Representative Richmond Hobson introduced a Prohibition resolution for congressional vote in December 1913, he also called for a united front from the nation's temperance societies. He wanted an entire week of lobbying, including "Prohibition sermons from all the pulpits of America," "resolutions in all Sunday Schools and Bible classes," with "telegrams of same the next day," and a "day of prayer."[65] Rallying churchgoers to political lobbying became a standard practice for prohibitionists, and in the 1900s and 1910s, formal petitioning came overwhelmingly from Protestant church organizations.

Protestant petitioning did not always cite morals or self-identified "religion" as the goal. During the temperance education push of the 1880s, for instance, Mary Hunt of the WCTU's "Department of Scientific Temperance Instruction" organized local branches to petition state and municipal school boards, and those petitions were to ask legislators to ensure that public school curricula reflect the "physiology and hygiene" problems caused by drinking.[66] In 1918, a United Brethren church in Oregon mailed a petition to Senator Wesley Jones, arguing that brewers wasted so many tons of grain, glucose, coal, cars, and men, and asked him to vote Prohibition war measures into place.[67] The First Baptist Church of Wentachee petitioned him about war- measure Prohibition as well, claiming that the United States was facing a "war emergency" that required protecting food security; to continue manufacturing alcohol from grain threatened "the loss of the cause for which we are fighting," a cause First Baptist identified as "Justice, Righteousness and World Democracy."[68] These arguments about waste, education, and security may seem like they fit into secular categories, but they were intractably entwined with Protestant religious mores. Additionally, any petition printed on church stationery is implicitly religious regardless of what specific topic it addresses or argument it makes—by declaring it the will of a specific congregation, it declares it to be a position formed by a community in conversation with their religious values.

Identifying America as endangered by alcohol was an important rhetorical strategy for Prohibitionist activities. Speaking before the United States House of Representatives in 1911, Richmond Hobson delivered a message that was later printed under the title *The Great Destroyer*. This speech made such threats explicit, arguing that if alcohol were not banned, then economic collapse, crime, and degeneracy (both physical and moral) would destroy America. Hobson framed this apocalyptically, arguing:

> In America we are making the last stand of the great white race and sub-stantially of the human race. If this destroyer can not be conquered in young America, it can not in any of the old and more degenerate nations. If America falls, the world will be undone and the human race will be doomed to go down from degeneracy into degeneracy till the Almighty in wrath wipes the accursed thing out.[69]

For Hobson, the Millennial Kingdom was one possible option but it was not a guarantee, and his eschatology wasn't always consistent. But before the Congress of the United States, Hobson emphasized a postmillennial future jeopardized by drinking, a utopia that could only be realized if America prohibited alcohol by law.

Hobson's language also demonstrates the white Christian national-ism embedded within many theologies of alcohol. In his construction, America had a special relationship with God and was poised to either help save the world or damn it. White Christian nationalism already had a long history in American Protestant theology—placing the United States as a central player in God's work on earth—and so Hobson's ren-dition wasn't especially unusual. It is however a good example of how easily that theology took specific moral concerns and interpreted them as universally important. Because God elected the United States to lead the world, any American shortcomings had global and ultimately cos-mic impact.

Another example comes from Elizabeth Tilton, who framed alcohol in similar terms in a booklet titled *Save America*. Tilton identified the United States as being in a war for "race survival" and drew upon the im-agery of Revelation to explain her position. If the "Red Cross Knights" (a reference to holy knights in Edward Spenser's *The Faerie Queene*) were the "saving remnant," then alcohol was "the dragon" of Revelation 12:17. Tilton framed this struggle as centuries old, arguing that the Pu-ritans started America's progress (progress that got "side-tracked" by abolitionism) and claiming that it was up to the present generation to lead America into ascendant sobriety.[70] Hobson and Tilton are representative of Prohibitionists' interpretations that alcohol devolved people into degenerates, increased crime, wasted resources, and was at its heart antithetical to God's plan for America and the world.

When evaluating Christian Temperance and Prohibitionism as Protestant projects, it's important to note the positions other Americans took—most notably, Jews and Catholics, the two largest groups of American non-Protestants in the era. Although some individual Jews participated in the Prohibition movement, by and large Protestants were unable to convince them to sign on. According to historian Marni Davis, this had less to do with sectarian identifications (such as the "Christian" part of "Woman's Christian Temperance Union") and far more to do with the fact that Jewish communities did not typically consider drunkenness to be an endemic problem in their own circles, and also because they resented the moral condescension that WCTU-style reformers aimed at anyone who drank even moderately.[71] In saying this, Davis is of course speaking in generalities, and some Jewish individuals chose to engage the Prohibition movement quite overtly. For example, the prominent rabbi Stephen Wise openly championed teetotaling on the grounds that the English eugenicist Caleb Saleeby convinced him that alcohol was a "race poison."[72] That said, race scientists often asserted that drunkenness was not a Jewish problem. The WCTU tried to open their organization to all faiths, but had little success attracting many non-Protestants into it. However, the support of folks like Wise allowed them to market their position as a moral universal rather than a specifically Protestant concern.

Catholics, on the other hand, often participated in the Christian Temperance movement. The Irish priest Theobald Mathew launched an anti-drinking crusade in Cork in 1838 and during the next 20 years helped shepherd it as a Catholic cause in both Ireland and the United States.[73] Catholic participation in Temperance politics was often uneasy, given the hegemonic goals many Protestant reformers openly espoused. Writing to his friend Martin Griffin, Father Ferdinand Kittell of Loretto, Pennsylvania stated that he had "voted the Prohibition national ticket in the campaign of '92" and that he "would become an out and out Prohibitionist" if it were not for certain factions within the movement, who "are continually harping about 'sectarian schools', and holding their meetings on religious lines."[74] In other words, the only thing holding Kittell back from fully supporting Prohibitionist politics was his interpretation that Prohibitionists were trying to insert Protestantism into more areas of public life than he was comfortable with. It is hard to fault Father Ferdinand for such a position since Protestant nativism had a long and antagonistic history of anti-Catholic positions and legal overtures by the time he wrote. Prohibition was part of a larger Protestant reform movement that sought to usher in the Millennial Kingdom; Jews and Catholics who participated in the legislative goals of these reforms did so because they felt alcohol posed a significant threat to individual communities or society at large, but they did not necessarily share in the same utopian eschatology of their Protestant cohorts.

However ecumenical the Christian Temperance and Prohibition movements may have been in membership, their end goals were forged from Protestant moral theologies, and their strategies reflected this. Postmillennialism is irremovable from the temperance ethos. Even if some individuals who participated in it held different, pessimistic eschatologies (premillennial Fundamentalists, for example), they were the seasoning on an optimistically utopian dish. Most reformers thought they could gain the results they wanted and see a better America emerge from it. Progressivism as a political ideal falls apart without the premise that better government is fully capable of creating positive social change; for lack of a better word, it requires a kind of faith. Additionally, the leading figures of the Temperance Movement were postmillennialist Protestants, and by virtue of their position, they were the ones who placed the goalposts—even when non-Protestants participated in the movement, they were usually aiming for Protestant outcomes.

Conclusions

This chapter has argued that Protestants—especially postmillennialist Protestants—generated and shepherded the Christian Temperance Movement into Prohibitionism, and that they treated alcohol as a complex enemy capable of damage. They saw drinking as a threat to American survival, private morals, social morals, liberty, Christendom, public health, public safety, sanity, productivity, and millennial progress, and they endeavored to do something about it. This is relevant to the Drug War in three ways.

The first way Christian Temperance and Prohibitionism relate to the Drug War is that reformers rarely drew a distinction between various substances. Alcohol was a type—the most common type—of narcotic poison. Temperance literature identified tobacco and opium as cognate threats as early as the 1820s. People were explicitly identifying alcohol as a "narcotic" by the end of the nineteenth century. The Drug War and Christian Temperance aren't necessarily separate things, then. There may be moments where it is analytically useful to think of them separately but their original critics didn't separate them. It may then be better to think of alcohol as one substance in the War on Drugs that has been decriminalized and legalized since its genesis. Furthermore, reformers' hostility toward alcohol and other substances shared the same rationale. What complaints people had of alcohol—its attendant immorality, criminality, racial degeneracy, health problems, and the threat to America—all of that was applied to other substances, too. Not one critique of alcohol covered in this chapter will disappear; all of them will resurface in the context of other kinds of substance use.

Second, the strategies that Prohibitionists and Temperance advocates employed (education campaigns, publications, organizing societies, individual persuasion, holding rallies, scientific arguments, legal and legislative intervention, and security claims) were all central to the antidrug movement as well. Many of the same Christian lobbyists who helped secure Prohibition (such as Richmond Hobson) also worked on the antinarcotic movement. The antidrug movement also reproduced the interfaith efforts that many Christian Temperance reformers had tried to attain, often with better success. The most important carryover was the ideological framework, particularly the blend of utopian postmillennialism with apocalyptic threat. America could change the world for the glory of God or else imperil it through unaddressed substance use. That ideal—birthed in Christian Temperance—was foundational for the Drug War.

Finally, it is important to pay attention to the moral language and the affective worlds it produced. The Leavitts, Willards, and Hobsons who threw themselves against alcohol with such passion—even sometimes willingly landing in jail—show how seriously reformers considered the problem. This was not a school levy or a commercial rezoning proposal, alcohol was a moral threat and a mortal threat. The idea that alcohol enslaved, and that this slavery produced perilous consequences for both the individual and the wider community, meant that those who sought to stop it often viewed themselves as heroic agents working to thwart a sinister and malevolent enemy. The postmillennialists among them (which was most of them) also saw themselves within a sacred, cosmic history. They participated in a divine plan to transform the world into the Kingdom of God. There are emotional stakes in that; being a player in sacred history can be energizing. Furthermore, the Kingdom advanced whether those outside of it recognized it or not; to transform one's public language into secular prose in no way cheapened this advance.

Judith Butler once noted that "if the public sphere is a Protestant accomplishment, as several scholars have argued, then public life presupposes and reaffirms one dominant religious tradition *as* the secular."[75] The moral criteria that Christian Temperance championed and elevated were born out of an explicitly religious context. They had biblical and theological reasons for caring about many of the things they did. As Temperance evolved into Prohibitionism, it began clothing itself in secular raiment, but its presuppositions and moralities were Protestant affirmations. There was a time in American history where people did not really consider it the job of government to control substance use, yet in our world today, such expectations are often taken for granted: *of course* governments control substance use. Christian Temperance is the bridge between those worlds. This movement took religious objections to drinking and lobbied for municipal, state, federal, and at times even international governments to control it. We acquired the legislative and police frameworks for regulating substance use from these religion-to-secular overtures.

2

Sin, Addiction, and Biomorality

Boise (1913)

In 1913 the Boise police arrested Fong Loon for murder. On the night of July 21, Fong Loon had apparently quarreled with a man named Fong Chung in the basement of a Chinese temple. According to Loon, Chung had pulled a gun on him, and Loon had therefore been forced to shoot Chung as a matter of self-defense. Investigators didn't accept his story and suspected there was more going on than what Loon was saying. Chung lay dying from his injury in St. Luke's Hospital for several days. Hoping to get more of the story, officials took advantage of this protracted death and sent a Chinese translator named Yee Wee along with a court stenographer to acquire Chung's legal testimony. Chung spoke no English and the Boise court officials spoke no Chinese—Yee Wee was the sole individual who understood both sides of the conversation. Chung died two days later.

It so happens that Yee Wee may also have enjoyed recreational opium, which turned out to be a serious problem for the Idaho courts. According to Yee Wee's translation, Chung had accused Loon of shooting him unprovoked at point blank range. Chung contended that the two men had no previous argument, that no one had been drinking, and that Loon's behavior was incomprehensible given its total lack of provocation. Loon simply walked into the room ready to fight and when Chung tried to deescalate the situation, Loon shot him in front of several witnesses. The court stenographer recording this conversation later described Chung's replies to Yee Wee as little more than animal grunts, casting doubt on their authenticity. More than a century later we are left with a mystery: Were the stenographer's doubts one more example of the casual anti-Chinese racism so commonplace in 1910s America, or did Yee Wee contrive a false testimony in front of a stenographer ignorant of

Chinese? Fong Loon's attorney had hoped to demonstrate that Yee Wee's alleged opium use naturally meant he was also a liar, but the trial court forbade Loon's lawyer from pursuing such questions.

The trial judge may have refused the admissibility of questions about Wee's opium use, but Fong Loon appealed his case and the Supreme Court of Idaho found that decision to have been a mistake. Justice Budge noted that Loon had been convicted of manslaughter (a serious offense for which Loon was facing a decade in jail) almost entirely on Yee Wee's story. The credibility of the translator was obviously a question of critical importance and the opium use was therefore relevant. Justice Budge claimed that opium produced two significant effects in habitual users: first, that opium use fogged the brain, meaning that potentially Yee Wee may not have remembered what questions were even being asked during the translation; and second, that opium indeed turned its users into liars. The court opined:

> We believe it will be admitted that habitual users of opium, or other like narcotics, become notorious liars. The habit of lying comes doubtless from the fact that the users of those narcotics pass the greater part of their lives in an unreal world, and thus become unable to distinguish between images and facts, between illusions and realities.
>
> In Wharton & Stille's *Medical Jurisprudence*, 3d ed., sec. 1111, it is said that "Of the mental symptoms," in the ease of a morphinomaniac or other habitual users of drugs, "the most characteristic, perhaps, are the moral perversions. The chronic morphinomaniac is often a confirmed liar. The truth is not in him. . . . There is something quite pathological in this mendacity; the lying is unblushing, inexpert, spontaneous,—a sort of second nature. . . . They have been so often narcotized, and thus cut off from actualities, living in a dreamstate, that they do not seem able to recognize realities when they see them."[1]

What the Idaho Supreme Court was arguing, then, was that medical experts identified substance abuse as a condition leading to immorality. This immorality was medical in nature—an opium user cannot help but lie since the lying was pathological. Justice Budge suggested that because of Yee Wee's moral incapacity it was possible that he merely imagined what sorts of things Fong Loon *could* have done in the situation and then conflated his own imagination with Chung's testimony. Given medical knowledge about immorality, Yee Wee's testimony couldn't be trusted. Idaho remanded the case and ordered a new trial for Fong Loon.

The *Fong Loon* case demonstrates the significance of what I call "biomorality," which refers to medical models of morality that identify it as a physiological function. Citing expert medical textbooks, Idaho threw out a murder conviction on the grounds that opium use made Yee Wee physiologically immoral. It wasn't just that Wee *chose* to be immoral, it was that opium had changed his physiology in such a way that he suffered innately from "moral perversion," as Budge phrased it. This kind of biologizing was typical for the early Drug War, and biomoral theories shaped approaches to both addiction and addicts. Biomorality informed medical treatments, legal strategies, and policy initiatives.

People today typically do not approach "morality" as a physiological category, yet earlier generations saw biomorality as so self-evident that they could confidently base court decisions on it. This chapter explains how and why biomoralists reached such conclusions. Interpretations of alcohol that considered it taxonomically related to narcotics were important supports for biomoral theory. Many early addiction theorists straddled both religion and medicine. The religious criticisms of alcohol were from the start equally applicable to opium misuse, and some people applied them to tobacco, too. As people became more familiar with habit-forming substances, the category expanded into what we now call "drugs," a category that is defined not by what the substances do physiologically (cocaine, heroin, and hashish affect the body very differently), but is rather a category putatively based on a substance's habit-forming potential. (A substance's social acceptability often matters more than its habit-forming capacity for whether people consider it a "drug.") The compulsive elements of addiction were still mysterious to nineteenth-century doctors and many reached divergent conclusions about how it worked. Some reduced addiction to merely a matter of willpower. Some people saw it as a kind of demonic force. Others interpreted it as a sort of madness. Nearly all interpretations though treated addiction and immorality as kindred.

As medical experts and reformers struggled to understand addiction, they frequently mapped their critiques of alcohol onto narcotics. Phrenology was particularly helpful for standardizing this view since phrenologists literally created maps. They treated the brain as the seat of human behavior and created a kind of cognitive cartography depicting which parts of the brain controlled which behavioral functions, including morals. Long after phrenology waned, some of their theories about narcotic use continued to inform understandings of addiction. Beyond phrenology, medical experts more broadly wed drug use to immorality—sometimes they claimed that substance use produced immoral behavior in people, and other times they argued that drug use was itself a symptom of more fundamental biomoral flaws intrinsic to the addict.

This chapter focuses primarily on the conceptual frameworks of addiction theories, but these ideas had consequences beyond just intellectual debate. Many of these ideas underpinned colonial interventions or criminal law. They also helped shape the US eugenics movement. Those who feared degeneracy (the degradation or devolution of individual physiologies, collective gene pools, or even civilizations) also engaged ideas about biology and morality; for them, biomorality was a key area of concern. Substance use would come to play a role in all of these and its discourse was consequential.

Narcotic Madness

There was considerable medical precedent when the Idaho Supreme Court decided that opium users lived in a permanent "dreamstate" where they couldn't distinguish reality from fantasy. Early nineteenth-century medical experts often interpreted the altered states of consciousness that some substances produce as a kind of temporary insanity. Nineteenth-century addiction theory was still underdeveloped, and not all experts agreed on the specifics. For American and British doctors, alcohol insanity and narcotic insanity were two sides of the same coin, with alcohol and narcotics frequently being classified together as different varieties of one thing. French doctors, on the other hand, treated alcoholism and drug addiction as separate categories, referring to drug addiction as "*toxicomanie*" (madness produced by intoxication).[2] American sources usually referred to addiction as a "habit" throughout much of the nineteenth century and referred to drug addicts as *habitués*. While many medical sources agreed that there was something compulsive about addiction, there was no consensus about what caused it.

Professional medical texts were not the only sources that identified narcotics as a source of madness. One of the most popular texts on this subject was Thomas De Quincey's lurid book, *Confessions of an English Opium-Eater*, first published in 1821. De Quincey's work held clout. For the next century, texts theorizing addiction frequently referenced it, treating it as a part of the data that informed their conclusions. De Quincey's descriptive language appeared repeatedly in books about addiction. *Confessions* described his opium experiences as "dreams," and more specifically, "Oriental dreams" filled with "an oppression as of madness" replete with "moral and spiritual terrors," along with the occasional "physical horror," too.[3] At the same time, he also saw opium as a source of potential revelation—but only for developed western minds. While De Quincey highlighted opium as essentially foreign in nature, he left some small space for civilized Europeans to make productive use of opium's mind-altering effects.[4] His depictions of opium dreams and moral terrors emphasized an accompanying emotional and contemplative chaos and his eventual misery produced a sad picture for readers. For those who wished to treat narcotics as a source of madness, De Quincey offered compelling evidence.

Jacques-Joseph Moreau's 1845 work *Hashish and Mental Illness* had a cultural impact similar to De Quincey's, proffering the notion that substance use creates temporary madness. Moreau wrote, "there is not a single, elementary manifestation of mental illness that cannot be found in the mental changes caused by hashish," by which he meant that the full spectrum of mental illnesses were available for sampling through hashish use.[5] Dr. Moreau had stylistic flair and Euro-American elites devoured his medical book. Moreau colorfully detailed both others' use of hashish as well as his own. Hashish caused manic fits of giggling, terrifying and tactile hallucinations, mercurial mood swings, and an inability to reason. Moreau wrote that he felt "millions of insects eating my head," described falling down "an immense, bottomless shaft, the well of Bicêtre," and claimed that he attempted to duel a bowl of candied fruit using a spoon as a weapon.[6] In a particularly significant passage, Moreau recounts that he felt compelled to sit at the piano and play a bit of the opera *Black Domino*, when

I interrupted myself after several measures because a truly diabolic spectacle greeted my eyes: I thought I saw the image of my brother standing atop the piano. He stirred and presented a forked tail, all black and ending with three lanterns, one red, one green, and one white. This apparition presented itself to me several times during the course of the evening. I was sitting under a canopy. "Why," I suddenly cried, "do you nail down my limbs? I feel as if I am turning into lead. Oh, I am so heavy!" They took my hands to raise me, and I fell heavily to the ground. I kneeled in the manner of the Moslems, saying, "My father, I accuse myself, etc.," as though I was starting confession.[7]

Moreau's own religious outlook is ambiguous in the text, but we can reasonably extrapolate how this passage would have registered to Protestant readers. The content of his madness is clearly demonic (as are some of the other visions he described); it invokes the language of crucifixion ("why do you nail down my limbs?"); and it merges a Muslim prayer posture with a Catholic confession that is delivered to no one. Not only did Moreau serve as an early, influential source for thinking about pharmacological insanity, he also invoked a dark religious gallimaufry in which many American audiences would have seen barbarism's sigils. Given that Moreau's book emerged at the high point of nineteenth-century American nativism, we could reasonably expect that at least some readers would have recoiled at the Catholic content of his visions. The spectacle of the doctor crucified before a devil obviously would have translated into a negative reading of hash for Christian readers, for there were very few circumstances in which nineteenth- or twentieth-century Christians of any stripe encouraged willful exposure to hallucinated demons. In short, De Quincey and Moreau produced detailed accounts of irrational, bizarre, and frightening behavior brought on by their substance use, thereby offering sober readers mediated knowledge of substance use.

Theorists often saw addiction itself as a kind of madness. Nineteenth-century observers formed many theories as they sought to understand it, but at the end of the day they were all grappling with the question of undesirable-yet-compulsive behavior. Many people were puzzled by the fact that someone might genuinely wish to abandon substance use yet could not step away from their drug. Some considered that this might represent a cognitive flaw, some degenerative quirk of mental failure.

Others thought perhaps it was a matter of volitional sin and that addicts were not really *unable* to quit, they were actually *unwilling* to quit. Some wondered if perhaps parentage had something to do with the matter. (Such confusion over the nature of addiction also ushered in a golden era for selling questionable and quack addiction cures.) Yet whichever way they leaned interpretively, addiction theorists overwhelmingly treated addicts' compulsions as a kind of partial or total insanity.

Many of the models for narcotic madness reproduced those of alcohol insanity. In nineteenth-century literature this often had to do with the idea that addiction fed a nervous energy depletion—opium, alcohol, and other substances were ways for the body to make up for something it lacked. The hallucinatory powers attributed to alcohol, opiates, madness, and religious visions also made these phenomena close cousins in the minds of many nineteenth-century Americans.[8] Taxonomically speaking, alcohol and narcotics were often understood to be the same thing. Writing in 1893 of "narcomania," for instance, addiction specialist T. D. Crothers explained that "opium mania is only one member of this family." Alcoholism, cocaine, or other substances would likely replace it if the addict were left to their own devices.[9] Classifying these substances together remained a common approach into the twentieth century. The 1934 book *Narcotics and Youth Today* was almost entirely about alcohol. Opiates and nicotine were mentioned only briefly as other varieties, which makes the title odd unless the author considered alcohol to be one subcategory of narcotics.[10]

Alcohol was often classified narcotically, though not always; sometimes it was classified as a stimulant, especially in the nineteenth century. Such categories were not fixed, and declarations that "item A" is a stimulant or narcotic often represented the author's best guess about how a particular substance worked rather than reflecting any permanent scientific classification. At any rate, the common placement of alcohol among the narcotics encouraged experts to interpret it as a model for understanding other substances. Just as halogens like chlorine and fluorine bind similarly at the atomic level, or an assortment of sharks can have similar skeletons, scales, and eggs, the various subcategories of "narcotic" implicitly had similarities beyond their mere sedative nature. By this kind of logic, if alcohol could be said to cause a certain behavior, then opium and other narcotics should be predictably similar.

When it came to how madness worked physiologically, nineteenth- and early twentieth-century medical discourse was in flux. Benjamin Rush and other doctors thought alcohol madness was produced by organ damage—sometimes that damage was located in the brain, sometimes the liver, sometimes elsewhere. Beecher observed that alcohol madness included emotional disturbances (particularly uncontrolled, irrational anger), irreligiosity, and physical pain upon being touched. Doctors were also preoccupied with the physical shaking and occasional hallucinations that plagued those suffering from delirium tremens. With great frequency medical and religious texts saw immorality—and by extension, criminality—as products of alcohol madness, and then read that onto narcotics, too.

We should be fair to those in the nineteenth century who were trying to unravel the mysteries of addiction since there can be some overlap between alcohol symptoms and those of opium and since some of their interpretations of addiction were not so different from how contemporary doctors with access to a great deal more medical research would understand the problem. Opiate withdrawal can include emotional distress, physical pain (including pain upon being touched), a compulsion to acquire more opiates to relieve the withdrawal symptoms, unpredictable behavior and chatter, and physical shaking or convulsions similar to those of delirium tremens.[11] Because alcohol and opium both have anesthetic properties, some of the consequences of their use as well as their withdrawal are similar. Opium has a stronger effect, which can be useful for dulling chronic pain, yet may in the long run create a heightened sensitivity to pain once quit.[12] Nineteenth- and early twentieth-century reports posited that during the earliest stages of withdrawal, addicts' pain sensitivity was so heightened that they would feel "every nerve in the body," leading them to recoil at breezes, feel their feet burning, or feel their bones.[13] Well into the twentieth century medical reports also accused addicts of consistently inventing or exaggerating their withdrawal symptoms. The description of such arcane bodily knowledge could easily be read as madness to those who had not experienced it firsthand.

Nearly every medical textbook today would acknowledge that substance use affects cognitive processes. Nineteenth-century doctors didn't have the medical technology necessary to study neuropeptides or opioid receptors, so their answer to *how* substance use altered thought and behavior quite naturally doesn't resemble contemporary explanations. It also wasn't entirely clear where concepts like individual personality or morality fit into cognition. Early addiction theorists felt certain that substance use affected both personality and moral capacity, and so it was perhaps a natural jump for many of them to assert that personality and morality were biological in nature since they could be pharmacologically modified. Phrenology was also interested in what a person's brain and skull shape could tell examiners about this, and phrenologists offered biomoral models that were consequential for interpretations of substance use.

Phrenology

Cognitive studies were still young in the early nineteenth century. The phrenological model treated the brain as the cognitive organ (a position not yet universally accepted), and more specifically, it treated the brain as a conglomeration of sub-organs that each performed different functions.[14] These sub-organs, more commonly referred to as "faculties," governed specific behaviors or drives, ranging from basic animal instincts (such as "instinct of self-defense" or "instinct of propagation") to higher-order attributes (such as "talent for poetry" or "comparative sagacity").[15] Lending credence to this model was the Phineas Gage case. In 1848 Gage had a metal shaft driven through his skull during a horrifying railroad construction accident. Gage survived but unsurprisingly he suffered permanent brain damage. Whereas Gage had previously been known as a man of "temperate habits" and one who was of polite, earnest, and kind-hearted character, the brain damage led to significant personality changes.[16] Phrenologists argued that this personality change was caused by the metal rod damaging the faculties for "veneration" and "benevolence." Because the metal rod had ripped these faculties away from his brain, Gage was now unable to treat people kindly or be respectful of moral norms. The Gage case is one reason among many that people found phrenology plausible, understanding the brain to be the site of multiple personality traits that could be harmed or improved within certain limits.

Phrenological models of mind competed well among other nineteenth-century interpretations, with many people accepting it as viable, valid science.[17] Because many understood it as valid science, it was therefore considered useful for drafting new policies, informing other branches of knowledge, or influencing various realms of human social life. For Christian interpreters, phrenology also offered important theological insights. God had shaped each part of the human anatomy to fulfill a certain function, including the mental faculties. Although some early phrenologists such as Franz Joseph Gall saw the mind as naturally oriented toward vice and in need of control, other phrenologists such as Johan Spurzheim saw the mind as fundamentally oriented toward virtuosity. Spurzheim also saw history as a progress narrative, with humans gradually developing toward better versions of their ancestors; this positive evolution could be observed in religion, too.[18] Indeed, certain parts of the mind were built specifically for religiosity; even Gall's list enumerated "moral sense" and "God and Religion" as mental faculties. Many other models also included "veneration" as a faculty.

What this means is that phrenology offered a geography for religion: Religiosity was a biological product of thought and could be mapped onto human brains. If those brains were damaged (such as with Phineas Gage), then religiosity could disappear. The devout exercised their religious faculties (including morality) and thus enlarged those portions of their brains, attaining greater degrees of religious and moral skill. Although some phrenologists might interpret this to mean that religion was a product of biological accident and that perhaps God was not so much a reality as a vestigial organ run amok, that was an unpopular reading for Americans. Instead, American phrenologists tended to see it as indicative of divine design; God had crafted an awe-inspiring organ to govern human behavior.

What makes phrenology relevant here is that it helps show the range of ways people understood madness and brain function. Biomorality was not the only game in town. Some Protestants, for instance, understood insanity as the product of "moral irregularities and excessive passions."[19] In such a model, mental illness is best explained not by biological disorder, but by sin—the immorality is that which causes insanity, not the other way around. Even in cases where biological origins were thought responsible for madness (such as brain lesions), caretakers often focused upon behavioral or moral reformation as treatment.[20] Americans often balked at European models of the body that reduced humanity down to flesh and flesh alone. American theorists who accepted biological models of insanity frequently tried to avoid coming across so reductively, with some even treating the mind as an immortal thing different than the brain.[21] In other words, for many American medical theorists, the brain was undoubtedly a biological structure that could be tampered with, impeded, deteriorated, or broken, but an inviolable mind existed independently of any biological structures. The mind and the brain are not the same thing in that case, rather, the mind is a kind of spiritual entity with which the brain interacts or mediates. At any rate, biological theories of madness and brain damage went hand-in-hand for many of these theorists; if a brain were harmed, it would malfunction.

Phrenology becomes most interesting in its contributions to interpreting substance use as well as how substance use affects religiosity. As historian David Stack has argued, phrenologists such as William Lovett saw alcohol as a substance which "irritated and excited the brain," whose long-term use caused serious cognitive damage.[22] Alcohol could "harden" certain membranes, leaving drinkers to their baser, animal instincts and obliterating the higher faculties that accounted for civilized behavior. Recall though that those highest order faculties for phrenologists were things like religiosity, veneration, and morality. The assertion that alcohol damaged the most sensitive parts of the brain first meant that religious faculties would be the first to go. In short: For those who accepted phrenology as valid science, its implications were that drinkers were medically less moral and less capable of religion.

These phrenological interpretations outlived phrenology itself. Phrenology contributed to antidrug and anti-alcohol positions in a number of ways, but the most significant intervention came via Richmond Pearson Hobson, who was a Spanish-American War hero, a congressman, an Anti-Saloon League orator, and eventually a major figure in antidrug activism. His phrenological interpretations are important for thinking about its reach and the way it shaped attitudes toward substance use. Hobson's anti-substance campaigns occurred in the early twentieth century, first with alcohol and then with narcotics. Although he rarely named his arguments as phrenological, it is clear from context that this was his cognitive model, and his personal papers include phrenological ephemera.

Hobson believed that alcohol and narcotics destroyed brain tissue. Of alcohol, he said that "there is no tissue or organ that is safe from its attack" but that the brain was especially affected.[23] Dogs that were given alcohol would deteriorate physically and mentally and then never recover. According to Hobson, this effect was worse in humans. In a circular letter written during his time in Congress, he argued that alcohol "attacks the blood, and especially paralyzes and gradually tears down the top part of the brain (the seat of character), causing degeneracy, which carries with it crime, pauperism, insanity, entails disease and untimely death and blights the lives of children unborn."[24] The phrenological model is clearer here than it is in many of Hobson's later arguments and it is important for understanding his interpretations of substance use, since his greater transparency in early speeches allows one to confidently detect his more subtle uses of phrenology in later materials. For Hobson, morality was located in the "top of the brain" and could be damaged by alcohol, leading to degeneracy that manifests in immoral and criminal behavior among other medical dysfunctions. Hobson's geography for moral degeneracy would have been at home in almost any nineteenth-century phrenology textbook.

Hobson took the same approach when interpreting narcotics. In a document submitted to both the Democrat and Republican Conventions in 1924 (a document well-received by both), he used the same phrenological model. In this case Hobson argued that "Narcotics are especially dangerous to the upper brain and the organs of reproduction. A person taking narcotics regularly impedes evolutionary progress and tends to degenerate backwards toward the brute."[25] The phrasing is specific enough to be recognizable as phrenology for those aware of its correspondent models yet indirect enough to not necessarily call strong attention to itself. It also mirrors the alcohol model exactly; not only is the "upper brain" the primary site of damage, but its attendant degeneracy and devolution exist here as well. Using very similar language in 1932, Hobson went one step further when explaining drugs to the students of Phi Delta Kappa at New York University, saying that

> The narcotic poison penetrating the upper brain naturally inflicts the deepest and swiftest injury upon the parts that are the tenderest, the most complex and unstable, which are developed latest in human evolutionary progress and distinguish the man from the brute. The transformation in character is swift in the young, and swifter with cocaine and heroin than with the other narcotics.[26]

For Hobson, the brain was a biological structure evolving in stages, with human moral and spiritual functions serving as the most significant distinguishing feature separating humans from baser animals. Additionally, it shows that Hobson treated narcotics as functioning in the same manner, but that some substances worked faster than others. Last, youth were more vulnerable as their bodies and minds had not yet matured into the fullness of stable or semi-stable adulthood. In short, the anti-substance positions Hobson deployed in his twentieth-century reform movements made robust use of phrenology as an underlying logic.

Biomorality

Regardless of whether one accepted phrenology or not, many (if not most) substance use reformers included morality as a biological concern. The notion that biology shapes or houses morality is inseparable from the early Drug War. Phrenologists like Hobson mapped it onto the brain, but other medical experts (including those with no evidence of phrenological sympathies) claimed the same principle: Immorality was a medical symptom. Anti-alcohol literature often identified morality as medical terrain, and this concept carried over into antinarcotic discourse as the early Drug War escalated. Dr. J. H. Kellogg argued in 1894 that just like alcohol, opium destroys "the mental and moral faculties. Self-control and self-respect are lost. Reputation, honor, friends, wealth—everything is sacrificed for the gratification of the artificial appetite."[27] Writing for *The American Journal of Psychology* in 1900, George E. Dawson referred to alcoholics and drug addicts as "improvident" and "generally deficient in [their] moral and intellectual perceptions." He added that

> the sense of personal honor is one of the highest attainments in evolution. Destroy this sense, and almost everything else comes easy. Theft or dishonesty of any kind is always attended with falsehood and deception, and is often attended with such a loss of self-respect that vice of every description is recklessly indulged in.[28]

T. D. Crothers, writing for the *Journal of the American Medical Association* in 1899, argued that opiates produced "a palsy of the higher psychic centers" in which "the personality of the former person is lost," and that this "psychic wreckage" symptomatically led to criminal behavior.[29] In some cases the causal relationship was reversed, with addicts electing to use narcotics because they were already moral degenerates.[30] In 1936, *The New England Journal of Medicine* explained that addicts used drugs because they wished to flee the human condition.

> No mortal healer is able to offer them better substitutes for the unbearable realities from which they seek to escape. . . . The ranks of psychopathic addicts claim many of this class for chronic "neurotics," alcoholics, narcotic addicts, and other social, moral and legal transgressors; for there are many people who are unsuited by native intelligence, ability, and training to assume more than a very limited degree of responsibility, independence, and maturity.[31]

None of those examples come from minor sources and they show how thoroughly biomoral models permeated addiction theory. Overall, the majority of American medical texts dealing with narcotics (and virtually all non-medical assessments of the subject) agreed that narcotic abuse either symptomatically led to immorality or was the product of it.

Biomorality was fundamental to the early Drug War and even if it has since waned as a medical model, the ethos of repudiation that it fostered—the urge to exile addicts for their failures to behave responsibly—continues today. Professional scholars may already be well-acquainted with the idea that medicine can be a site of moralization, but such concepts are not always well-known beyond academia. To be sure, medicine represented a major component of early Drug War discourse, practice, and rationale. Medicine should not however be mistaken for a neutral site of pure truth.

In their study of religion and the AIDS crisis, Anthony Petro offers a helpful example of this principle that may be more accessible to some. Petro argues that "morality doubles as both a religious and secular concept, often becoming the site of translation between the two. This is particularly true for moral claims about health."[32] Petro's argument is compelling: When the AIDS crisis broke in the early 1980s, observers noted the close ties between infection and gay sex. Because gay sex was still popularly understood to be deviant (particularly in US Christian communities), AIDS was thereby cast as "a disease of sexual immorality." The moral objections to gay sex derived in large part from conservative Christian theology. One of Petro's main points is that medicine's neutrality is sometimes more aspirational than real—public health responses were extraordinarily hard to separate from religious moral expectations. Treatment solutions, research funding, and health advice were dominated by federal policies shaped to favor those conservative Christian moralities. There was no reason for the Reagan administration to support treatments for a disease that only occurred in people who failed at the moral obligations that people demanded of them. Although AIDS and drug addiction are different phenomena, morality's ability to translate religious conviction into public health policy is similar.

If biomoralists are right and morality is indeed governed by cognitive biology, then damage to addicts' biomoral centers constituted a health problem as well as a social one. In early substance use discourse, the concepts of immorality and madness are cousins. Both require a normative model of cognition in order to be legible. Insanity is defined by its relationship to normative thought (the insane cannot think or behave "normally"). If substance use causes insanity, and if that insanity leads to immorality, then substance use therefore needs to be controlled for the benefit of individuals, communities, and nations. Not only does halting drugs preserve individuals' mental and somatic integrity, it also preserves societal stability. Mad or immoral addicts break rules, including legal ones. They lie. They steal. They visit ladies of the night. They debauch youth. They swear. They undermine the economy. They gamble on horses. They threaten American society, and the reason is that the substances which destroyed their capacity for sane, moral goodness also make slaves of them. This was the argument that biomoralists made for controlling substance use.

Biomoral theories meant that while many reformers were willing to accept that addiction constituted a medical problem, their solutions trended toward the punitive as time went on. Addicts were pitiful, but they were also dangerous. By the twentieth century many people assumed that accidental medical addiction was a thing of the past and therefore drug addicts had become addicts through their reckless and immoral choices. Although some doctors and reformers would have preferred to treat addicts gently, the weight of public opinion—and eventually the police force of law—gradually pushed in the direction of prison, sterilization, and other forms of institutional restraint as solutions for addiction.

Religious opinions shaped how this biomoral crisis played out. Protestant moralities typically expected industriousness, conscientious care for one's body, the proper use of money, rationality, veneration of and respect for God, and the avoidance of vice—especially vices of illicit physical pleasure. Addicts fell short of these and other moral expectations. Biomorality allowed reformers to portray these contingent moral positions as secular, scientific truths. If morality and religiosity were indeed physiological functions of the brain, this essentially transmuted religion and morality into non-subjective medical facts. Religion and morality become products of biological well-being in this model. Dominant moral norms—those things for which people were accountable to one another—were derived from religion, but as manifestations of physiology they suddenly became scientific truth that existed independent of doctrine or dogma.

The Nature of Addiction

In the nineteenth and early twentieth centuries, medical, theological, and social theorists endeavored to comprehend the nature of addiction. What was it that drove people toward this madly compulsive behavior? Why did drunkards and opium habitués throw away their money on poison? How could material substances produce such disturbing psychological states? These were points of debate. Because theorists had already begun wrestling with the nature of alcoholism in decades prior, those working in the late nineteenth and early twentieth centuries already had some existing models to work with; alcohol addiction theories were conscripted into service for narcotics. However, there was little consensus on how addiction functioned in this era, and some doctors did not even consider addiction to be real.[33]

The earliest nineteenth-century addiction theorists often saw the body as a balance of humoral fluids and nervous energy, and/or as a machine that operated on mechanistic principles.[34] ("Nervous" here means "of the nerves" rather than "anxious.") Medical theorists frequently treated opiates and alcohol as agents that numbed, drained, or deadened the nervous flow, and some suggested that addiction was merely an overindulgence, and a dangerous one at that. By 1840, these notions of nervous energy had filtered through the early Christian Temperance Movement, and by 1880, the New York neurologist George Beard was using "neurasthenia" to explain addiction. What Beard meant by "neurasthenia" is that some bodies had insufficient nervous energy. Neurasthenic bodies autonomically sought to remedy this shortage using artificial replacements for that missing power, which neurasthenics experienced as cravings.[35] According to Beard, if nervous deficiencies were successfully treated, then this would allow addicts to recover, since the underlying medical reason for neurasthenic cravings would no longer exist. To draw an analogy, this model could be compared to a locomotive: When a train travels too slowly, adding coal into the furnace will improve the heat and therefore the steam production. Once the locomotive reaches its proper speed, the engineer no longer needs to feed it. Beard's neurasthenic model saw the body as operating similarly. Bodies need a certain amount of nervous energy, and the compulsion to consume substances was the body's natural way to make up for an energy deficit; finding a natural nervous equilibrium would therefore cure addiction.

Morphine use increased after the mid-nineteenth century along with a correspondingly greater interest in addiction phenomena. From the 1870s onward, addiction occupied a more prominent place in medical debate and Beard's model was not the only one in use.[36] That lack of consensus was partly due to the fact that addiction theory was still relatively new, and because there was no uniformly accepted medical model of how bodies worked as a physiological whole. Additionally, doctors were sometimes suspicious that other, divergent positions were either quackery or financially motivated chicanery, genuine problems that the American Medical Association sought to address as early as 1849.[37]

Medical interpretations of addiction tended to emphasize several features: the centrality of the nervous system to addiction, the process of habituation, and moral deterioration. In 1903, for instance, *Journal of the American Medical Association* suggested that "any new drug that can affect the nervous system seems to obtain its habitués," citing opiates and cocaine as interpretive models.[38] In an influential book, Dr. Albrecht Erlenmeyer suggested that while alcoholism tends to be found most often in the lower classes, "morphinomania" tends to be found within the upper. "The morphine vice" is derived from medical ministrations that extend too long, and as "a protoplasmic poison," morphine "by its actions on the higher nervous centres [. . .] undoes the finished results of evolution," which is to say that "the individual becomes more and more like the brute or automaton."[39] In a study of opium addiction, Dr. Frederick Hubbard wrote that "the subtle influence of the drug is felt in every fibre of the nervous system," and that withholding the opium produced complicated spasms, distress, which meant addiction was a nervous disease and was not therefore "subject to the will."[40] Directly contrary to Hubbard's argument, the *Maryland Medical Journal* suggested that addiction was the product of a "weak will" and usually occurred with drugs that offered "pleasant dreams, delightful sensations, and are stimulating."[41] Some theorists saw addiction as symptomatic of inferior heredity.[42] Some theories suggested that for some addicts all substances were interchangeable—as an 1885 health book argued, such addicts "are not opium or chloral habitués, nor inebriates from alcohol, but they are habituated to artificial narcotism."[43] The range of these explanations demonstrates that doctors were somewhat mystified by the relationship between narcotics and willpower, but also shows that most theorized some sort of cognitive damage led to the alienation of free will.

In the twentieth century it became more common for medical experts to suggest that addiction was uncontrollably compulsive. Writing in 1913, Dr. George Pettey argued:

> Thousands of the most wretched and helpless of all human beings are being constantly and openly stigmatized as degenerates, willful perverts, inveterate liars, and fiends, and are having numerous other epithets of reproach and condemnation heaped upon them for continuing a course of conduct to which they are impelled by forces that it is totally beyond their power to resist.[44]

Pettey cited several of the leading experts (including Erlenmeyer) to validate his claim that withdrawal symptoms illustrated the levels of bondage within which substance use chained addicts, and to criticize the dominant notion that addicts could simply give up narcotics if they only wanted to.[45] In 1920, Dr. Ernest Bishop made a similar observation, arguing

The conception of drug addiction as a "habit" has, however, in the past so overwhelmingly dominated the attitude of writers both medical and lay, that consideration of withdrawal signs as physical phenomena, and the analysis of their origin and mechanism on the basis of physical disease and constant body reaction has received all too little attention. The tendency has been to casually regard or belittle them as a part of the essential picture of narcotic addiction, and to place overwhelming emphasis upon mental desire as an explanation of the drug addict's inability to discontinue the administration of opiate drugs.[46]

According to Bishop, one reason people misunderstood addiction as voluntary was because they misunderstood substance use as intrinsically pleasurable. When people are first introduced to opiates, the sensation is one of satisfying relaxation and lightness. But Bishop noted that these feelings disappear as time goes on, and after awhile the relationship addicts have to their substance becomes inverted—they do not feel pleasure when administering their drug, only feel relief from the misery and pain that they experience without it. Bishop and Pettey represented a viewpoint that addiction was compulsive and contradicted a position still commonplace in their day that addicts were voluntary pleasure seekers.

However, even among those who recognized addiction as a compulsive, uncontrollable behavior, there were some who treated addiction as coterminous with moral decline. Writing in 1923, 15 doctors coauthored an article for the *New York State Journal of Medicine*. They argued that

Contrary to popular belief, the majority of narcotic habitues are criminals, with criminal records in the courts. In fact, narcotism is so involved with criminality, that to relax police vigilance over the one is to enhance the other. [. . .] When a criminal addict is confined in a penal institution, he should be placed in the section devoted to mental defectives, for there is almost always some mental defect or inferiority associated with addiction, and the medical man is best qualified to direct its treatment.[47]

Such claims were common. Similar theorists frequently argued that criminality and addiction were overlapping conditions. Crime frequently was seen as a product of biology in this era and morality represented a special concern for criminology.[48] It is no surprise then that substance use, which was seen as a demoralizing agent, should be so closely tied to criminality. The fact that addiction was irresistibly compulsive made it more dangerous; as a cultivator of criminal immorality, substance use transformed addicts into agents of chaos who needed to be controlled since they could not control themselves.

Addiction Treatment

Medical commentators disputed whether addiction was treatable. The idea that addiction could be treated required viewing it as an uncontrollable compulsion rather than a self-chosen habit. Those who viewed it as a volitional choice advised addicts to just stop using drugs—the only cure was for an addict to simply quit. For those who thought addiction resided somewhere beyond patients' freewill, the question of curability was debatable—some said yes, others said no. Many theorists in this era argued for a tepid "yes," suggesting that addiction *was* treatable, but that most patients would never actually make it to victory.

Addiction treatment was a lucrative business. Many addicts did not wish to be as they were and were willing to sacrifice financially for a chance at freedom. In 1887, a laudanum addict in Ohio mailed $15 to a doctor in the Bahamas in exchange for a cure, promising an additional $10 upon successful treatment.[49] ($25 in 1887 would be over $600 today.) A decade later rehabilitation centers came into vogue, marketed on the premise that addicts who tried to recover at home had too much room to relapse and were unable to overcome their moral shortfalls alone.[50] Specific treatments varied. A plan described in 1904 involved a lengthy stay at a rehabilitation hospital, which included several days without alcohol or narcotics, followed by diarrhetics, Turkish baths, strychnine, codeine, and mandrake.[51] Some tried to cure addiction with hypnotics: Patients would be administered substances like chloral or hyoscine and kept asleep until the withdrawal symptoms wore off.[52] Psychological treatments also emerged, ranging from hypnosis to counseling; some counselors assessed addiction as an inability to face or cope with reality.[53] Rehabilitation homes—an evolved version of the asylum—were one common approach to addiction treatment, but so too were mail order medications, most of which were fraudulent.[54] Some of the more famous treatment centers, such as the chain of centers known as the Keeley Institutes, sold their own addiction medicines.[55] The early era of the Drug War witnessed no consensus as to how addiction could be successfully treated.

In the American context, medical experts often considered that gradual or sudden relinquishment of the habit was the only way out of addiction. In 1918, the *American Journal of Nursing* proposed that addiction was treatable so long as toxicities are allowed to dissipate. Nurses and doctors were tasked with "assisting [addicts] out of their slavery to alcohol or drugs," but needed patience, for

> According to the laws of psycho-physical parallelism, every mental action has a corresponding physical reaction and vice versa; consequently the person whose body is poisoned by the intemperate use of alcohol and drugs cannot, for the time being, think or act normally.[56]

In this approach, only time can treat the problem, and the end of withdrawal indicates the end of addiction and madness.

There were also many naysayers who understood such treatments to be temporary at best. According to John O'Connor, a surgeon from the New York City Department of Corrections writing in 1927,

> Whether we regard drug addiction as a disease or as a habit we find ourselves confronted with the same inescapable conclusion: there is no permanent "cure" for the unfortunate who has become addicted to narcotics. There is no medicine that can develop an immunity to recurrence of the craving that sends the addict again and again to the unscrupulous vendors who ply their hellish traffic with mind only for the enormous profits to be wrung from their all too willing victims.[57]

The only real cure according to Dr. O'Connor was to prevent addiction before it began, using education and legal controls as strategies.

In 1929 the editorial staff of the *New England Journal of Medicine* also saw addiction as an incurable problem via medication.

> We can definitely answer here that no disease of psychogenic origin, such as alcoholism, is cured by any medicine. The alcohol habit can only

be cured by the patient himself, exactly the same as any other habit is stopped. The cure must be in large part voluntary, although much can be done by removing the source of the patient's habit.[58]

NEJM went on to add that "drug cures" are a slightly different matter since "one may substitute, at least temporarily, a drug of lesser habit formation in order to rid the patient of a stronger one. On the other hand, the principles of curing a disease of psychogenic origin should apply to drugs exactly as they apply to alcoholism." *NEJM* wasn't claiming that addiction was incurable, it was rejecting purely mechanistic causes; in some cases medication might make abstinence easier, but addiction was only conquered through a patient's own willpower.

Maintenance treatment represented another approach in the United States until 1919, when its legal status changed.[59] (This treatment continued to be practiced elsewhere in the world.) Maintenance treatment is the administration of reduced narcotic dosage to addicts, usually in cases where addicts are considered too far gone for saving, and usually continuing for as long as the addict wishes. Occasionally the term also applied to situations where continually reduced dosage was intended to wean an addict off narcotics. Withdrawal symptoms can be brutal and sometimes dangerous, particularly if it is sudden and immediate rather than a gradual tapering off. Period sources noted that withdrawal symptoms can include depression, violent spasms, uncontrolled vomiting, and death. *The Lancet* claimed in 1916 that regardless of whether the patient was normal or degenerate, these withdrawal symptoms of morphinism are inescapable, since they are the result of "material cause and effect."[60] Some doctors felt that to impose such suffering on addicts— especially when they thought the addiction unbeatable—violated their professional ethic to "do no harm." Maintenance treatment was thus a way to honor the "do no harm" principle while discouraging runaway addiction (and by extension, overdoses), and it made sense as a solution for those who considered addiction to be incurable.

Religious Approaches

Medical doctors were not the only ones theorizing addiction; theologians (both lay and formal) had their own interventions. Many considered medical science a relevant source of knowledge for understanding addiction and they merely brought religion into the picture in order to contextualize substance use spiritually. Others rejected medical interpretations outright, favoring religious interpretations exclusively. It is tempting to say that hybrid medical-spiritual interpretations dominated the field, but the historical record is not robust enough to evaluate this question as definitively as one might like. Most religious texts intervening in narcotic addiction acknowledged its habitual nature but did not offer any theories about how addiction worked. Furthermore, the medical-religious split is not easily made. Many doctors incorporated Christianity in their texts and many Christians without medical training still included medical knowledge in their understanding of drugs. The distinction here between "medical" texts and "religious" ones is therefore more an evaluation of the dominant themes and intended use of a source—that is, whether a work was meant to inform medical students or energize Christians. Most of the religious sources examined here accepted medical science as a valid interpretive lens. These medical explanations for addiction (often centered on nervous energy) did not undermine what was to be a long-lived religious reading of addiction: Narcotic abuse is volitional sin.

The celebrated nineteenth-century Presbyterian preacher, Reverend Thomas De Witt Talmadge of the Brooklyn Tabernacle, offers a good example of the addiction-as-sin model. In a jeremiad about tobacco use, Talmadge compared it to opium, hashish, and chloral addictions, arguing that tobacco acted upon the nerves until it took more and more of it to bring the user to normalcy. He also treated tobacco use as a volitional choice, though, insisting that his congregants free themselves of it, and suggesting that "One reason the evil thrives is because so many ministers smoke."[61] Talmadge recounted his own struggles with nicotine, explaining that in days gone by he had confronted his temptation when a Philadelphian tobacconist offered him unlimited free cigars if he would move there to preach. According to Talmadge, this moment of temptation was his moment of awakening wherein he instantly gave up smoking forever. Given the explicit comparison of tobacco with opium, chloral, and cannabis, as well as the identified equivalency of nicotine with these other narcotics, Talmadge implied that all addictions can be abandoned in this way.

Another theological intervention came from Charles Bunting, a caretaker at the New York Home for Intemperate Men (a Christian rehabilitation center), who argued that to use narcotics or alcohol was not only to march under "the banner of Satan," but it was in fact to "change the bodies, made to be temples of the Holy Ghost, into cesspools of filth and iniquity." According to Bunting,

> The object of the Home was not to seek the cure of the intemperate by medical treatment nor was it intended to be an asylum for permanent residence. It was opened with the full assurance that though such men might be helped by mere moral or physical agencies, such agencies were insufficient and could not of themselves save them. We seek to impress upon the drunkard who comes under our care, the fact that drunkenness is a sin against God, to be repented of and forsaken, therefore, the Gospel Remedy is applied to the alcoholic and narcotic habits, which are regarded and treated purely and simply as sins.[62]

This cure required total severance from alcohol, morphine, and opium. Bunting denied that addiction was hereditary, claiming instead that "we do not believe drunkenness is inherited any more than any other evil; therefore the inmate has his mind disabused of that idea by placing the responsibility where it rests, alone upon himself."[63] Cures therefore had to deal solely with "the mind and soul," which Bunting explicitly demarcated from "the body."[64] In other words, the body was not the self but rather the shell that houses the self. Dedication to substance abstinence was rigorous and required at least some form of Christian devotion:

> No one is allowed to remain who does not, within a proper time, manifest willingness to listen to such counsel and instruction. We have no desire to force our religious belief upon anyone, nor do we ask any to adopt a special creed or denominational system; but we do expect all to be present at the religious exercises, and to be honest in their efforts to break away absolutely and permanently from their evil habits. . . . Immediately upon coming to the Home, a form of questions is asked the applicant, *one of which is particularly emphasized*—"Do you earnestly desire to permanently reform and become a Christian man?"[65]

Addiction here is framed as antithetical to Christianity: There are no Christian addicts because for Bunting this was a contradiction in terms. In evangelical fashion, the book was packed with testimonies as well; each story recounted how the determination to abandon sin led men out of alcohol, opium, and morphine addiction. Bunting ran his recovery center on the premise that addiction was willful sin that could be fixed by abandoning it and embracing Christian virtue, and those unable to "manifest willingness to listen to such counsel" were asked to leave.

The New York Home for Intemperate Men was not the only one to mandate drug-free Christianity. Dr. J. G. Kerr, a medical missionary in Macao, explained that the opium habit deteriorated the body and so deadened it that other medicines were useless for treating illnesses. Kerr thought this was bad, but not so bad as its spiritual effects, writing, "we, who possess the wisdom revealed in God's Word, know the spiritual nature of man is infinitely more important, inasmuch as it is immortal."[66] Kerr continued, saying

> missionaries in China, by almost universal consent, exclude opium smokers from Church membership . . . Because opium vitiates and debases the moral sense. Purity, truthfulness and uprightness are not characteristics of a slave to opium. Deprive him of his accustomed daily allowance of the drug and his craving for it overrules all considerations of morality and religion. . . . The degradation of the moral nature renders it impossible for the spiritual nature of man to rise above the corruptions inherent in human nature and he cannot therefore rise in the scale of being as every one must who sincerely takes upon himself the vows of a holy God.[67]

In Kerr's estimation, then, Christianity and addiction are incompatible in that opium ruins the capacity for addicts to perform the moral devotions requisite for conversion; the corruption of human nature therefore cannot be escaped.

In a more positive spin, others pitched addiction as curable by conversion or miraculous intervention. A narrative in an 1871 issue of *The Christian* presented the author demanding of an addict shaking at the altar, "if you cannot trust Christ to save you from this sin and to take away your appetite for this poison, how can you trust Him for your soul's salvation?"[68] After a week of personal wrestling the addict found that he did trust Jesus, and as his soul was saved, his addiction vanished as well. In 1914, a woman wrote *The Gospel Trumpet* to reveal that she had been a morphine addict for 35 years but had been delivered of it after attending a revival in Anderson, Indiana, and then suffering through the withdrawal cold turkey.[69] A similar case comes from John Livingston Nevius's missionary activities in China. Although nineteenth-century American Protestants were somewhat less likely to accept demon possession phenomena as real when compared to evangelicals today, Nevius was among those who did. In his final published work, Nevius recounted the story of Heo Tai-ts, who was an opium addict and demoniac. Only after Christian intervention is he able to recover; Christians exorcise his demon and after he is freed of it he is finally able to abandon his opium addiction. This process continued in the region, with addicts being freed from opium as they convert to Christianity and/or are freed of demons.[70] In all styles of this narrative, however, narcotic abuse is a sin incompatible with Christianity.

Perhaps the most important theological intervention is the notion that addiction was a form of slavery. (The word itself derives from the Latin term *addictus*, denoting a kind of enslavement.) As we have seen, the Temperance Movement made ample use of this trope in anti-alcohol discourse. Claims that narcotics enslaved addicts should not automatically be taken as metaphor. Such language may sometimes have been metaphor but often it was not. Sometimes it was both. It was common in this period for people to think of the body and mind (or soul) as separate things. What specifically was being enslaved remained an open question. If drugs enslave the body, they relegate the soul to a space of victimhood where it is no longer in control. If the soul itself is what gets enslaved, then that is far worse. Most sources were circumspect on this question and refused to explain exactly what they mean. Sometimes narcotic substances were treated as demonic, and thus evil is what makes drugs a slavemaster. In other cases interlocutors present narcotics merely as material substances (not that this is necessarily better). The consistent language of slavery created a discourse in which substance use annulled one of the central virtues which Americans championed as their birthright: liberty.

When Christian antidrug materials proposed that addiction was demonic they rarely theorized how. It is often unclear whether substance demons were meant to be metaphorical or literal truth; many instances are vague enough to permit both readings, and in general Protestants of this era were divided as to whether demons were literal spiritual entities still plaguing humanity. Even as a metaphor demons remain a useful image, though, especially since the idea of substance slavery has much conceptual overlap with the concept of the compulsive immorality frequently associated with demonic possession. For an 1881 example that seems more likely to have been metaphor, Dr. Leslie Keeley claimed that "Opium is the Mephistopheles of the age!"[71] Keeley linked this Mephistophical nature to the horrors of narcotic slavery, writing

> Half a million men and women in America slaves of a drug! The thought of slavery is, in itself, abhorrent; but when we remember that this is a slavery the most damnable on earth; a bondage to a soulless, merciless tyrant; a captivity whose daylight is Despair and whose hope is Death, the impressive fact fills our minds with pity and woe![72]

Slavery here is one of many forms, but the unparalleled depression wrought by this master makes it the worst kind. This was not just a nineteenth-century take on the matter, either; the trope of narcotic slavery persisted well into the twentieth century. Writing in 1927, a history professor at American University argued that

> Democratic Constitutions cannot be safeguarded by growing hundreds of thousands of drug addicts, whose moral and mental reactions and whose command of will and energy are wholly given over to the subtle influence of a drug that leaves the victim more or less of an automaton—but an automaton who has one burning desire, to get as many others as he can in a like condition.[73]

Professor James uses the word "automaton" instead of "slave," but the concept remains the same, and the stakes are clearly marked: Narcotic slavery threatens national security. Writing in 1918, Dr. Charles Stokes argued that addicts posed a danger to military integrity (they were unfit to serve) as well as industrial labor. Addiction taxed not just mental acuity but the whole body, leading to decreased productivity and, in the case of the psychopathically addicted, workplace violence.[74] The slavery theme dominated interpretations of narcotics, presenting the body as a potential puppet to a malevolent force locatable either in the substance itself or in the demonic realm, and which produced terrific problems for society.

Conclusions

No consensus existed during the nineteenth and early twentieth centuries for how narcotics worked upon the body. Common themes emerged, however, in the forms of slavery and insanity. Most explanations assumed some relationship between the mind and the body although the exact nature of the relationship was contested. Symptomatic immorality emerged as a problem germane to other social concerns, both domestically as well as in colonial and international settings. The dreadful possibility that there might be no cure—or at best only a flimsy one—also prompted wider social reactions, particularly in education.

Religious interpretations of the body frequently presented it as sacrosanct, something that ought not be violated by narcotic enslavement. Whether an inviolable mind existed independent of the body was an open question, but the brain was universally understood to require good care. By whatever mechanism addiction worked, medical and non-medical observers considered the derailment of proper brain function to be a serious problem. For American Protestants in the nineteenth and early twentieth centuries, this was spiritually dangerous, since the mind was the primary site of salvation, prayer, and communion with God. It was also the means by which one read scripture, although given the problem of chronic immorality that they believed addiction produced, period commentators might have treated this as a secondary problem since a better knowledge of morals could not benefit readers in such circumstances.

Protestants did not agree in this time period as to whether demons existed as real entities with personalities or whether the scriptures that referenced them were more metaphorical than literal. Period sources frequently refer to addicts as "fiends," yet rarely do they make their theology explicit when they use the term, and this may well have just been a colloquialism.[75] Regardless of where individuals came down on the matter, narcotics performed the same functions as demon possession. If a body were enslaved to a substance such as morphine, the self that was attached to that body no longer held uncontested control over its actions. The identity of that self grew sickly pale as the drug either dominated it temporarily or ate away at it permanently, replacing good character with immorality. Insane addicts were thought to behave irrationally, absurdly, and sometimes criminally. Whether people called that demonic or not, their understanding of it was basically the same thing. If, as Shakespeare wrote, "a rose by any other name would smell as sweet," then a demon by any other name is as defiling. Drugs posed the same threat that demons do regardless of whether they were specifically named as such.

"Religion" is not easily contained or compartmentalized. Nineteenth- and early twentieth-century theorists framed addiction in moral terms, either marking addiction as a cause of immorality or marking immorality as a cause of addiction. This morality derived from a transdenominational Protestantism and was religious in origin, even when those moral norms were not couched in religious language. Many Christian Prohibitionists and antidrug activists removed explicitly religious language from their public policy proposals, imagining that by erasing the language they presented a neutral policy. At the same time as these interventionists cited biomorality as a cause for alarm, they also anchored morality itself to transdenominational Protestantism.

These medical and religious objections to substance use led to serious domestic concerns about narcotics. Phrenology and other medical models of addiction held implications for two spheres of American identity: postmillennialist destiny and eugenics. Degeneracy theory approached substance use as a dangerous Charybdis that could swallow up American progress, with drugs deteriorating biological and societal integrity. Substance use was retrogressive when it came to perfecting American racial stock, which eugenics sought to improve. Postmillennialism did not require eugenics, but as an optimistic progress narrative it could easily work alongside it.

3

Degeneracy, Eugenics, and the Great American Race

Chicago (1909)

In 1909, the physician William Healy found himself deeply embedded in two experimental institutions, both representative of the cultural idealism and faith in government's capacity to solve social problems that was so characteristic of the Progressive Era: first, the Chicago Juvenile Court (founded in 1899 and the first of its kind in the United States), which sought to end youthful criminal recidivism; and second, the new Juvenile Psychopathic Institute, which endeavored to research juvenile criminality using new insights from psychological theory.[1] Healy was deeply committed to these, hoping that proper research into the causes of juvenile delinquency could not just resolve the financial burden of crime, but also make a sincere difference in the lives of children.[2] Juvenile courts such as Chicago's claimed their role as *parens patriae* (a legal phrase meaning "the state as parent") and attempted to walk a middle ground between dismissing children's crimes as non-prosecutable and trying children the same way they might adults, including execution.[3] Children, aged 7–17, who appeared in Chicago's Juvenile Court were mostly Catholic and mostly immigrants, and were tried for crimes ranging from "mischief" and "incorrigibility" to theft and prostitution.[4] When groups were brought in together, probation officers would sort out the "good boys" from the "immoral" ones, considering immorality a necessary condition for delinquency.[5] Substance use—tea, cocaine, morphine, tobacco—ranked among those moral problems that delinquency reformers cared about.

In the 800+ page book resulting from his work with the JPI, Healy's hope was that eventually his research would help demonstrate that "better nurture and better education" had therapeutic benefits.[6] *The Individual Delinquent* (1915) would become an influential work in both criminology and psychoanalysis. Healy's lifelong view was that youths' criminality was neither fully "nature" nor fully "nurture," but rather that heredity and environment both featured prominently in moral downfall, for which addiction was both a species and a catalyst. Substance use could lead to immoral choices but it could also itself be the product of a deeper biological degeneracy.

The JPI wasn't Healy's own idea; rather, the reformers of Chicago's Hull House originated and funded the plan.[7] Hull House defies easy religious categorization and it is perhaps best described as an idealistic experiment in disrupting class barriers with emphasis on serving the poor and recognizing their humanity.[8] As progeny of the Progressivist ethos, the Hull House reformers held to a capacious view of mission— they were motivated by a sense of moral duty to create a better society by addressing not just poverty, but also mental illness, children's welfare, crime, drugs, vice—any issue they felt hindered society's well-being was worth their attention.[9] (As a "settlement house" they were also part of a national movement that historian Sarah Imhoff identifies as "bound up with Protestant postmillennial theologies.")[10] Jane Addams, perhaps Hull House's most famous advocate, considered caffeine and drug running among the vicious problems affecting Chicago's delinquents.[11]

Healy fit comfortably within the Hull House sphere and saw adolescent well-being as his calling. He largely agreed with reformer Julia Lathrop that criminals embraced crime because of bad circumstances and environment, yet he was not himself ready to reduce everything down to environment—heredity mattered too.[12] In Healy's estimation, morality was at least partly a biological phenomenon and different races possessed different moral capacities.[13] Yet "degeneracy" threatened to unseat white moral superiority. In this context, degeneracy meant that through bad heredity, bad environment, or assorted catalysts, people could be atavistically reduced into primitive stages. Juvenile delinquency represented not only a social problem to Healy, but also a kind of laboratory where he could observe—and perhaps even intervene in—degeneracy.

Healy's interest in degeneracy was wide-ranging, and substance use represented only one aspect of it, both as a symptom of degeneracy and a cause. Addiction was sometimes learned; sometimes people became addicts because they were never taught moral restraint; and sometimes people were born with a hereditarily defective nervous system that compelled them toward substance use. Two boys in his 1915 book stand out as significant examples of this: one whom he called "Case 29" (henceforth "Jack") and one whom he called "Case 35" (henceforth "Tom"). Jack and Tom were adolescent addicts.

Fifteen-year-old Jack was a cocaine addict and an inveterate liar. Although he was both short and gaunt for his age (5'0" and 98 pounds), his skilled duplicity and wispy moustache helped to convince others that he was an adult. Jack was potentially also a cocaine dealer given that he was arrested with multiple packets on him. Jack's home life was chaotic and he often slept elsewhere. His mother was severely alcoholic and his father absent. He knew the street life well and was "glib" as he recounted terrible stories to Healy. He also suffered from some very uncomfortable sexually transmitted diseases. Before becoming a cocainist, Jack also made use of other stimulants such as coffee. For Healy, Jack represented a particularly degenerate strain of human genetics: "a distinctly inferior type" who lacked willpower and moral capacity. Cocaine served Jack by offering him an artificial boldness to supplement his already degenerate state.[14]

Tom was 10 when he first came to Healy and 14 when *The Individual Delinquent* came out. Tom had many problems. In 1908 he fell and suffered a severe head injury that required him to be hospitalized for three weeks, recovering with crossed eyes, pupils that opened at different apertures, and bad headaches on one side. Healy reported that at age 14, Tom weighed 53 pounds, was 4'7", had club-shaped fingertips, overused his facial muscles, and spoke with a staccato. His home life was even more troubled than Jack's. Tom's alcoholic father committed suicide, as had another man living in Tom's house. His sister also tried to kill herself. His mother was usually absent since she had to work to support the family, but when she was home she abused Tom. Tom became a thief and by 10 was a caffeine addict, drinking 7–9 cups of coffee daily, although he had cut back on this by age 14.

Healy wanted to redeem both boys' characters as much as nature would allow. Any competent therapist today would immediately recognize the profound trauma at work in Jack's and Tom's home lives and trauma's relationship to their behavior. Healy would have agreed with them in part, yet he would have been ill-content with present-day counselors' approaches, for there was no getting past degeneracy's hand in both boys' misbehavior. Healy argued that Jack's inferior heredity was observable through the "stigmata of degeneracy," since he also had anemia, a "shifty and tired expression," an asymmetrical chest, a family history of alcoholism, and physical and sexual developments that were out of sync with each other. Similarly, Tom's speech impediment and fingertips were stigmatic, too. So far as Healy was concerned, their abuse of coffee and cocaine evidenced their maladapted heredity, and while the boys' home lives certainly mattered, to some extent their bad behavior was biologically predestined. What counted as "moral," though—the degenerate hereditary failures that both boys suffered—derived from Protestant norms.

Eugenics, Drugs, and Biomorality

Eugenics is most often remembered today for its coercive sterilization programs, yet while these were of course significant, they represent only one part of what eugenics actually was. "Eugenics" was more or less a special kind of race science. The term comes from the Greek "*eu*" (good) and "*genus*" (birth) and the movement peaked during the early twentieth century. Eugenicists sought to perfect human heredity in order to build a better species, promoting "supernormal" people to reproduce with one another and discouraging certain categories of "subnormal" or "unfit" people from procreating. Although eugenics could theoretically be applied to the improvement of any race, in practice most eugenicists cared primarily about whiteness. Sometimes they made this explicit; in the US context, eugenicists often framed their argument as being about "the Great White Race" or sometimes "the American Race." They encouraged people to mate carefully and in many states they managed to get compulsory laws that required sterilization of people too "unfit" to reproduce. Inferior moral capacity represented one form of unfitness.

Various American institutions such as prisons, asylums, and hospitals had legal cover (and in some cases legal obligations) to sterilize those deemed "unfit," a position that was controversial even at eugenics's height. Yet to reduce eugenics down to just sterilization or law both frames it in ways contrary to what eugenicists thought they were doing and obfuscates its wider cultural impacts. In his eugenical parenting guide, for instance, medical doctor W. Grant Hague explained that

Eugenics, simply defined, means "better babies." It is the art of being well born: it implies a consideration of every subject that is concerned in the well being of the race. Such subjects are: motherhood, marriage, heredity, environment, disease, hygiene, sanitation, vice, education, culture,—in short, everything upon which the health of the people depends.[15]

Sterilization was indeed part of eugenics, representing a branch of it often termed "negative eugenics," but Hague's explanation sits closer to where many eugenicists spent their cognitive energy. Sterilization removed bad characteristics from the gene pool, but eugenics placed a capacious emphasis on public health, welfare, and the future of American progress. It was sometimes a personal practice, such as when people made choices about diet or recreation that aimed at supporting the health of their society. Eugenics was an ethos, a measure of individuals' worthiness, and at times a way of living in the world. Both negative and positive eugenics mattered for the Drug War. Positive eugenics emphasized raising morally righteous children who would avoid addiction (and for that matter avoid addicts, too), whereas negative eugenics emphasized preventing future addicts from being born.

Insofar as eugenics represented an ethics of "good births" and the reproduction of moral citizens, it also drew upon the language and logic of its precursor, degeneracy theory. The term "eugenics" itself derives from race scientist Francis Galton's 1883 book, *Inquiries into Human Faculty and Its Development*, but for years degeneracy theory had already been floating around scientific circles and was only different in that it was slightly less interventionist.[16] The term "degeneracy" signaled a few things. First, it meant biological degeneracy, in which bodies decayed, underdeveloped, regressed, and/or malfunctioned; congenital disabilities (both mental and physical) were taken as evidence validating this principle. Second, it meant moral degeneracy, in which individuals ceased striving to better themselves and instead behaved in uncouth or vulgar ways. Third, it meant social degeneracy, in which civilizational progress ceased to advance and society began moving backwards to its lesser forms. Oftentimes degeneracy referred to all three of these categories working together as a malfeasant mélange of human dysfunction. At least since the 1850s, degeneracy theorists had linked substance use—especially alcohol and tobacco—to racial decay.[17] By the 1890s that interpretation was all but standard in both Europe and America.[18]

By the turn of the century, narcotics were playing a more significant role in eugenics texts. In his 1898 book, *Degeneracy: Its Causes, Signs, and Results*, the Chicago medical professor Eugene Talbot argued that "toxic agents" were Americans' chief degenerators.[19] Talbot suggested that there was good statistical evidence that alcohol was the leading cause of degeneracy but emphasized to his readers that tobacco and opium were degenerative, too. In fact, Talbot considered opium more dangerous than alcohol because alcoholics could abstain without severe consequences, whereas opium addicts could not. He also feared that addicts might have children who would grow into maturity, writing

> Opium does not have as great tendencies to interfere with the structure of the ovary and testicles as alcohol, hence the greater danger of the opium habitué's children surviving. Opium, when smoked, stimulates the reproductive apparatus, and thus would greatly increase the number of degenerates due to this habit but for the defects due to the inheritance of the habit and their consequences.[20]

It might surprise contemporary readers to discover such disapprovals of childbirth; infant survival is today rarely thought of as a "danger." Talbot must be read in the context of early eugenics, where he was hardly the only one wishing for children's deaths.[21] Talbot's problem with children surviving was hereditary degeneracy: Children born to degenerates or children born *as* degenerates (as in the case of opium births) tainted the gene pool.[22] In this line of thinking, degeneracy is not just an individual's problem, it is a social problem that affects the entire population.

Biomorality, to reiterate, refers to the notion that moral behavior is controlled partly or entirely by human physiology. For biomoralists and particularly eugenicists, heredity was what would make or break civilization, what would propel America to the forefront or lead to its degenerative demise. The unfit were known through their stigmata: illiteracy, hemophilia, promiscuity, addiction, epilepsy, and so on. Under biomoral degeneracy theories (of which William Healy's was a milder variant), substance use was either a symptom of degeneracy or else its cause. Relatedly, Healy and Hull House were actively engaged in trying to reform Chicago drug culture, particularly with keeping cocaine out of youths' reach.[23] By examining eugenics beyond just its sterilization laws, Healy's arguments about drugs and degeneracy take on new meaning. Those invested in sterilization probably would have looked at Jack and Tom as good candidates for it, but they served as cautionary tales to non-sterilizing eugenicists, too. Some eugenicists believed that an acquired addiction might produce new defects in offspring, but for those who followed the logic Healy did, addiction was already itself a kind of stigmata representative of deeper degeneracies. Addicts were by definition inferior to other people and a taint on American bloodstock.

Healy embraced a worldview that considered moral reform to be ideal for those caught in vice and moral control necessary in cases where reform proved impossible. Overall, eugenicists spent far more time discussing physical and cognitive disabilities than they did drug addiction, and segregating the disabled from everyone else was already a common practice before Healy wrote *The Juvenile Delinquent*. Scientists and reformers often treated the disabled as particularly prone to immorality, and institutional segregation—particularly to rural locations—helped to keep their wantonness in check.[24] Eugenicists interested in controlling addicts and addiction drew upon long-standing theories that institutionalization could help correct addiction (an idea going back to the nineteenth century), or, at minimum, keep addicts from passing their defective genes on to future generations by limiting their sexual activity (an idea more in vogue during the early twentieth century).[25] Farm labor was exactly what Healy felt could help degenerate addicts like Tom.[26] For Healy, though, farm segregation was a stopgap. "Defectives and inferiors" could not be controlled simply by legislation and brief institutionalization.[27] Asylums and prisons could only do so much, for when the problem was hereditary it was unbeatable through such methods. Like Talbot, he also described it as sometimes "fortunate" when defective children died.[28] What this really gets at is that for many eugenicists, addiction was best understood as the product of a more holistic biological taint in need of erasure. Antidrug legislation and the institutionalization of addicts were both good, but the problem could only be fixed when Americans began procreating more conscientiously, choosing to mate with morally righteous, intelligent, able-bodied people and intentionally excluding the immoral or disabled from consideration. Eugenics's successful intervention in legal policy was certainly important, but the way it intervened in wider themes of lived morality was equally so. One of the places to pay special attention to it is its discourse about the kind of people addicts were.

Race Suicide, Substance Use, and Christian America

Degeneracy theory and its later incarnation in eugenics were also fundamentally about race. Race scientists endeavored to identify different races' capabilities, identifying their strengths, weaknesses, and unique traits, typically identifying European races as the most able and civilized of the world's peoples.[29] While race scientists fixated upon these essentialized differences, the applications for race science tended toward two questions: How can white race(s) be improved and protected from contamination, and how can race science help us govern better? Eugenics sought to take theories of heredity and degeneracy and use them to reshape both domestic and global society.

"Race suicide" represented a special concern for eugenicists, who proposed that if the overall health and well-being of a particular race diminished too much it was possible for that race to decline into total extinction. Many scientists, reformers, politicians, and theologians worried that white race(s) were neglecting their biological integrity. In 1905, for instance, then-president Theodore Roosevelt informed a national organization of mothers that "the first and greatest duty of womanhood" is to bear and raise children "sound in body, mind, and character, and numerous enough so that the race shall increase and not decrease." Citing race suicide by name, he couched Americans' fecundity as a requisite defense of civilization and morality, arguing that good, fertile Americans who choose not to reproduce "merit contempt as hearty as any visited upon the soldier who runs away in battle."[30] In the United States, "race suicide" was most concerned about either the breeding stock of the "Anglo-Saxon" race or the "American" race. Defense against it was multiform and ranged from attempts to legally block biologically inferior or immoral people from immigrating to encouraging people to intentionally consider heredity when selecting spouses.[31]

It was commonplace for eugenicists to argue that America was racially Protestant. In his highly influential book, *Our Country*, Josiah Strong argued in 1885 that Anglo-Saxons had essentially invented a "pure *spiritual* Christianity" distinguished from the "formalism" of Catholicism and "absolutism of the Pope" upon which civil liberty rested.[32] Strong argued that "Christianity, the press and steam" represented the "moral, mental, and material" progress of civilization—a progress that could potentially continue for centuries with America at its helm—yet such progress had its enemies. Those enemies included religious degeneracy on the part of Protestants; alcoholism, opium, chloral, and chloroform addictions; illegitimate religions like Mormonism and Catholicism; and immigrants who don't privilege Christian civilization.[33] For Strong, America was fundamentally Anglo-Saxon—a racial category he considered by nature Protestant—which was under fire in "the final competition of races."[34] The 1914 book, *The Standard History of the World by Great Historians*, reproduced similar assumptions, explaining that "The Scandinavian races . . . and their Teutonic kinsmen, the German races . . . and the United States of America, are almost the only Protestant nations of the world; thus showing that the old instincts still run in the blood and cause these races to seek light, freedom and progress, and not to give way to the luxury of emotion or to the satisfaction of repose."[35] While praising his own successes, Harvey Washington Wiley expressed thankfulness "to have been the son of moral, intelligent, and physically perfect parents," going on to explain that "descendants of the Scotch and Irish Presbyterians, or Protestants in the General Sense, in Great Britain, and of the Huguenots of France, have always shown themselves to be a superior people. Not only are they a healthy race, long-lived, and industrious, but their children have been brought up with strict discipline." Wiley wanted America to have more "heroic Calvinists" like Jonathan Edwards and less "flotsam and jetsam of humanity" like those found in poorhouses.[36] Although he stopped short of identifying the United States as "Protestant," in his 1935 "eugenics catechism" Huntington Ellsworth argued that those descending from the New England Puritans "furnish leaders out of all proportion to their numbers" while also being "only about half as likely to be criminals or to receive public relief." He felt Quakers and Unitarians were similar. The children of clergymen had "2,400 times as great a chance of getting into *Who's Who* as had the son of an unskilled laborer."[37] Huntington's argument was that Protestant religiosity unconsciously selected morality as a eugenic trait when it came to reproduction, thus Protestants had a better sense of leadership and moral integrity.

The idea that racial difference involved moral, intellectual, and religious divergence was quite common and long-lived. W. D. Weatherford's 1912 book, *Present Forces in Negro Progress* (published by the YMCA), argued that superstition was a "weakness of negro character," and represented "the great[est] bar to the Negro's advancement."[38] Those invested in race science often treated the United States as Christian in essence, and since race carried religious implications, it seemed natural to them that America should bar non-Christian races from entry. In 1881, for instance, *The Chautauquan* argued that Chinese immigrants were "destitute of what Americans call 'conscience,'" refusing to pursue "mental or moral improvement." Instead, Chinese immigrants lived selfishly, sharing their recreational opium with children and embracing alcoholism. *The Chautauquan* presented Chinese and African immigration as "a political question" that it wasn't prepared to answer, but that "whether God intends that America shall be inhabited finally by a yellow or white-skinned variety of human beings, is uncertain, but to us there is no doubt that he intends to have it inhabited by Christians."[39] For all of the article's performative ambivalence about the question, *The Chautauquan* was indeed arguing that racial others ought not be permitted entry into the United States since this would taint its Christian essence. The standard interpretation in this era was that Africans and the Chinese were fundamentally heathen and prone to immorality; few among *The Chautauquan*'s readership would have read it differently.[40]

The Chautauquan's instinct to treat America as essentially white and Christian would remain representative of eugenical attitudes for decades to come. A moral, Protestant, white, normatively abled America is who they wished to protect from "race suicide," and they often made this explicit.[41] This is relevant for the Drug War in three ways. First, eugenics framed disability and immorality as defects malignant enough to warrant excluding degenerates from mainstream society and certainly to exclude them from consideration as romantic partners. Because addiction was so often seen as a biomoral defect, eugenics included substance use as a disqualifying condition. If race suicide was really a threat, then good Americans were duty-bound to reproduce with eugenic matches. Second, concerns about fitness and degeneracy also extended into white governance of racial others. These ideas mattered quite a lot for policing substance use, especially in colonial settings. Third, by portraying a moral Christian America threatened by vice, self-centered heathens, and the moral failures attendant to degeneracy, eugenicists worked with an ideological binary where substance use stood among those things antithetical to the United States itself. Law matters and serves a disciplinary function, but one of the areas where eugenics discourses about degeneracy and race suicide also mattered was in how it shaped Americans' wider attitudes toward addicts.

William J. Robinson's 1917 eugenic marriage guide offers a strong example of this. Robinson explained:

> Addiction to drugs, whether it be opium, morphine, heroin or cocaine, is a strongly dysgenic factor. . . . A few cases of drug addiction are external; that is, the patient may have a good healthy constitution, no hereditary taint, and still because during some sickness he was given morphine a number of times he may have developed an addiction to the drug. But those cases are rare. . . . in most cases it isn't the drug addiction that causes the degeneracy; it is the degeneracy or the neuropathic or psychopathic constitution that causes the drug addiction. And such cases are bad matrimonial risks.[42]

In other words, the only circumstances in which someone might reasonably consider an addict (presumably including recovering addicts) as worthy of consideration is if addiction were medically explicable.

Similarly, children were taught in schools to regard addiction not only as symptomatic of bad heredity but also to consider addicts as parasites. To be clear, children were already being taught to think of addicts as "weak-willed" catastrophes by the time of temperance curricula reforms in the 1880s (more on this later).[43] The languages of "degeneracy" and "fitness" were already in use, too, although it is not clear that the terms yet had their eugenic meanings for temperance authors. For instance, the 1884 *Practical Work in the School Room* taught that alcohol made people "unfit to think and work" as well as "unfit to serve themselves, their neighbor, or God," yet this may or may not have been meant to imply degeneracy theory. Similarly, its suggestion that tobacco made users selfish, lazy liars, and led smokers into drinking and corrupt friendships, demonstrates no explicit links to degeneracy theory, yet still harmonizes quite easily with it.[44] By the 1890s, however, textbooks were becoming more explicit in presenting addiction as a hereditary problem. The 1898 *Text-book of Anatomy, Physiology, and Hygiene* informed students that addiction ranked among degeneracy's inheritable traits. Degenerate addicts, it warned, might also produce children with stigmata other than addiction (such as insanity or idiocy) and vice versa—the children of the insane might become addicts.[45] As scientists increasingly began to view the relationship between addiction and heredity as a sure thing, textbooks also became more explicit about how addicts burdened everyone else. In the "Racial Hygiene" chapter of his *Narcotics and Youth Today* textbook, Robert Corradini explained,

> Alcohol can kill a few, taint many, and produce a host of socially, morally, mentally and physically unfit, for which the rest of society is penalized. We must maintain many of them at terrific expense—as public charges—in institutions, while they are holding back society from normal progress which should and could be made, were it not due to these social barnacles. If the habitual use of narcotics could be eliminated, it would greatly reduce the number of inmates in the institutions for the physically and mentally unfit, besides vastly increasing the general health of the population.[46]

Corradini argued that while addiction was hereditary and could be passed on from parent to child, the use of alcohol, cocaine, codeine, opium, and morphine would disrupt the normal functioning of sex organs in ways that produced malformed offspring. Narcotics were therefore a "race poison capable of damaging not only the individual user, but the race as well."[47] Eugenics's relationship with culture wasn't just about law, it was also about training Americans that they owed their race sobriety—anything else threatened racial purity. By the time Corradini's book emerged in the 1930s it was common for addiction to be considered a hereditary problem preventable through better birth control.

Eugenics is best remembered for its sterilization agenda, which was often coerced or non-consensual and certainly one of its most damning features. The eugenics side of the Drug War certainly shared in this. In

1911, for instance, Iowa passed an act mandating that supervisors of various institutions (asylums, jails, etc.) evaluate their charges at minimum once per year and sterilize or "unsex" (neuter) them if they were found to be defective or degenerate; it specifically included "drunkards" and "drug fiends" among those to be sterilized.[48] The bill passed the Iowa House 64 to 13, and the Iowa Senate 32 to 0.[49] Iowans celebrated this law. The local paper in Leon opined that "the welfare of our race depends on such preventative legislation."[50] Iowan Baptists also wanted additional laws to prevent alcoholics and criminals from getting married.[51] Like many of the early eugenics laws, Iowa's was soon replaced by one with less remarkable language, one that required less *mandatory* sterilization of specific classes, but that still allowed institutions safe cover to sterilize addicts as they wished. Roman Catholics may have typically opposed sterilization laws like Iowa's, but many Protestants found it quite acceptable and—in some cases—commensurate with what American Christians were morally required to do.[52]

Protestant Eugenics and White Christian Nationalism

If one could travel back to the United States as it existed in the late nineteenth or early twentieth centuries, the blending of whiteness, Christianity, and nationhood into one amalgam was quite standard and widespread.[53] To be sure, American Protestants were frequently invested in converting racial others to Christianity, but many wanted to maintain the United States as a white, Protestant nation. They sought to protect whiteness from contamination along many fronts, including the contamination caused by substance use. This was both religious and political at the same time.

In his 1922 book *Race Decadence*, the University of Chicago medical professor William Sadler claimed that the problem of drinking and "drug habits" required "a clear understanding of applied eugenics." Sadler was explicitly concerned about the deterioration of "civilized peoples," which he specified meant "the 'stock' of the white races." Zooming in on his real concern—the United States—Sadler worried that American devotion to Christian principles had weakened, and that Christianity as "the guiding star of national destiny" really needed "a great spiritual awakening." Degeneracy was a multifarious enemy for Christian America, and substance use ranked among its sinister manifestations. Americans' mental capacity, prowess, and hereditary morality were in decline. He also noted that cocaine, caffeinated drinks, strong condiments, excessive meat, and tobacco produced "moral condemnation," although it is unclear what exactly he meant by this phrase.

There's no question that Sadler connected substance use to crime. He stopped short of attempting a causal proof, but permitted correlation to do that work for him. In a section titled "The Moron Problem," Sadler explained that 84 percent of Chicago's prostitutes (who he implied were mostly born out of wedlock—yet another mark of degeneracy) smoked cigarettes and a smaller percentage used cocaine and morphine. Elsewhere he claimed that more than 50 percent of the prison population had addiction problems, with at least 5,000 addicts institutionalized in jails or asylums at the taxpayers' expense. For Sadler, addiction, immorality, and American decline were only ameliorable if Americans were willing to embrace mandatory sterilization and revive their Christian moral heritage.[54]

John Harvey Kellogg represents another influential example of how white Christian supremacy and eugenics merged to discourage substance use. Kellogg lived for years as a Seventh-Day Adventist, although he eventually left the denomination (but not Christianity) later in life. For many Adventists, bodily health that centered upon "Bible hygiene" was a sacred moral duty, and by the 1860s one of Adventism's most important founders, Ellen White, prohibited coffee, tea, tobacco, alcohol, and drugs to protect Christians from the endemic "disease, deformity and imbecility" to which these contributed.[55] Kellogg, who was quite close with White, took the same position, emphasizing its eugenical aspects more explicitly as scientific discourse gave this stronger voice. Indeed, Kellogg would become one of the most prominent eugenicists in the United States, working with people like David Starr Jordan, Paul Popenoe, and Charles Davenport to organize "Race Betterment" conferences and programs, as well as encouraging sterilization laws in Michigan and elsewhere.[56] Elite eugenicists, including Jordan, Davenport, Sadler, John D. Rockefeller Jr., Irving Fisher, Madison Grant, and Henry Ford, would visit Kellogg at his Battle Creek Sanitarium.[57] Kellogg was one of many who supported forming a "eugenics registry," a living document that would track Americans' hereditary fitness and might lead to racial improvement over time.[58] By the twentieth century, he was convinced that religious discipline (and Christian morality in particular) was a central defense against degeneracy and a boon to race improvement—at least for whites.[59] Kellogg was convinced that white races ruled the world because of their superiority and that, while he wished African Americans well, the African race was slowly dying off due to its hereditary immorality. He also feared that white races would be enslaved by Asians if something weren't done about it.[60]

Kellogg was vocal about his antidrug positions. He prefaced his 1909 book *Man the Masterpiece* with a screed about the "race decadence," immorality, and degeneracy that threatened America. Kellogg pinned rising crime, sickness, moral perversion, tooth decay, physical degeneracy, and insanity on Americans' defiance of God's expectations for healthy living, explaining

> We must recognize as a solemn reality that religion includes the body, and that the laws which govern the healthful performance of the bodily functions are as much the laws of God as are those of the decalogue. . . . The world needs a John the Baptist to proclaim the gospel of health,—a voice crying in the wilderness of disease, degeneracy, and death, and pointing the way upward and away from the awful fate which threatens the race.[61]

He went on in the book to describe tobacco as a "relic of barbarism" originating with American Indians before it made its way into white use and as the substance most damaging to heredity. Tobacco users' children were "robbed of their rightful patrimony" since they were intrinsically misborn—weak, nervous, insane, sickly, and sometimes dwarves. Similarly, drinkers were "not the greatest sufferer" of their vice—their degenerate children were.[62] The children of drinkers, smokers, chloral users, and opium users were not all raving lunatics locked in asylums—Kellogg contended that thousands of drug-born degenerates roamed free with their bad heredity unrecognized yet ready to snap at any moment.[63] In short, Kellogg was one of many Christians campaigning against substance use as a threat to America, Christianity, and racial purity, all of which imbricated each other.

War hero, congressman, Prohibitionist, and later in life an antinarcotics activist, Richmond Pearson Hobson was a little more postmillennialist in his opposition to substance-fueled degeneracy than Kellogg. Like many religious moderates of his day, Hobson accepted evolutionary theory and indeed had worked it into his faith: Evolution was God's plan for developing and eventually perfecting humanity. In a letter to John D. Rockefeller Jr., Hobson argued:

> These definite findings of science are opening the way for the greatest reform in the life-history of the human species, the elimination of beverage alcohol, a reform that will remove the sources of decay and permit the race to rise in accord with the evolutionary processes of nature to fulfill what is clearly God's purpose for the race. The paramount duty of the generation to which you and I belong is to bring about this reform with efficiency and the least amount of delay.[64]

Rephrased, his argument can be summarized thus: God set evolution in motion and tasked humans with the preservation of that process so that humans might continue to evolve into something holier. Alcohol obstructed civilization from reaching that goal. When paired with Hobson's other statements, this passage illuminates more fully the threat he saw in substance use, including narcotics. Although Hobson was not much of a theologian and was sometimes inconsistent, post-millennialism often colored his opposition to intoxicants. In 1915, he wrote,

> The degeneracy will greatly give way under the operations of nature's law of evolution, the higher and nobler faculties of mankind will rapidly develop. It is then that peace and good will be hastened upon the earth and the prejudices and hatreds of the ages will be more rapidly dissipated; liberty and free institutions will advance until they become universal and this century will witness more stupendous progress in the advance of civilization in the uplift and welfare of humanity than has been witnessed in any ten [centuries of] the world's history.[65]

Elsewhere he explained that as a "habit-forming drug" and the chief cause of degeneracy, alcohol stood counter to the "spiritual nature of civilization," robbing both men and the nation itself of an authentic "relationship with God." He offered phrenological biomoral explanations for how exactly it doomed people to an ignorance of peace, justice, and their Father.[66]

Hobson's language should be read as that of the Millennial Kingdom. If human evolution leads to the dissolving of hatred and the elevation of peace and goodwill, these are some of the eschatological goals in postmillennial thought. For someone like Hobson, degeneracy and evolution were antipodes, although humanity can participate in its own forward motion by modulating "the operation of nature's law." Substance use deeply violates those "laws of nature" though, degenerating both individuals' minds and bodies, and in fact civilization itself. Hobson wanted firm controls placed on substance use for this reason. But given the white Christian nationalism he expressed throughout his life, and given that controlled evolution fit within his theology, it necessarily sacralizes the protections he wanted for those "laws of nature." On their own, "laws of nature" sounds like a neutral, scientific term, and perhaps in some cases people used them that way. But for Hobson and those like him, the scientific language of "degeneracy" and "laws of nature" were code for the divine historical process of millennial progress. That language gave him cover to speak to various audiences at once, operating out of Protestant norms but simultaneously speaking to a wider crowd.[67]

Progressive-Era postmillennialism often paired eschatological expectations with human action—God expected Christians to do some of the work. In his 1914 book, *Single Standard Eugenics*, Thomas Shannon complained that some Christians relied too much on the Atonement to automatically solve everything and that it was somewhat irrelevant when it came to eugenics. "Evangelistic efforts come too late for the unfortunate, confirmed and hopeless defectives and degenerates of this generation," Shannon wrote. Shannon also contended that 90 percent of race degeneracy was due to tobacco, alcohol, and other immoralities.[68] He offered readers two solutions: First, degenerates needed to be segregated from the rest of society so that their incurable defects would not be passed on to future generations, and second, people must awaken to and practice eugenics in their own lives. This looked like moral living, avoiding substance use, marrying eugenically, and devoting themselves to both God and the American flag.[69] Shannon offered his readers a picture of what the future would hold if "Mr. Public Conscience" would only fully awaken on moral purity. Alcohol, tobacco, and vice would vanish, the food supply would improve, prisons and asylums would be converted into factories (whose workers would not form unions or strike), and the government would come to spend $5 billion annually on Christian missions.[70]

In short, postmillennialists who accepted science as a revelatory source frequently accepted race science and degeneracy theory as theologically significant. Eugenics thereby fit into utopian ideals for a Millennial Kingdom, and Christians had a duty to enact reforms that would improve heredity. Sometimes this meant deciding who could marry whom (some twentieth-century churches required fiancés to produce medical evidence that they were a eugenically fit match), sometimes it meant sterilizing the unfit so they could not reproduce, and sometimes this meant improving social conditions that affected heredity.[71] Substance use represented one of these eugenic degenerators in need of redress. However, one of public Protestantism's features—perhaps even its defining feature—is its capacity for setting the terms of morality beyond its own borders. As the dominant Protestant eschatology in nineteenth-century America, perhaps it is natural that postmillennialism would color wider attitudes toward duty. Even those who did not count themselves as faithful Christians often shared an expectation that everyone had a part to play in national progress toward a brighter future. Eugenicists often made positive references to "the eugenic millennium," an indication of how much overlap these concepts had.[72] One important instance of this comes from Harvey Washington Wiley, whose personal story shows a clear trajectory from confessional postmillennialism to a secularized version of it. Wiley was also a particularly important curator of Americans' antidrug ethics.

Harvey Washington Wiley and Secularized Postmillennialism

Harvey Washington Wiley, the first head of what would eventually be named the Food and Drug Administration, was one of the Drug War's leading proponents—he shaped public opinion, helped design new regulations for substance use, and prosecuted companies he considered to be drug peddlers. He was slightly quieter about his eugenicism than other leading figures, but eugenicist he was—he served on the central committee for Kellogg's "Race Betterment Conferences" and considered substance use a dysgenic threat.[73] His beliefs also provide some interesting interpretive work since postmillennialist Protestantism informed his early understanding of how America should operate, but he shifted his religious orientation later in life. His work was also consequential. The 1906 Pure Food and Drug Act—which was partly designed to address the problem of hidden narcotics in household medicines—was his brainchild. Wiley resigned his FDA position in 1912 but continued supporting health causes. He was well known and throughout his life people in positions of authority still contacted him for advice and input on substance use. Wiley penned articles for popular magazines such as *Good Housekeeping* (of which he was an editor) and the *Ladies' Home Journal*, which were widely read, and in so doing he helped contribute to the popularity of eugenics and antidrug perspectives.

Historians have typically omitted discussions of Wiley's religion, but those who address it identify him as "religiously fervent," or they note that he was deeply invested in the Stone-Campbell movement during his youth but became less orthodox in adulthood.[74] This is about as far as discussion of Wiley's religious life goes. Surely some of this is due to the paucity of Wiley's own comments about it; his autobiography speaks to the Stone-Campbell upbringing (but says little of religion after), and if he could be considered Christian in the later parts of his life, then his writings for *Good Housekeeping* suggest heterodoxy. Wiley didn't intentionally try to annoy Christians, but he emphasized that scientific consensus should overrule any claims found in the Bible.[75]

Wiley's mid-nineteenth-century records reveal a character that could indeed be deemed "religiously fervent," but his later writings indicate an abandonment of formal religion and an agnosticism that was de facto atheism. In an 1892 address at a Washington social event that was something like an early "Toastsmasters Club," Wiley offered a cognitive theory of religion. He didn't outright deny the existence of an afterlife and expressed hope that there might be one, but he also thought it likely that humans had simply evolved in ways that programmed them to be religious and that there was no good evidence of a spiritual reality.[76] Yet in his earliest texts, his ideas about society and human bodies were unequivocally formed in a postmillennialist, theologically liberal framework. Wiley considered public health to be an important area of human life that would see improvement as progress drove human biology closer to its millennial state. His later views—even after his agnosis—do not significantly deviate from these earlier interpretations, except for the absence of explicitly religious framing.

Specificity may be helpful here. Late in 1869, Wiley delivered a sermon in a university chapel titled "What the Age Will Demand of the Coming Man." Wiley anchored his thoughts in a postmillennialist model of history, arguing that

> Men live for a day and die, but humanity never dies. Each one is a link in the great chain of which the one end is firmly fixed in Eden's garden and the other safely anchored in the haven of the Millennial day. As the dead world still lives hid with Christ in God so the unborn future is keenly alive in the will of the Great Life-Giver. All attempts of isolation are so many efforts to thwart the purpose of the Almighty, and all apotheosis and worship of the Present are treachery to the Past insult to the Future and sacrilege of Eternity.[77]

In the context of the whole sermon, what Wiley meant was that humanity is more than the individual and that our species does not exist solely in the present. While Wiley didn't deny that individuals matter, he clearly cared more about "humanity" than "humans." He especially cared about humanity's future: Eden lay behind and the Millennial Kingdom lay ahead and people must consider how best to reach it. Making intertextual references to Ephesians 6 and 1 John 2, Wiley further suggested that "a true work of preparation is . . . a hardening of the muscles a training of the nerves and a buckling on of the armor that we may help to fight the battle of humanity against three allied foes the world, the flesh, and the Devil; or less figuratively disease, ignorance and vice."[78] In other words, the biblical mandate to overcome the world, the flesh, and the Devil was to be found in moral, intellectual, and medical progress. Evil wanes as progress waxes. Wiley's presentation of better health as foundational for millennial advancement was commonplace for the time.[79]

This battle to overcome disease, ignorance, and immorality was a societal matter and therefore demanded attention to public health, including the end of substance misuse. Wiley observed that "there is no surer test of the moral condition of a civilized nation than the longevity of its citizens. The reason is simple and ample, for temperance and self-control pillars of the moral temple are cornerstones in the cathedral of Hygiene."[80] Hygienically securing the nation was not to be found solely in one cause such as alcohol abolition, but rather in a holistic approach that considered the types and qualities of food people consumed, the maintenance of physical fitness, and the removal of toxins from human bodies. Civilization only advanced if health and biomorality advanced. In other words, Wiley felt American Christians must have an ongoing concern for replacing vice with morality, reforming public health, and investing in the natural sciences, which he considered a "supplement" to the Bible.[81] His position was quite typical for American postmillennialists.

For Wiley in 1869, the human body was a site for civilizational progress, and his twentieth-century words and deeds replicate this position exactly. He stopped talking about human health as an advance toward the Kingdom, yet he continued to predicate national welfare and social advancement upon it. There are multiple ways that people use the word "secularism," but one of those meanings is the evacuation of religion from public spheres, and another refers to when societies start to drift away from explicitly religious epistemologies.[82] Either could describe Wiley and so it might be helpful to think of his approach as a kind of secular postmillennialism.[83] His goals were the same as his previously Christian postmillennialism, and the way that people can accomplish those goals remained the same, yet God did not occupy any serious role within the schema.[84]

Wiley aimed to advance civilizational progress partly through law and partly through education. In a 1919 article titled "Making the New American," he explained that "For eight years I have been endeavoring, in the pages of GOOD HOUSEKEEPING, to lead the people of this country into a better method of life."[85] He continued by identifying how important wholesome food and disease prevention were and explained that "the whole attitude of these activities has been the production of a better American citizen." Wiley specified this "better American citizen" was the child who had not yet been born, but who

> has a better heredity than his forebears. He also has a better environment. . . . The child who is born into this world will have a better destiny . . . The first privilege of the future child born in America is a good heredity. . . . The supreme right of the child is a good physical, mental and

moral hereditary impulse. To this end the control of the State over marriage, which already exists everywhere, should be much further extended
than it has been heretofore. Marriage is not an inalienable right. It is an
institution for the welfare of the state. How carelessly it has been controlled, is seen in the idiots, imbeciles, morons, insane, epileptic, scrofu-
lous, and syphilitic wrecks of humanity. . . . Born with the impulse of a
good heredity his instincts shall be virtuous and his ambitions fashioned
by reason. Fortified with morality he will always be inclined to fight vice
and embrace virtue. . . . The new American will be as free of social and
political faults as he is of physical and mental defects. He will bring a stability to the Republic. . . . He will seek the unexplored realms of science.
He will add new knowledge to our store, knowledge which will no longer
be used to destroy mankind.[86]

This is a postmillennial approach to American civilization that requires
no God for its success. Heredity can be perfected and advanced by
eugenically controlling human reproduction. Insanity and unfitness can
be culled from the United States, and future Americans will be devoutly
moral and intellectual as a result, purifying its politics and governance.
In the end, the United States is transformed into a paradise of social
and physical perfection. Wiley is one specific example of a wider phenomenon; many secular eugenicists held such positions.[87] Wiley is only
unique in that he had a bigger pulpit from which to speak and thereby
shape eugenics-inflected, antidrug opinion.

In the early years of the twentieth century, Wiley considered drug addiction to mostly be a problem of ignorance. In a *Ladies' Home Journal*
article penned while he was still chief chemist for the Department of Agriculture, he complained that when someone is sick, all of their visitors
seem to have a foolproof remedy suggestion, which often involves patent
medicines found at the local druggist's.[88] Prescription laws did not yet
widely exist; nearly all medicine was what we today would call "over the
counter." Consumers risked medical addiction because these medicines
often secretly contained narcotics. Wiley disliked the ease with which
narcotics might be purchased and the readiness with which even physicians recommended them. These orally administered narcotics often ruined "the vitality" of the digestive tract, and Wiley suggested that while
De Quincey might be very poetic about his written experiences of it,

opium and other narcotics represented a serious threat to willpower and self-management. Crafting a stalwart American race required making narcotics harder to legally acquire, along with educating both doctors and patients about narcotics' effects. Additionally, Wiley pushed for medical professionals' control over health entirely; "laity" (as he put it) ought not to be evaluating their own health or self-medicating. "The eradication and elimination of these drug habits" would help Americans by producing better health, mental solvency, "happier childhood" with "stronger youth," and sturdier elders who had less pain.[89] Although some addicts surely only had themselves to blame, Wiley also mistrusted America's laissez-faire attitude toward commercial practice, and he considered corporate greed a culprit that needed to be fettered. He pursued the end of substance use not only through education, but through law, too. It was not enough to merely convince people that their own health buoyed the nation, but laws needed to reflect that priority as well.

Wiley helped propel the Pure Food and Drug Act of 1906 through Congress, but passing and then executing it was a challenge: Industrialists managed media narratives to support pharmaceutical interests.[90] The act synchronized well with Wiley's style since its concern with drugs was the same concern as that with adulterated food products: It sought to end fraudulent corporate practices which tricked consumers into using unhealthy or outright dangerous products. In the case of drugs, patent medicines made dubious claims about what the product could accomplish and often omitted any mention of dangerous ingredients. For example, "Ryno's Hay Fever and Catarrh Remedy" was basically just pure cocaine, even though the container said nothing of it.[91] Such legislation also fit Wiley's conception of government, which he believed was charged to prevent race suicide. Good citizens, he contended, could only be made when the nation properly educated its members as well as cared for children "before birth."[92] *Scientific American* lauded Wiley for his attitudes and efforts, arguing that because of him, "the babies of a nation are no longer drugged into degeneracy and death."[93]

Wiley's juridical interests included not just crafting new regulations but also exercising them. Coca-Cola has famously been remembered for having once contained cocaine. What has fallen out of popular memory, however, was the sharp criticism in the early twentieth century of its caffeine content. Wiley was a central agitator in the campaign against caffeine abuse and had a deep personal investment when Coca-Cola went to trial over allegations of selling caffeinated danger. By "deep personal investment" I mean to say that he created not one but *two* scrapbooks of the trial, scrapbooks which appear to have been made solely for his own edification. This strongly suggests that the trial represented something meaningful for Wiley.

The government's 1911 case against Coca-Cola was founded upon criteria in the Pure Food Act of 1906. Wiley charged Coca-Cola with libel, arguing that the cola was adulterated and misbranded due to added caffeine and artificial coloring. Wiley lost the case. The district court in Chattanooga found that while Coca-Cola contained caffeine, it could not be considered "adulterated" since the caffeine occurred naturally in cola; the court determined that the coloring issue would need to be decided by jury.[94]

This trial is not significant because of its legal outcome, which was anticlimactic. It is significant because of what it says about substance use and the category of "drugs." When historians examine this early antidrug period, they often focus only on today's narcotic bugbears: heroin, cocaine, marijuana, and so on. This elides the wide spectrum of substances that early reformers cared about. Wiley didn't prosecute Coca-Cola because of a labeling technicality, he prosecuted Coca-Cola because he thought caffeine was dangerous and poisonous. He had no case on those grounds though, since caffeine was legal everywhere. Wiley prosecuted a libel case because it was the only legal route available to him.

Wiley was not the first to target caffeine nor was he the last. An 1886 issue of the *Boston Medical and Surgical Journal* described the dangers of "chronic tea poisoning," which include damage to the nervous system, digestive system, and anemia.[95] In 1897 the *Journal of the American Medical Association* published an article titled "The Evils of Tea-Drinking," in which the author denounced "these days of Tea-worship" and in which "the apostles of temperance are too prone to forget that there are other intemperances than alcoholic ones, and of these none is more vicious than the pet vice of refined and polite society, tea-debauchery."[96] The article explained that 2–4 percent of tea consists of "thein, caffein and guaranin," and that these alkaloids "produce insomnia, restlessness, mental depression and general nervous derangement," and occasionally even death.[97] Kellogg used nearly identical language and arguments.[98]

JAMA published a case study in 1908 in which a man consumed whiskey (though he never became drunk), but after quitting alcohol chose to consume caffeine instead. After several days he went mad in ways mimicking Moreau and De Quincey. He believed God had told him his wife has died. He heard disembodied words "in running water" and held conversations with motors, who spoke words "profane, some vulgar, and some very religious." He entered an ecstatic state replete with psychic powers, he encountered spirits, and he communed with God, who planned to "take care of" him.[99] The doctor concluded that this temporary insanity (which cleared up after a few days) was due to caffeine, whose effects include "mental confusion, hallucinations, and delirium." William Healy noted caffeine as a problem for both Jack and Tom, and in fact blamed it for some of Tom's degeneracy. There was no consensus on the matter, but these sources were typical for the anti-caffeine wing of the medical establishment. Many doctors denounced caffeine as a toxic, deleterious substance that ruined digestion, nervous systems, and threatened victims with insanity and death.

Wiley accepted all of these premises and contributed his own reading as well: Caffeine stole energy from other parts of the body. As he phrased it in the editorials section of *JAMA*,

> believing as I do, in the eternal principles of energy, and that you cannot get something for nothing, I am unable to see how the stimulation produced by a drug like caffein can secure any energy except at a corresponding expense . . . Fatigue is the signal of danger showing the need of rest and recreation. Caffein extinguishes the red light but does not close the switch.[100]

Wiley went on to condemn Coca-Cola and to rebuke some professors who had reported findings that suggested caffeine was not particularly dangerous. He continued throughout his career to oppose it, arguing that coffee and tea had "no food value" and that the caffeine was dangerous for children, yet was sold to them indiscriminately.[101] He even authored a pamphlet titled "The Drugging of Children," which featured a silhouette of the devil whipping a little girl with the word "Caffein" written above it.[102] Wiley's concern for children consuming caffeine was a rhetorical point that others borrowed from him, often citing him in the process.

The Woman's Christian Temperance Union's periodical, *The Union Signal*, argued against caffeine on many occasions. In 1909, they informed readers that the caffeine used in the soft drinks sold to Americans came from four sources: kola nuts, tea, coffee, and South American bird shit—a claim that was surely intended to disgust readers into avoiding caffeinated sodas.[103] *The Union Signal* also ran a series of anti-caffeine articles that today would be called "paid content," meaning that they appeared to be news but were actually advertisements for the Postum Cereal Company (now Post Cereals). These argued that the public had a right to know the truth about coffee, which was that it was addictive, enslaving, and that "one in every three coffee users has some form of incipient or chronic disease," which posed "a terrible menace to a nation of civilized people." Grape-nuts were thus a better breakfast choice.[104] The *Union Signal* and Wiley's goals converged at the point of social engineering. Wiley wanted to build society into eugenic perfection, and substances like caffeine, alcohol, tobacco, and opium obstructed that end and even contravened it. The WCTU wanted a moral society where individuals reflected Christian principles and advanced the Millennial Kingdom toward its culmination.

The anti-caffeine positions that Wiley and others fought for also highlight how ideological the category of "drugs" can often be. Caffeine, which is addictive, sometimes still gets listed as a "drug" today, but usually only as a technicality. As with other habit-forming substances, though, caffeine addicts can expect an unpleasant withdrawal process if they try to quit. Few people today really care about who uses caffeine, though, and most are content to let others make their own decisions about it. It is quite common for people to joke on social media about how dysfunctional they are without coffee, but far fewer joke about needing cocaine or ketamine each morning before going to work. Any ninth grader can buy a pumpkin spice latte and few baristas would feel uncomfortable selling them one. Our contemporary attitudes toward it were not a guaranteed historical development, though, and reformers like Wiley would probably be depressed to see how ubiquitous caffeine is to twenty-first century American culture. If they could travel to the present day, they would mourn our wasteful embrace of degenerative, caffeinated race poisons and perhaps judge us quite openly for it.

Eugenics and Shame

For eugenicists addiction was something to extinguish, a mark of bio-moral defectiveness. Antidrug eugenicists participated in American legislative politics, and some people like Wiley got quite far toward their goals. Legislation is not the only kind of social power though. Eugenics functioned as a hermeneutic of social belonging, one that made pariahs of addicts. Perhaps some people escaped their addictions, but could they ever escape the degeneracy that spawned it? Under eugenics' bio-moral models, addictions were stigmatic. Since degeneracy operated at a genetic level, recovered addicts could never really be free of the taint. Eugenicists also argued that drug use can permanently damage genetic material, which further exacerbates an irremovable stain—there will always be the specter of what damage the tobacco or cocaine may have done to potential offspring. Antidrug eugenics had legal teeth to be sure, but one of its most potent contributions to the War on Drugs can't be easily traced and that's what it did to social reputations. Eugenics spoke with the authority of science but also played in the politics of shame.

There's overlap between eugenicists' readings of addiction and their readings of disability—they often thought of addiction as itself a hereditary condition or as the product of a disabling condition (e.g., neurasthenia). Disability was often treated as shameful in its own right, and families were often embarrassed about disabled members.[105] Shame is a reflexive phenomenon; it is a dialogue between the judgment and expectations that others have of someone else—and the failure to live up to those expectations—which can translate into the internalized experience of shame upon recognition of that failure.[106] Disability historians Sharon L. Snyder and David T. Mitchell name the eugenics discourse about disability the "master trope of human disqualification," which is right.[107] Eugenicists' criticism of addiction as a hereditary fault—one they explicitly linked to criminality, epilepsy, cognitive disabilities, and inferiority—placed it in the same category as disability. It stood among the symptoms of American decline as a threat to Christian civilization and racial purity.

Shame is hard to track. It is often a private experience, one that by its nature people are often loath to discuss. Eugenics's antidrug discourse demands its consideration though, particularly given how central emotion is to the lived human experience. Even though it is less visible than other emotional experiences, there is some suggestive evidence of shame's importance for addicts living under eugenics's hegemony. One piece is that addicts were typically secretive about their substance use.[108] There are many reasons why someone might be secretive, but it seems exceedingly likely that for many addicts the secrecy stemmed from embarrassment or humiliation. Some writers commented on this, such as when Arthur Woods explained,

> the drug user becomes an irresponsible member of his social group, and as far as his influence goes it lowers the standards of the group. There is further the sense of isolation resulting from the chasm between the addict and the normal world. The addict tends to feel a social stigma and think of his rôle as a person decidedly different from that of the nonuser. He conceives of himself as peculiar, probably inferior . . . it is this sense of living in a different social world that helps promote his isolation.[109]

Woods basically agreed with addicts who shared that self-assessment. At times he wrote sympathetically of those caught in medical addiction, yet he also expressed that "in one perverted sense narcotics endow people with a sort of diseased will of tyrannical force," yet one "which leads to their own destruction."[110]

Woods wasn't an outlier: Eugenics discourse insisted upon addicts' unfitness, worthlessness, or social parasitism, positions that curated substance users' shame. Wiley, for instance, explained, "There is no more pitiable sight to me than to see a boy of ten to seventeen smoking a cigarette. I at once lose faith in his future. I see in his development only an inefficient and perhaps invalid citizen."[111] Woods and Wiley are representative. Sometimes people expressed pity or sympathy for addicts, but it was quite rare for commentators to withhold judgment. Pity and sympathy were nearly always mixed with evaluations of addicts as defective people.

Addicts' shame experiences have been preserved in a few accounts. John Hawkins, a doctor writing about addiction in 1937, offered some case histories that show shame to be significant. One morphine addict, a man who had once been a newspaper editor, told Hawkins that he had privately wanted to send cards to some of his former friends at Christmas. He decided not to "out of consideration for their feelings." Another addict could only pay for her morphine through prostitution. In regular society, she carried herself in a way that masked her job and her habit, and she gave to charities even when she couldn't afford to do so. She hated her addiction and the prostitution, but feeling she could never escape them, she settled for merely hiding her circumstances. Commenting on this phenomenon, Hawkins explained,

> The great majority of this class fear detection almost constantly, and once they allow their dose to increase to such proportions as to make the performance of their duties impossible or detection almost certain, they desert their work to avoid the censure of their employers and friends. Finding themselves a helpless, hopeless slave to drugs, without income and with a strange desire to separate themselves as far as possible from their families, their friends and their former associates, their plight is pitiable indeed, and it is not remarkable that a large number of them leave their native haunts and fairly "fall" into occupations far from respectable.[112]

Was a eugenics discourse about degeneracy and the purification of society solely responsible for this experience of shame? No—but it was an important piece of it. A century prior, someone could use opium habitually and expect some rebuke, but by the 1930s that same condition drove people away from those they knew and loved, afraid to even send Christmas cards. It's important to keep legal and institutional regulatory power in mind, but we also need to recognize that eugenics discourse had less tangible consequences for the lived experiences of addicts. Nobody truly lives outside of moral frameworks. When those frameworks render someone dangerous or disgusting—to the extent that the state should sterilize them so that nobody else will ever be like them in the future—it gets personal.

Conclusions

Degeneracy theory and eugenics had much to say about individual lives but the bigger concern was always civilization itself. In the context of American eugenics, some eugenicists thought in global terms, but the United States was usually their first focus. People like Wiley, Kellogg, Sadler, and Hobson wanted to see it evolve into a nation ruled by a perfect white race and they believed that this was possible with the right engineering. Substance use posed a threat to this, however, since it led to sickness, madness, and immorality, all of which could be passed down to future generations. Conversely, degenerates were also the people who were most likely to misuse substances. The lack of willpower or unwillingness to conform to moral standards meant that degenerates were easily turned into addicts. Such addiction worsened their degeneracy, leading to a total moral abandon that produced crime, deceit, and large-scale social problems.

It would go too far to say that postmillennialism is responsible for the Drug War. It would also go too far to say that *any* single force or catalyst led to the Drug War. The War on Drugs was (and is) a complex convergence of different interests, ideologies, idealisms, practices, prejudices, obsessions, antagonisms, and reactions. Although postmillennialism may not be the sole rationale for the Drug War, it was an important ingredient for its development. Christian nationalists identified the United States as fundamentally and permanently Christian—to lose this quality would be to lose America. For those who took a postmillennialist view, oftentimes America was also ordained to lead the world toward the promised Kingdom. That Kingdom would be realized through human progress, and scientists kept unlocking new secrets of God's universe. The laws of heredity were one such area of advancement.

Postmillennialism shaped American eugenics in important ways and the two ideas worked well together. Both saw history as a progress narrative with an attainable future utopia. Both saw moral improvement as a necessary condition of that progress. Both typically approached morality as a universal and often self-evident category. For Christian eugenicists, heredity, biology, and cognition were all mechanisms that God created to build humanity. The Millennial Kingdom was not an individualistic heaven, it was a utopian civilization where the greater good of all was the primary concern and eugenics could help the world get there. Counterintuitively, postmillennialism doesn't have to be Christian. Like many people, Harvey Washington Wiley changed as he as he got older. During Wiley's formative years, he learned to think about the future as a golden utopia waiting for humanity to unlock it. He lost faith in the literal millennium of scripture but he still pursued the same postmillennialist agenda of civilization and progress that first informed it.

Wiley wasn't alone in this process. Any eugenicist raised in the United States grew up in a world shaped by Protestant hegemony. Morality isn't something one fully chooses, it is something that one is socialized into. That's not to say that morality is just a matter of passive reception. It can be negotiated and sometimes even rejected, but both of those usually require conscious effort and self-awareness. The optimism that came with postmillennialism—the idea that a brighter day was just beyond the horizon and that America could keep advancing ad infinitum—would have surrounded them as kids regardless of their own affiliation. Not every American eugenicist came from a Christian background (let alone a postmillennialist one), nor was every adult eugenicist a white Christian nationalist. At the same time, eugenics was explicitly about white racial purity and it was so indebted to postmillennialist attitudes about individuals' potential to reform civilization that they made jokes about their own "eugenic millennium." Perhaps some will disagree with me, but I understand American eugenics to itself be a manifestation of public Protestantism, one that helped to translate contingent moral norms into wider positions about public health.

Degeneracy theory and eugenics were consequential for the development of a global Drug War, and not solely because of heredity. As degenerative substances, narcotics threatened to upend societies and posed a threat to everyone, even those who did not themselves use drugs. This was particularly true with regard to children. Children are a kind of moral signifier, representing the most innocent of the vulnerable, and would remain a constant trope from the earliest days of Christian Temperance to the present. Eugenics discourse about children and future generations was rarely about specific children, though, rather, it was about the imaginary child. The child was a symbol of vulnerable innocence for antidrug activists, and a potent symbol at that.

Children weren't the only people who reformers considered vulnerable. Race theory suggested that European races were better off and more advanced than the other peoples of the world, that they were in general more capable, had better self-control, and were more clever. If substance use threatened to damage white society, race theorists and eugenicists considered people of color to be even more vulnerable. In the nineteenth and early twentieth centuries, colonial powers emphasized a duty they identified as "The Civilizing Mission." For many colonial powers—including the United States—this civilizing mission had a religious component to it. Civilizers believed that Christianity offered a foundation to societies superior to other religions, especially "savage" ones. Missionaries were therefore a major force in this battle to bring "the child races" up to speed. However, missionaries were also frequently aware of the larger discourses surrounding narcotics. Many used degeneracy theory to argue against substance use and also quite often treated substance use as an impediment to conversion. In response to these positions, missionaries often intervened in colonial policy, asking authorities to prohibit substance use for indigenous peoples; it is here that we turn next.

4

US Colonialism and Substance Use Prohibition

Honolulu (1917)

In Honolulu on December 30, 1917, the Hawaiian prince Jonah Kalanianole petitioned Congress not in his role as delegate to the House of
Representatives but in his capacity as president of Ahahui Puuhonua O
Na Hawaii (the Hawaiian Protective Association). Kalanianole and the
other officers of APONH—themselves a mix of white missionaries and
Native Hawaiian leaders—somewhat surprisingly begged Congress to
suspend home rule.

Home rule, which is the direct government of a colony by the people
living there, was something that many colonized peoples longed for and
which Hawaiians had some measure of as far as Kalanianole was concerned. Claiming to speak for the entirety of the Hawaiian race, APONH
insisted that although Hawaiians both wanted and deserved home rule,
their present circumstances were dire enough to warrant its temporary
retraction. According to their "memorial and resolution," alcohol and
the Central Powers threatened severe harm.[1]

APONH couched their argument in cosmic terms. The petition began
with a florid and mythic recounting of the Christian God's work in the
world using a style reminiscent of Polynesian cosmogonies, described
humanity's ascent out of chaotic darkness into an ever-unfolding light of
knowledge, morality, and destiny. APONH went on to argue that Hawaii
had always sought improvement, which was why King Kamehameha II
and Queen Kaahumanu had abolished heathen idolatry, invited missionaries to Hawaii, and solidified Hawaiians as a Christian people. Yet
according to APONH, the civilized nations such as the United States
had brought Hawaii problems, too. APONH averred that those nations
brought "deadly vice" with them, which "[multiplied] with an alarming
rapidity the physical, spiritual, moral and social problems of its people."

The evilest of these, they argued, was alcohol. Hawaiians had resisted drinking, forming the first of America's temperance societies in an attempt to avoid that "demon." Not everyone escaped drinking, though, leading to insanity, immorality, poverty, lawbreaking, and cultural damage. Now that the United States had entered the war, there was no room for error: Congress must ban alcohol in Hawaii by decree, preserving both Hawaiians' dreams of Christian civilization as well as American military integrity. In another petition from April 1918, APONH argued that "the Hawaiian Race is about to be a race of the past," vanishing into extinction because of drinking.[2]

Kalanianole's argument is fascinating for multiple reasons. First, he and APONH reproduced a very conventional argument about race and substance use, one that would have been recognizable to their intended audience. Since the earliest days of colonialism, European powers argued that their legal sovereignty over foreign lands rested on the necessity of converting indigenous people to Christianity.[3] Christianity meant civilization, and uncivilized peoples needed missionaries and foreign governments to help them advance. Although this concept dates back to at least the fourteenth-century Northern Crusades, the nineteenth and early twentieth centuries saw the idea revitalized in important ways. Theories of civilizational development—presumed to be scientific—implied a moral responsibility to colonize and improve "savage" or "barbarian" peoples. But by the late nineteenth century, missionaries and temperance societies deplored European and American abuses, criticizing how "Christian nations" consistently introduced opium or alcohol to indigenous "heathen" peoples. Furthermore, it was a common assertion that American Indians on the continent were vanishing because of alcohol abuse; the replication of this argument in Hawaii would have signaled a close analog for white readers.[4] Not only did American colonialists apply race science to argue that non-white people were less able to handle such substances, they saw substance use as an obstacle to the civilizing mission.

A second reason Kalanianole's argument is interesting is the role he played in the Hawaiian colonial power structures. Kalanianole and APONH claimed to represent all Hawaiians as though Native Hawaiians were unified in all things. He championed a postmillennial Christian narrative and denounced indigenous Polynesian religion. He identified

Hawaiians as fully integrated and supportive of the United States and American sovereignty. He further claimed that Hawaii is today Christian because King Opukahaia "persisted" and "persuaded" missionaries to come to the islands, thus positioning their conversion as an explicit and deliberate act of self-agency. Although Polynesian social norms typically would have granted Kalanianole some level of respect and authority, absolutely none of the aforementioned proposals would have been amenable to *all* Hawaiians.

In short, Kalanianole participated in and replicated the colonialist arguments supporting Hawaiian subjugation. Although he argued that Hawaiians are fully civilized—democratically oriented, patriotic, and Christian—his historical account is one in which Hawaii's success was only possible through missionary activity and western rule. Noenoe Silva's study of Hawaiian colonization tells a different story, though. Native Hawaiians often resisted and resented western conquest. Missionary interventions were invasive, often attempting to ban Hawaiian religious and medical practices through law alongside the restructuring of Hawaiian labor practices and land use.[5] American legislators forbade Hawaiian children to use their native language in schools.[6] American businessmen borrowed US troops to overthrow Queen Liliuokalani—the last regnant Hawaiian monarch—and install themselves as new rulers. Put another way, the American occupation and annexation of Hawaii was a project of cultural genocide, an approach that allows a people to survive but which attempts to destroy their defining culture and replace it with another. Many Hawaiians living in 1917 would have had personal memories of American conquest. Missionaries had been arguing for a century that Hawaiians were barbaric, backwards, and in need of white Christian morality and rule.[7] Kalanianole's petitionary claims thereby reproduced the central theme in white American narratives about Hawaii—that it was a place still in the fragile process of civilizing—and valorized US sovereignty in ways that would have offended at least some of the people for whom he claimed to speak.

Kalanianole's cooperation with American rule is representative of colonialist approaches more broadly and helpful for understanding substance use prohibition in this context; it is a model example of how some prohibitionists of indigenous background campaigned for stricter metropolitan control. Postcolonial theorist Julian Go notes that it was fairly typical for American colonialism to conscript local elites into their projects; by placing members of the colonized in visible positions of dignity, American colonizers sent a symbolic message that the colonized were guiding their own destinies.[8] Kalanianole was not appointed per se, as was the case in some other colonial contexts; he was elected by voters living in Hawaii, most of whom were Native Hawaiian.[9] Yet Kalanianole spoke with the colonizers' idioms and championed goals that fit dominant white American norms. (Indeed, his intended goals replicate those of the Anti-Saloon League, the Secretary of the Navy, and congressional resolutions.)[10] The second APONH petition from 1918 averred that Hawaiians must learn "what it is to be grateful" and "to respect his superiors and know his place and station in life," as well as learn how to labor and better manage finances. Such requests are a trophy to paternalism. Despite those arguments we should not assume that Kalanianole simply acquiesced to white American norms passively.

There's no reason to think he wasn't entirely on board with these narratives. As anthropologist Lila Abu-Lughod argues, present-day Americans often imagine that foreign others are being compelled or coerced when they make choices that Americans believe are contrary to those others' interests.[11] Kalanianole's acceptance and encouragement of white Christian hegemony at the expense of indigenous Hawaiian culture would seem to reproduce this problem: His behavior does not easily mesh with contemporary moral norms about what he *should* have wanted for Hawaii. We cannot conclude from this though that he was just a puppet, that he was insincere, or that he had been tricked into collaborating with colonial policy; this is part of the complicated work of deciphering colonial politics. Kalanianole claimed to speak for all Hawaiians and to defend their interests, but he represented one paternalist, pro-American faction. American metropolitan authorities were generally happy to recognize particular individuals as authentic envoys for indigenous peoples when those individuals championed colonial goals. This allowed authorities to then use those envoys' normative demands to validate the work that colonialists already wanted to do. When Kalanianole asked Congress to abolish alcohol by federal writ it thereby reproduced a typical process for controlling substance use in US colonial contexts, and Kalanianole got at least part of what he wanted: Woodrow Wilson prohibited alcohol in Oahu by executive order roughly two months later.[12]

Colonial concerns about substance use contributed to the Drug War in major ways; in fact, it is unclear if it ever could have unfolded the way it did without them. Colonizers used race science and anthropological arguments about civilizational development to justify conquest and rule.[13] Some kinds of substance use seemed to produce immoral and uncivilized conditions—at least to many religiously oriented colonizers. European colonial governments often thought differently; the British and Dutch in particular made large profits from trading opium in the Far East, as did Japan. Missionaries—particularly American and British missionaries—found such commerce repugnant and petitioned governments for change. Some elite missionaries such as Charles Henry Brent managed to wrangle colonial governments into committing themselves to drug control by treaty agreements. In the diplomatic aftermath of World War I, the fledgling League of Nations found itself tasked with orchestrating and effecting these treaty agreements, creating an entire division just for opium control. It is the missionary element of colonialism, however, that generated the most significant antidrug fervor.

Anthropology, Cultural Evolution, and Race Science

Anthropology contributed to the civilizing mission by offering a formula for civilizational development known as "cultural evolution," sometimes also called "stagism" (not to be confused with a Marxist theory of the same name). Cultural evolution theory developed hand in hand with race science and proposed that human cultures develop in various stages, but argued that some races advanced faster than others. Development could be sped up, however, with the right interventions. People could be taught higher stages of civilization, and advanced culture could also indoctrinate less developed peoples through diffusion. Although not all anthropologists accepted this theory (Franz Boas stands out as a famous exception), by the end of the nineteenth century it held considerable currency.

In 1888, J. W. Powell, the Smithsonian's director of ethnology, wrote a fairly typical version of stagist theory for *The American Anthropologist*. He claimed that human evolution was a long process, but that all human societies pass through three stages, identified as "savagery," "barbarism," and "civilization." (Other anthropologists sometimes replaced "savagery" with the term "primitive.") Such taxonomies had already been in existence for decades.[14] Powell proposed that specific subsections of culture such as "language" and "philosophy" could be identified along civilizational spectrums; some languages were more advanced than others, and while philosophies began in mythology near the "savagery" end of the spectrum, they eventually evolved into "science," which was civilized.[15] Powell also argued that savage peoples could become civilized through cultural contact and exchange, writing that

> when savage or barbaric peoples associate with civilized peoples they learn the civilized language and often abandon their own. For a long time the new language is imperfectly spoken and is mastered but to a limited extent. There is a sense in which it may be said that the language in passing from the higher to the lower people is degraded, but the civilized man is not degraded because the savage attempts to speak his tongue and the power of expression of the savage is greatly improved thereby. Wherever Christian civilization comes in contact with savagery, monotheism and the people speedily learn to believe in a Great Spirit God, but such belief is always more or less tainted with polytheism and other abhorrent superstitions. [. . .] In all cases, activities borrowed from a higher by a lower culture result in progress.[16]

Although Powell notes that other theorists proposed that some races are progressive and some retrogressive, he himself argued that all races everywhere progress—they just do it at different speeds and with different ease. Cultural diffusion was a useful strategy to him; just as people learn to speak official languages, colonized savages would learn to advance toward monotheism if Christianity were present. Powell's version helps highlight the stakes for American colonial projects. "Lesser races" had not yet attained civilization, but they could if colonizers helped them.

Cultural evolution essentially took the racial politics of the nineteenth century and stamped them with a scientific imprimatur. European and American thinkers had for centuries theorized white supremacy through different means; here, anthropology offered a supposedly scientific rationale for it. By observing the differences between European and American societies and how non-Europeans conducted their lives, cultural evolution proposed that one represented "civilization" and the other "savagery." As religious studies theorist Jonathan Z. Smith wrote, though, "difference is rarely something simply to be noted; it is, most often, something in which one has a stake. It is above all a political matter."[17] To call a style of music or an approach to land management "savage" was not without its stakes, it was a claim to white superiority and often the basis for reforming whatever "savage" quality was under consideration. Additionally, that hierarchy of superiority and inferiority not only justified relocating sovereign power to a European or American metropole, for colonialists it demanded it. To leave "lesser races" to govern themselves was irresponsible and immoral.

Internal Colonialism and American Indians

Of course cultural evolution only approved conditions and ideologies already at work; it is not as though Europe and the United States waited for science to green-light colonialism before they engaged in it. Indeed, the American Indian reservation system was highly influential in shaping anthropological theory—ethnologists spent a good amount of time trying to discover what "primitive" people could teach them about cultural evolution. The reservation system was not created for scientists, though, it was meant to corral American Indians into compact places as a way to open up land for white settlement and to make them feel safe from a racial other whom they considered dangerous. It was also one of the earliest sites of the American civilizing mission.

White American attitudes toward American Indians were complicated in the years of the early republic. On one hand, many were terrified of Indians. Before the Revolution, the colonial Pennsylvania government had offered bounties in exchange for Indian scalps, and at the time of the Revolution, many rebels were convinced that wide-scale war with American Indians was unavoidable.[18] This fear of Indians lasted well into the nineteenth century; historian Philip Deloria suggests it wasn't until after the 1890 massacre at Wounded Knee that people believed Indians to be "pacified."[19] Even so, American missionaries began moving into Indian societies in the first decades of the nineteenth century, hoping that by their very presence they could help convert and therefore civilize the Indians.[20] Teaching American Indians to adopt vigorous white labor practices and to learn English represented another civilizing goal, one that the federal government was willing to pay missionaries to perform.

The federal government reached into American Indian life in significant ways and with gradually evolving and ever-increasing power structures. As religious historian Sylvester Johnson notes, between the 1819 passage of the Civilization Act and the 1840s, the US government spent the equivalent of 4.5 billion contemporary dollars on sending Christian missionaries to convert American Indians.[21] In 1824, John Calhoun created the Indian Office as a sub-department in the Department of War, and in 1830 the Indian Removal Act saw the forced removal of American Indians to new reservations west of the Mississippi.[22] In 1832, Congress created the post "Commissioner of Indian Affairs," a position with sweeping power over Indian relations, and in 1849 the Office moved into the newly formed Department of the Interior as the "Bureau of Indian Affairs" (BIA).[23] Between the 1840s and 1880s, the federal government created, guided, and regulated the reservation system. The initial hope was that reservation borders would generate some modicum of peace and amnesty between American Indians and white settlers, but in the course of westward expansion, American Indians found their territory shrinking further and further as white Americans demanded more land or repartitioned reservations in unhelpful ways. Tribes gradually also found themselves forced onto reservations they did not wish to inhabit, with US troops capturing and returning Indians who escaped them.[24] Although the realpolitik of reservations was far more about containing a racial other, civilization represented an important ideological underpinning: Reservations and the attendant governance of Indian life was guaranteed to erase the Indian threat by transforming them into civilized societies that reflected and inhabited white norms.

"Cultural genocide" was a term developed when international lawyers began trying Nazi war crimes after World War II; although the term itself is anachronistic in this setting, the concept would have been recognizable to Americans who were invested in the civilizing mission and most of them would have found it approvable. During the nineteenth century (and especially the latter half), the general consensus was that American Indians were "savage" and incapable of self-rule. Part of "civilizing" Indians necessarily required destroying particular aspects of their society; it was the things that made them different from white, Christian Americans that rankled contemporary critics.[25] A particularly noteworthy example comes from General Henry Pratt, who founded the famed Carlisle Indian Industrial School in Pennsylvania specifically in an effort to "kill the Indian, but save the man." Pratt's view was that only by intentionally destroying Indian culture could the Indian race survive, and the school was very deliberately designed to do exactly that. Children were removed more than 1,000 miles from their families, often for years, where they were forbidden to speak Indian languages, wear Indian clothing, or practice Indian religions. Pratt felt these policies were generous acts of support for Indians, yet this "civilizing" process was often traumatic for students and caused lifelong psychological trauma.[26] White discourse about Carlisle unsurprisingly focused on the students who felt positive about their experience, though, emphasizing the possibility and plausibility of advancing savage races toward civilization. Education represented a primary front of the civilizing mission, one that white colonizers lionized in both its institutional and informal formats.

Restricting Alcohol

The civilizing mission also demanded an end to substance use. Between its reservation system and educational strategies, the federal government held significant influence over the day-to-day lives of Indians. Laws to prevent Indians from drinking alcohol date back at least to Jefferson's presidency, expanding through a century-long series of legal strategies designed to expand prohibition under the BIA's watchful eye.[27] Anthropologist Gilbert Quintero has compellingly argued that constructions of Indian alcohol consumption were both born of colonialism as well as perpetuated it. Quintero writes that

> knowledge about Native American drinking constructs and reinforces differences between this group and others on a number of different biological, social, and cultural levels. This derives from the fact that all theories of Indian drinking are colonial forms of knowledge to the extent that: (1) they create, standardize, and make into social facts perceived biological, racial, cultural, and social oppositions between the colonizer (white, Euro-American) and the colonized (red, Native American); (2) they are

systematically utilized in specific contexts to disempower the colonized by characterizing Indian people as dysfunctional, pathological, or weak, thereby reinforcing the power of the colonizer.[28]

Given how nineteenth-century scientists approached alcohol in general, and given how race science's arguments positioned Indian inferiority, it should be unsurprising that alcohol was such a concern for the Bureau of Indian Affairs. Colonial experts saw alcoholism as a racial problem, interpreting and representing American Indians as biologically predisposed to addiction and lacking self-discipline. That narrative suggested that because of such racial weaknesses, white Americans needed to take greater control of American Indian societies if Indians were to ever become civilized.

One need not accept the race science position that American Indians are biologically more susceptible to addiction to recognize that for some specific, individual Indians, alcohol certainly would have posed problems. (The proposal that American Indians are genetically predisposed to alcoholism is more propaganda than fact; there isn't much evidence to support this.)[29] Like every other population group that consumes alcohol, some Indians did find themselves hooked. These stood out to white observers, who made note of the Indians who fit their narratives and ignored the ones who did not. Because some Indians did become alcoholics, civilizers often fixated on them as representative models of Indian degeneracy.

To many white Americans, fully civilizing American Indians seemed like an accomplishment that lay over the horizon. In the March 1913 edition of *The Red Man* (a journal published by Carlisle), the editorial section wrote that "the gradual, and, it is hoped from now on, accelerated evolution of the race into healthy, self-supporting, self-respecting, Christian men and women, will come as it has with the Indian's Pale Face brother." The editorial further suggested that Indians could not yet be trusted to manage their own property, since they tend to lose everything and become destitute, and that "a large portion" of Indians "are illiterate and incompetent."[30] *The Red Man* further took the position that "as a Nation, we can guide and protect him, but in the end the Indian will have to work out his own salvation."[31] Converting Indians to full citizenship required not just Christian conversion and practice, but "the gospel of hardwork [*sic*] and frugality" alongside the rejection of "waste" and "idleness." Federal oversight would continue to be necessary until they advanced enough for self-government. This also required protection from "bootleggers" and "the liquor traffic."

The Red Man devoted an entire issue to Indians and alcohol the next year. The issue included an article from the Reverend Sherman Coolidge, who in addition to being clergy was also president of the Society of American Indians, an activist group that lobbied for Indian causes from an assimilationist perspective. The article itself derived from Coolidge's address to a 1913 Anti-Saloon League rally in Columbus, Ohio. Coolidge had been born in Wyoming, but went east at age seven without knowledge of English or Christianity. He got by on a kind of pidgin sign language until he acquired enough English to interact with others. While attending a boarding school (presumably one of the Indian schools modeled after Carlisle), Coolidge began attending a Presbyterian church, where he converted to Protestant Christianity and pledged to become a minister. Coolidge understood his mission as one of both evangelism and reconciliation; he wished to convert other Indians to Christianity, but he also wanted white Americans and American Indians to "understand each other."[32] Coolidge is a complicated figure; on one hand, he refused some of the dominant ideological positions of his day, such as the idea that reservations were benevolent or that Indians were vanishing. On the other, he accepted race science and stagist discourse, suggesting that Indian survival and progress could only be accomplished in the absence of alcohol. He wrote "no diseased or drunken people, no diseased or drunken race can develop, and we want the Indians to become efficient, peaceable citizens of the United States."[33] He accepted the premise that most American Indians remained undercivilized and that sobriety was a precondition if they ever hoped to advance.

From Alcohol to Peyote

Coolidge's position—much like Kalanianole's—was a standard approach to substance use from those invested in the civilizing mission: Only through strong government oversight could natives be protected from intoxication. Alcohol may have been the primary substance to fear, but other substances needed attention too, including peyote. Peyote prohibition ranks among the messiest realms of the early Drug War. Although every area of the Drug War had multiple voices, peyote was conceptually more complex given its religious utility and its indigenous medical use. That complexity was complicated further when colonial voices failed to produce any coherent picture of what peyote even did. It was also unclear who had the right to prohibit peyote; Tribal councils, states, congressmen, the BIA, individual policemen, and reservation superintendents all claimed jurisdictional authority at one point or another. On the other side were pro-peyote Indians who had diverse understandings of how peyote should be used, supported by liberal anthropologists and even some colonialist allies. Anti-peyotists held the majority position though, and given how robust the discourse was when it came to equating peyote with alcohol and opium, it's really quite remarkable that federal peyote prohibition never coalesced in this era. Peyote prohibitions frequently emerged, but only in a geographic patchwork and within competing jurisdictional claims to authority.

Peyote is a potent psychedelic flower that grows on cacti in Mexico and in small portions of the United States. It is what religion scholars sometimes call an entheogen, meaning that it is a psychoactive substance that generates a feeling of spiritual significance, and in peyote's case, is often accompanied by visions. Some entheogens are mild (marijuana is sometimes classified at the low end of the spectrum) and some are more intense; peyote would be near the intense end. In addition to its psychedelic effects, peyote also causes gastric distress (vomiting is typical), minor ataxia, and an adrenaline increase that can mildly increase heart rate, body temperature, sweating, pupil dilation, and insomnia.[34] Peyote has a long history of religious use in North America; it was already embedded in Aztec religion when Spanish conquistadores and inquisitors invaded Mexico, and, based on archaeological evidence, had been in use since at least 5000 BCE.[35] After Mexican independence, however, suppression of peyote diminished, and by the turn of the twentieth century it was almost unknown to botanists and bureaucrats in both Mexico and the United States.[36]

People sometimes imagine indigenous traditions to be stable, stationary, and unchanging. They also sometimes imagine that American Indians all operate monolithically, either uniformly agreeing to the same positions and outlooks across a pan-Indian identity, or else at least operating as such within tribal boundaries.[37] Peyote illustrates how problematic such assumptions are. There are many reasons why the religious use of peyote spread as it did in the nineteenth century. The Indian Removal Act compressed tribes from coast to coast into tighter spaces, placing them in contact with each other. Railroads revolutionized commercial transport, allowing goods to be shipped more easily and cheaply. Federal policies, missionaries, and reservations reshaped and restructured Indian life, often in destabilizing ways. As American Indians processed, adapted, and evaluated this cultural and social upheaval, some chose paths of innovation; peyote was one such path.

Pan-Indian peyote religions began coalescing in Oklahoma during the 1880s, taking off particularly well among the Kiowa, Comanche, and Caddo.[38] Although it is possible some of these tribes may have been aware of or even familiar with peyote at earlier dates, it was not until the 1880s that they began using peyote widely. Railroads out of Laredo facilitated peyote's introduction into what was then known as "Indian Territory." At times, Indians used peyote as a kind of medicine; at others, it was primarily a religious substance that offered access to a sacred otherworld. Medicine and religion are of course not mutually exclusive categories, so for most peyotists it was likely a little bit of both. There was no standardized, ritualized format one had to follow; while local communities sometimes shared patterns of peyote use, there was initially little in the way of prescriptivism and people often practiced peyote religion as they saw fit.

Peyote began to spread, partly through intentional evangelism (such as that of Quanah Parker) and partly through its introduction into other pan-Indian religious movements, such as the Ghost Dance.[39] By the early twentieth century it had long since made its way beyond Oklahoma, finding adherents across the western United States. Although practices varied from locale to locale, many peyotists embraced a kind of bricolage, drawing upon both indigenous and Christian idioms. Peyotists also often emphasized its Christian nature, explaining it as an incarnation of the Holy Spirit and validating that position through specific biblical references. These bricolages varied among different communities. The Osage leader Black Dog, for instance, appointed 12 people to be disciples in Pawhuska, Oklahoma, but Crow peyotists in Montana identified feathers as the 12 disciples.[40] At times, practices varied enough to provoke ire from other factions; Osage representatives told the BIA that their own peyote practices were temperate and helpful and in fact provided a cure for alcoholism, whereas the Winnebago's approach was self-serving and decadent.[41] (The claims that peyote cured alcoholism were repeated across other reservations, too, and today peyote is still sometimes used this way.)[42] Peyote religion was a flexible, uncodified thing.

Internal tribal regulations and external government interventions represented two different avenues for peyote suppression. Many government regulations emerged not through formal legislation but rather through the caprice of individuals working for the BIA. Much of this had to do with sloppy interpretive work; because "drugs" is not a natural classification but rather a taxonomic dumping ground for substances deemed bad or harmful, and because BIA officials and missionaries saw peyote as "evil," people were quick to argue that peyote was essentially the same thing as alcohol or narcotics. Although a more realistic narrative about peyote eventually cohered, individuals working with or for the BIA were still unclear about peyote well into the 1920s. (For example, in 1923 a police sergeant in Ponca City, Oklahoma confiscated "an opium bean" and turned it over to a nearby reservation superintendent. There is no such thing as an opium bean and it is clear from the text that the officer thought peyote and opium were the same thing.)[43] However, in the earliest years the confusion about what peyote is and does contributed significantly to its notoriety.

Part of the confusion about peyote had to do with the multiple names by which it was known. Although "peyote" is the standard term today, it was also often called "mescal" at the turn of the century, as well as by various native terms found in the diverse languages spoken by early peyotists. For English-speaking Americans it was a short jump from "mescal" to "mezcal," which is a type of liquor distilled from agave (tequila is one variety). Peyote buttons were also frequently referred to as "mescal beans." White Americans trying to make sense of peyote were often confused by this association, imagining—perhaps understandably—that mescal beans and mezcal were the same. Peyote was occasionally confused with other substances as well.

When it came to peyote's physiological effects, outsiders assigned it a range of properties. Some of the earliest BIA notes concerning it come from E. E. White, the reservation superintendent at Anadarko, Okla homa. In 1888, he argued that it "impair[ed] their minds and physical strength," that Indians were dying from it, and that if left unchecked, peyote would "soon greatly decimate them," claims that became common among BIA officials.[44] In 1898, Havelock Ellis claimed that it revealed "an orgy of vision" and an "optical fairyland," and it diverged from other substances in that it could be productive for someone with a well-ordered mind.[45] Writing to Wilbur Crafts in 1908 from the reservation at Colony, Oklahoma, the missionary Walter Roe claimed that peyote caused "an abnormal awakening of the imagination, during which the brain runs with fierce rapidity, and is out from under control," and that it "saps the nervous energy and will power, so that those who use it steadily and freely, gradually lose energy, clearness of thought, and persistent purpose."[46] In 1912, a party of Omaha Indians went to Washington to argue on behalf of peyote; the BIA met with them alongside some medical doctors, one of whom claimed that peyote was "an intoxicating poison" that was "of the same nature" as morphine.[47] A 1910 report argued that peyote reproduced the same effects as alcohol, except that it also caused experiences of time dilation, which meant it was also quite a bit like cannabis.[48] In a 1909 news brief titled "Opens War on Mescal Bean," an East Coast paper claimed that peyote contained both opium and cocaine.[49] In 1916, a Utah chemical lab reported to the governor that Utes were using peyote and that it had the same effect as opium.[50] In a notarized 1912 affidavit, a peyote apostate named John Semans claimed that the substance excited people sexually.[51] Others argued similarly, claiming that peyote meetings frequently devolved into orgies.[52] Some claimed it led to death, drunkenness, addiction, madness (even to the point of suicide), intestinal blood hemorrhages, lethargy, and degeneration. Some claimed abandoning peyote produced withdrawal symptoms like those of opium withdrawal.[53] At the same time, other interlocutors claimed that none of this was true except possibly the part about temporary lethargy. In summary, before the 1920s, explanations of peyote were often exotic, wrong, and wildly inconsistent.

Much as with other substances, peyote critics argued that irreligion—or at least, degenerated religion—was a symptom of use. In part this was because critics assumed peyote led to immorality (such as the apocryphal tales of orgies). However, because peyote is an entheogen and pro-peyote Indians treated it as such, missionaries and BIA agents found themselves up against a new competitor to conventional Protestant or Catholic Christianity. Although some missionaries felt ambivalent about peyote use, detecting some good among the bad, the majority of missionaries were wholly opposed to it. They often identified deviant religion among peyote's symptoms.

Plenty of missionaries involved themselves in the peyote issue. Two early missionary critics played a significant role in shaping the dominant narrative: Walter C. Roe and Henry Vruwink of the Seger Reservation in Colony, Oklahoma, a reservation largely populated by the Arapaho and Cheyenne. Roe and Vruwink corresponded regularly with the BIA, published peyote criticisms for general audiences, and campaigned for peyote prohibition. In 1908, Harvey Washington Wiley identified Roe as a leading expert on peyote, and by the 1920s, the BIA championed them as paragons of wisdom, reproducing their arguments in official, distributed booklets about peyote.[54]

Walter Roe wrote Wilbur Crafts in 1908 to alert him to peyote, apparently in response to a suggestion from a mutual friend. Roe gave Crafts a rundown on what he thought to be the physical effects of peyote, but emphasized the religious problems it caused far more intently. Roe wrote,

> Morally, its effect is much worse in some tribes than in others. Beginning from the South and working northward, the worship which has grown up about its use has been mingled increasingly with the use of the Bible and a very crude and ignorant presentation of the truths of Christinaity [sic] [. . .] Among the more southern tribes, as Comanches, Kiowas, and Caddos, it has simply assumed the form of a modified barbaric religion, usually engineered by the educated young men, and distinctly harmful in its moral effects upon the tribe. One of the worst results of its use is that it erects a very strong barrier in the way of the presentation of the Christian religion to any tribe that has adopted its use, and is an attempt on the part of the more enlightened of the Indians to establish a racial and tribal religion as against what they call the white man's religion.[55]

One of Roe's chief critiques then was that peyote produced at best a defective Christianity and at worst a "barbaric" religion that necessarily meant cultural retrogression. His claim that Indians promoted peyote as an alternative to "white man's religion" would also seem problematic to anyone with an assimilationist or civilizing mission perspective since they would have considered "white man's religion" inherently civilized and Indians as racially incapable of producing something better.

Roe later went on to write an explanatory article in 1912, which would be reproduced in congressional debates about peyote prohibition into the 1930s. Roe claimed that during peyote's "journey northward it has steadily dropped off pagan elements and grafted on Christian ones, until, as among the Winnebagos of Nebraska, it poses as a Christian denomination, administering the sacraments, and even claiming the right to marry."[56] He theorized that besides creating physical pleasure and offering status to ambitious young Indians, peyote also represented "a religion which claims to be the Indian form of Christianity, and therefore makes a strong appeal to the racial instinct." In terms of its moral consequences, he claimed,

> It is certain that any practice which excites the imagination and relaxes the will, as the use of peyote does, must result in sexual immorality, and the facts bear out this reasoning. I have been told repeatedly by those who have given up the practice that the so-called "Mescal feasts" were often the scene of unbridled libertinism. (In some tribes, e.g. the Winnebagos, the cult teaches that peyote and liquor are incompatible and thus some restraint is exercised over drunkenness, but unfortunately, in most cases, the effect does not last. Certain undoubted instances of moral reform in such tribes I would attribute to the influence of the Bible and Christian teaching intermingled with their worship rather than to the drug.)[57]

Roe concluded with a potent argument that cinched together his evaluations of peyote, religion, and policy. He averred that

> if Christianity, the accepted religion of the most civilized races of the earth, has any superiority [. . .] over the pagan or hybrid forms of religion practiced by aboriginal peoples, then anything that prevents the acceptance of the better and the retention of the worse is a detriment to those affected. This is true of the mescal worship. By this intermixture of a drug habit with a pretence of Christian teaching the young men of many

tribes are being led into an absurd cult incompatible with Christianity and the work of missionaries of all churches is seriously interfered with.[58]

In other words, peyote represented a toxic, degrading influence that led indigenous peoples back into barbarism, not forward into civilization. Christianity was supreme and the BIA must force peyote religion out of existence if Indians are to make progress.

Henry Vruwink took rather similar approaches and cited Roe in his work, which makes sense given that they often worked together. In a 1915 document titled "Peyote or Mescal" (a document that would be cited by Christian periodicals for the next decade), Vruwink reproduced many of Roe's arguments. He did, however, emphasize much more strongly that peyote was essentially the same thing as alcohol. Drawing upon Indian testimonies—many of which were collected by the YMCA for use in lobbying campaigns—Vruwink explained that Indians only used peyote as a substitute for alcohol. In all caps he declared, "PEYOTE WILL SURELY MAKE YOU DRUNK."[59] Drawing upon those testimonies also allowed him to argue that peyotists consumed $60–$100 worth of it in each sitting. (This is an impossible amount; using the BIA's highest price estimates for the 1910s, this would mean every Indian was consuming 12,000–20,000 peyote buttons per session.) Vruwink challenged peyote Christianity, arguing that connecting peyote to Jesus was to embrace "idolatry and blasphemy which makes the intelligent Christian shudder." Vruwink also posited a rationale for why Indians kept using peyote when it was obviously evil, arguing that:

> In view of the fact that peyote is such a detriment industrially, economically, physically, mentally, morally, and spiritually, why do so many Indians continue to eat this drug? There are various reasons. Some eat it because they dare not stop, they are not brave enough, being afraid of the ridicule and threats of the peyote members. Others eat it because they cannot stop; they are drug fiends, bound hand and foot. Still others will not stop because peyote means pleasure, profit, leadership. Most Indians eat peyote because of the pleasurable sensations. It is primarily a lust of the flesh, indulgence at the expense of all that makes manhood and womanhood.[60]

Vruwink's argument then was that Indians used peyote for selfish, deviant, or ignorant reasons, that it was addictive, and that peyote was wholly illegitimate.

In a later booklet titled *About Indians*, Vruwink suggested that peyote hindered Indian salvation and progress. Writing about "my Cheyennes and Arapahoes," he produced a list of their problems. While disease ranked high on his list, the moral conditions worried him more. "Chastity in boy life has been a joke; in girl life, until recently, it was scarce, indeed. Whiskey is ruining scores; licentiousness, hundreds; and the drug peyote, its thousand. My people are lost—body, mind and spirit."[61] Vruwink laid out the stakes in this:

> There is no such thing as sustained morality generation after generation, excepting where that morality is built on a religious basis. [. . .] The Indian is essentially religious; he must drink from the supernatural spring, be that spring bitter or sweet, wholesome or poison. The old springs have been filled up by the coming of the white man. Earnestly my people have been searching for a new spring—a spring essentially Indian in character. The Plains Indians have found it. [. . .] Approach nearer and you will hear their weird yet beautiful mescal songs. [. . .] We know the chemistry of the plant quite well. It is a drug as much so as cocain or morphine. Today it is the greatest menace, not only to the progress but also to the very existence of the Plains Indians. It is weakening their minds, undermining their physical constitutions; it is damning their souls. My people are lost, and there is no power in the earth to save them save the power of Jesus Christ.[62]

Vruwink—like so many other reservation missionaries from Arizona to Minnesota—saw peyote as antithetical to any progress, a progress that could only be attained through gradual Christian conversion.

Prohibition Strategies

Any serious consideration of early peyote prohibition needs to account for William E. Johnson, a staunch advocate for alcohol prohibition whom the BIA tapped for the role of "special chief officer" in 1906.[63] Johnson was a minor celebrity among prohibitionists and had the backing of important organizations such as the WCTU, the Anti-Saloon League, and the YMCA. In a 1920 reflection upon Johnson's legacy, the famed Newfoundland doctor Wilfred Grenfell called him "a good soldier of Jesus Christ."[64] Johnson was of Presbyterian background, with two great-aunts who had been missionaries among the Cherokee.[65] According to his biographer, it was in the context of an 1889 Nebraskan prohibition campaign that Johnson committed himself to the cause, using an Ira Sankey hymn to jest that the anti-prohibitionists were the army of Satan.[66] After a brief stint investigating alcohol in the Philippines, he returned to the United States and wrote an excoriation of "benevolent assimilation," arguing that the United States was instead abusing Filipinos by selling them liquor.[67] In short, Johnson was a pugnacious firebrand with a rigid moral pedigree and therefore an intuitive choice to lead the BIA's anti-alcohol endeavors.

Johnson took his charge to stop Indian drinking seriously, and stopping the flow of illegal alcohol onto reservations was a complicated and time-intensive job. Individuals living near reservations sometimes sold or bartered alcohol to Indians, and the sporadic, non-systematic nature of this distribution made it hard to police. Reservation Indians also sometimes made use of alcohols that were not intended for beverage purposes, such as wood alcohol, cooking extracts, or Sterno fluid.[68] Although white saloonkeepers would never have been permitted to open a bar inside a reservation, in states without prohibition laws it was legal to establish one just outside of them; in 1908 the Uintah reservation had 13 saloons along its border.[69] Given that municipal, county, and state laws about alcohol varied wildly across the west, strategies to keep alcohol away from Indians were tricky. Johnson had no problem pushing for new legislation in places where current legislation didn't suit his purposes. When he discovered in 1909 that Nebraska law only forbade selling alcohol to Indians who didn't hold US citizenship (a criterion that no longer applied to any Indian living in Nebraska) he began lobbying in Lincoln for new legislation that made it illegal to sell to citizen Indians as well.[70] Heart and soul, Johnson was committed to ending Indian intoxication.

Because peyote was so frequently assigned the same properties and derelictions as alcohol, Johnson considered it to fall within his purview. By 1907—one year into his appointment—he was already going after peyote.[71] In close conversation with top BIA officials and the Secretary of Agriculture, Johnson also creatively reinterpreted an 1897 federal law about alcohol. In Johnson's framing, the 1897 law "forbids the furnishing or delivery to an Indian, or the introduction into an Indian country or upon an Indian allotment, 'any article whatsoever, under any name, label or brand, which produces intoxication.'"[72] The law was undeniably written with alcohol in mind, but the language of "intoxication" permitted broader interpretations. Johnson began policing peyote as "dry whiskey" with DC's blessings.

Johnson tracked down the sources of peyote and their means of distribution, seeking to curtail both. Johnson concluded in 1909 that apart from individual Indians who distributed out of advocacy for peyote, there were only two significant commercial peyote distributors, both in Laredo.[73] The two stores—Wormsers Brothers and the Villegas Brothers—sold most of their peyote through the postal service or deliveries made by rail. In April 1909, Johnson arrived in Laredo and "corralled" the druggists.[74] He told both the Villegas and the Wormsers that providing peyote to Indians counted as a federal offense under the 1897 law and pressured both to stop selling it. He then purchased and burned all of the peyote they had in stock, instructing other special agents to "destroy everything you get."[75] While the Villegas Brothers cooperated with Johnson, the Wormsers were apparently cagier about it. Johnson was livid; in October he confided in a friend that he planned to "dig up some old cases against Wormsers Bros. and prosecute them to the limit if I find they are really making shipments of peyote to anybody."[76]

The impasse Johnson faced with them emerged from the racial criterion of the 1897 law. Congress had forbidden providing intoxicants to Indians, but the law said nothing whatsoever about intoxicants for white Americans—a point that the BIA was aware of and which they admitted to the Wormsers when pressed.[77] Records suggest that the Wormsers may have continued to sell peyote to presumably white Americans. This infuriated Johnson, who insisted that there was no such thing as a white market for peyote—a point he had made clear to the Wormsers in May when they asked him about selling to white pharmacists who were requesting it. Johnson contended that peyote was medically worthless and any druggist looking for peyote was faking and that he really wants them for an illicit traffic. [. . .] The peyotes have no medicinal qualities whatever. This has been demonstrated by the Army medical authorities in Washington. I had a letter from a firm the other day which wanted peyoyes [*sic*], claiming they wished to manufacture cocaine and opium from them. There is no opium or cocaine either in these articles.[78]

Johnson made the same argument to shipping companies, such as Wells Fargo and Pacific Express. On April 28, 1909, he informed Wells Fargo that "as this market is confined wholly to Indians, any and all shipments must necessarily be for illegal purpose, and the express agent who receives these articles for delivery [. . .] therefore becomes liable to prosecution."[79] He also told them that Pacific Express had already agreed to refuse peyote shipments on these grounds. On May 13, he told Pacific Express that he wished "to give proper notice of the intentions of the government to those who were at this time entangled with this traffic before bringing criminal prosecutions," and let them know that Wells Fargo had agreed to halt shipments.[80] (The careful reader will note that he thereby informed both companies that their competitor had already agreed to cease shipments.) Under his federal purview for prohibitionist police work, Johnson reinterpreted and used race-based alcohol law to threaten private businesses into compliance with his anti-peyote goals. When the two main vendors stopped selling to Indians and the shipping companies refused to carry it, it severely disrupted the peyote supply, forcing peyotists to create new distribution chains. One man's autocratic reading of race law effectively obstructed peyote religion nationwide for years.

It is unclear why Johnson was so convinced that there could be no white market for peyote. He was familiar with the medical literature about it, and some doctors had indeed advocated or experimented with its potential therapeutic use.[81] Even while informing the Wormsers that there could be no white market, he shared that pharmacists also had already contacted him. Although it postdates his letter to the Wormsers, in 1910 he himself helped traders in New York sell peyote to a German pharmaceutical company that wished to experiment.[82] He was also aware of random white people elsewhere who had interest. Johnson arranged for some mild espionage during his pursuits, so he sometimes obtained copies of peyote requests. For instance, in 1909 an "L.A. Slane" wrote to the Villegas Brothers from Hoonah, Alaska, asking for peyote, which Slane hoped to use to catch "thousands of ducks and geese."[83] How Slane hoped to dose thousands of waterfowl with peyote will probably forever remain a historical mystery, but the point is that with an Irish last name and an Alaskan address Slane was very likely white. It is probably the case though that Johnson was convinced that there *ought not to be* a white market. With Indian religious use representing the dominant driver of peyote commerce, Johnson perhaps found it easy to set aside white requests for the substance as rare outliers, particularly if a narrative about an exclusively Indian market offered him a way to singlehandedly declare all peyote to be illegal.

The BIA argument about peyote's illegality only lasted until about 1916, when a South Dakota district court decided that the 1897 law did not cover it.[84] Anti-peyotists thereafter intensified lobbying for new restrictions that would explicitly outlaw peyote. Missionaries, Christian lobbying groups, BIA employees, and anti-peyote American Indians frequently wrote letters and petitions. Periodicals ran articles denouncing peyote and its many purported horrors. In turn, many western states with Indian populations passed anti-peyote legislation. Utah, for example, outlawed peyote in 1917.[85] In 1920, Kansas outlawed *lophophora williamsii* (peyote), and in an act of confusion, *agava americana* (agave), from which they thought "mescal buttons" derived. (They don't.) Montana followed suit in 1923, outlawing both peyote and agave as well. These state laws were tricky to enforce, however. Ever since the 1832 Supreme Court case of *Worcester v. Georgia*, state laws were not held to apply to Indian nations, insofar as there were jurisdictional boundaries between Indian and state territory.[86] This meant that individual states could pass whatever peyote regulations they wanted, but absolutely none of those laws had any real teeth when it came to policing reservations. Jurisdictionally the only time a state law could affect Indians with peyote is if they were caught with it while off the reservation.

Jurisdictional principles didn't always stop BIA officials from attempting to enforce state laws, though. In 1923, the superintendents at the Tongue River reservation and the Crow reservation in Montana corresponded about how to best approach peyote suppression together. Writing to O. M. Boggess at Tongue River, Charles Asbury argued that they would need to be vigilant about catching Indians with their peyote while they were still outside of reservations. He wrote:

> We realize that if it came to a show-down, it [peyote law] could not be made to apply on Indian land still held in trust. Our County Attorney here is rather liberal in the matter of jurisdiction, and we are going to try to keep on the lookout for shipments in and for people carrying peyote to or from your reservation, and if we can get one or two cases, it will have a very wholesome effect. I take it you will not be offended if we should happen to arrest some Cheyennes coming in with a supply, if we get them here on the Crow townsite.[87]

In his reply, Boggess countered with a different proposal.

> First, because of the fact that no Peyote can arrive in the State of Montana without having crossed patented land, it is evident that all persons introducing it have violated the State law and that for this reason, all new arrivals of Peyote should be considered contraband and should for this reason, be at once removed from the reservation and the person introducing it should be punished under the State law for having crossed patented land with it. Second, because of the fact that persons caught with Peyote on the reservation will doubtless claim it is an old supply, received before February 15, and for the further fact that we owe deference to any law passed by the state of Montana, a date should be set at which all Peyote still on the reservation should be either destroyed or turned into the Agency office for destruction.[88]

Asbury recommended to the Commissioner of Indian Affairs that Boggess's response was indeed the right one. He claimed that "if we can seize the peyote and destroy it, either in transit or in the possession of these people, and have the right to search their premises for it, we would soon make it very difficult to carry on this cult."[89] This response was fairly typical for reservation superintendents; the righteousness of suppressing peyote religion seemed so transparently clear that any tool they could use to squelch it was justified.

Superintendents had to abide by BIA policy, but this still allowed them considerable breadth in their authority to regulate Indian life. Even before the Montana legislature outlawed peyote, the reservations there had some of the most heavy-handed attempts at suppression—Asbury himself described it as "sometimes stretching our authority."[90] Asbury treated peyote as wholly illegitimate, considering it a serious vice disguised as religion and detrimental to "these people who are just emerging from savagery."[91] In 1922, his proposed policies for the Crow reservation declared it "the duty" of "every employee, white or Indian" to "seize and destroy Peyote found on the Reservation or in possession of an Indian enroute to the reservation." Because Cheyenne Indians were promoting peyote, any "visiting Indian suspected of introducing Peyote" could be ordered to leave the reservation. (With the criteria consisting solely of "suspicion" it seems unlikely that very many Cheyenne were permitted to visit after the regulation went into effect.) Crow Indians who broke these rules could be punished with a month in jail and manual labor, and attendance at peyotist religious ceremonies was to be taken as evidence of guilt.[92] In nearby South Dakota, officials at the Rosebud reservation used more draconian strategies—anyone caught violating the peyote ban would have their bank accounts frozen for six months as punishment (with additional months added for each successive violation), tactics they learned from Oklahoma.[93] If one considers the kind of authority BIA officials wielded then, reservation administration made an entire front of the Drug War all on its own.

When it came to obtaining state or local control of peyote—or attempting to gain federal prohibition of it—the BIA, Christian lobbyists, and domestic missionaries frequently supported one another, cooperating to craft an anti-peyote narrative conducive for prohibition. In 1919, for example, the BIA circulated a questionnaire to reservation doctors, superintendents, and missionaries, asking them to submit answers so that they could get a holistic look at the peyote problem as it existed across all reservations. The questionnaire was written with leading questions clearly designed to provoke particular answers. For instance, the survey included questions such as "give specific instances of cases within your knowledge where the use or administration of peyote has been harmful or degrading"; "from your information and observation do you believe the plea that peyote is used as a religious sacrament is genuine, or that it is advanced as a cloak to prevent legislative enactment against its use"; and "are the Indians who use peyote any more or less industrious, thrifty, advanced or civilized than those who do not use it?"[94] This framing allowed the BIA to collect responses that affirmed the narrative they wanted, particularly since the people answering their questions were not neutral figures but mostly people who already agreed with them. A BIA official in Texas, for instance, claimed in his reply that he had never attended a peyote meeting and only had a little second-hand knowledge, yet he still went on to write that peyote-eating Indians are "lazy and dull," that peyote was "worse than whiskey," and that the religious angle was likely a scam.[95] An officer in Reno similarly reported that there was no peyote use on his reservation, but insisted that any argument about it being religious was merely "a subterfuge."[96] Writing from Montana, the missionary S. A. Vennick responded,

> I have no evidence clear enough to show a degrading influence, outside of the fact that all users, whether using it in a religious meeting, or privately, lose interest in religious activities, relying on their "pipe dreams," for their religious life. Albert Anderson comes rarely now to YMCA or Church, Frank Bethune never, Curly has not been out in a long time. Willie Fighting Bear (Ft. Berthold) attacked the agent, deserted his wife, and seemed ready to aggravate anyone when he would come to any gathering.[97]

The BIA compiled these reports and included them in a government-published booklet titled *Peyote: An Abridged Companion*, a document that also contained writing from Charles Roe and Harvey Washington Wiley. According to *Peyote*, the survey results showed a clear consensus: Peyote caused physical degeneracy, gross immorality, and the religiosity was only a ruse to obstruct legislation, with the exception of a few delusional "full bloods" who "believe sincerely in the cult."[98]

The 1919 survey has caught the attention of peyote historians (and for good reason), but it is not the only example of Christian activists and the BIA working together. In 1916, the Gandy Bill came up in Congress as an effort to prohibit peyote at the federal level. The bill had support not just from the BIA, but also the YMCA, Sherman Coolidge's Society of American Indians, the WCTU, and an array of conventionally Christian organizations.[99] There are other examples, too. Fearing peyote as a damaging and degrading substance, the YMCA began collecting testimonies denouncing it in 1911; some of these were obtained by the Reverend R. D. Hall, but many of them are sworn affidavits notarized in assorted western locations. Although there is no proof of it, it seems certain that the YMCA arranged for these and covered the costs—there is simply no plausible reason that half a dozen anti-peyotists in three different states would randomly decide to have their testimonies notarized at their own expense and then mail them to Hall. Hall transferred copies of these documents to the BIA with the explicit intention that they would go toward supporting peyote legislation.[100] The affidavits themselves came primarily from Indians who had formerly used peyote but since abandoned it, and they were frequently sensational. The affidavits describe peyote infanticides, orgies, madness, stomach holes that make people puffy when they drink water, frightening visions of devils and Jesse James, and so on. Multiple testimonies claim that God led the author away from peyote idolatry and back to true Christianity. These testimonies appeared in congressional records (among other places) until 1935. In 1918, an emissary from the Society of American Indians presented the whole collection to Congress during discussion of an Indian appropriations bill, arguing that "we realize that it [peyote] is a menace to our people, because they can not become educated or Christianized nor prosper unless they are sober. We seek citizenship for them, and they must be clothed in their sound mind to meet the obligation."[101] Christian reform organizations and the BIA were thus able to select helpful testimonies from Indians seeking to cooperate with anti-peyote politics, and by placing these in prominent records they endeavored to shape an alternative narrative to the pro-peyote arguments centered upon religious freedom.

American Indians' Suppression Efforts

This returns us to the question of authentic agency, and the power relationships involved in such testimonies are complex. For most tribes peyote was nearly always a minority religion and also quite new. For Indians who adhered to indigenous religions—and far more often for those who had converted to assorted, denominationally oriented Christianities—peyote was often a suspicious and potentially unsettling interloper. To those who considered it dangerous, offering anti-peyote testimony to the BIA or the YMCA was potentially a solution to the problem. At minimum such testimony might convince other Indians not to partake of it, but many anti-peyote Indians also hoped to help officials prohibit peyote by force; some of these anti-peyote testimonies were produced explicitly for use in white discourse. Anti-peyote interlocutors were often aware of this fact; indeed, many were counting on it. Much like Kalanianole, they couched their peyote criticism within a civilizing mission framework, claiming the authority to speak on behalf of all natives while simultaneously asking for portions of that native population to be externally controlled. As with Kalanianole, there is also no reason to suspect the anti-peyotists of duplicity or insincerity. Rather than rejecting a white colonial hierarchy, some accepted it and attempted to work within its confines for goals they found reasonable.

Additionally, some anti-peyotists attempted to regulate peyote themselves at tribal or reservation levels. Among the Pueblo of Taos, New Mexico, Governor Dómencion Córdova held considerably more authority than most other tribal chiefs would be afforded.[102] The BIA applauded the governor's view on peyote, writing, "we are fortunate in having an Indian Governor in this Pueblo who is in sympathy with the suppression of this vice."[103] Córdova saw peyote as a threat and its use was strictly forbidden, which led to conflict with peyote converts. On March 4, 1922, Córdova

> ordered certain Peyote fiends before the council to [answer] charges of misconduct while under the influence of Peyote as well as for violating the Pueblo law against the traffic in and use of this drug; found them guilty and fined them; they refused to pay their fines and the officers seized their blankets, drums, etc. to hold as security until fines were paid.[104]

When peyotists were still practicing their religion the next year, Córdova increased his punishments: Three peyotists were fined $700, $800, and $1,000 and publicly whipped.[105] The BIA was pleased with this outcome, arguing that "they are supposed to be and are all members of the Catholic Church and the Catholic Church does not approve of these practices any more than we do."[106] In cases such as the Taos Pueblo, the BIA was happy to support peyote bans that came via tribal governance.

Perhaps a more typical approach than exorbitant fines and public flogging can be found in a 1937 Sioux council wherein chiefs attempted to outlaw peyote on the Rosebud and Pine Ridge reservations. The chiefs present were irritated that while South Dakota law forbade peyote, it couldn't regulate it on the reservation. Although one chief noted that peyote had good results for combatting alcoholism, the weight of the conversation leaned hard against it. One speaker, Standing Bear, argued, "It is one of the lowest things that our people ever went into. It is not, of course, as bad as that Messiah craze some years ago. That is the way I look at it."[107] (Presumably he meant the Ghost Dance.) Another speaker, American Horse, argued that peyote undermined the three regular Christian denominations working among the Sioux, going on to say,

> I know that it is very detrimental to the people at large. I observe that this peyote is something that doesn't belong to the Sioux tribe. It has originated elsewhere. [. . .] we should appeal to the Commissioner of Indian Affairs to take such proper steps as possible.[108]

The tribal council approved two regulations they felt were moderate enough to pass muster: First, they forbade that peyote be used as medicine; and second, while peyote could continue to be used in religious ceremonies, the quantity must be limited to only one peyote bean or "glass of peyote soup."[109] In a surprising twist, however, the BIA under Franklin Roosevelt had completely reversed directions on peyote. Officials wrote back to South Dakota and told them the council had "gone too far" since peyote was protected under religious liberty.[110] Roosevelt's Commissioner of Indian Affairs John Collier believed the past administrations had overreached and that the BIA must take a much lighter hand with peyote suppression.

Conclusions

The dominant racial ideologies operating in nineteenth- and early twentieth-century America treated indigenous peoples as hopelessly backward and in dire need of help. White supremacy, supported by both race science and postmillennialist models of progress, approached colonized peoples as being capable of reform through the civilizing mission.

American paternalists imagined American Indians to be a child race that could be elevated and developed into something greater so long as civilized, white Americans took charge of their affairs and taught them how to be better than they were. They also saw this mission as both challenging and precarious; indigenous people needed to be protected from manifold detractions if the civilizing mission were to succeed.

To white civilizers, substance use meant road blocks and degeneration. Many people—even those who were powerfully invested in American Indian progress—thought natives faced extinction. Their narratives proposed that if Indians were to survive in a modern world, they must pay attention to both health and behavior. Only moral, industrious, educated Indians could expect to survive in the United States. So far as scientists, legislators, bureaucrats, and missionaries were concerned, alcohol ruptured every category of native progress. Alcohol also served as the conceptual model for other substances, so what was true of alcohol was true of all intoxicants. If peyote truly was "like being drunk only it's lots worse" as one anti-peyotist put it, then this posed even more serious challenges to survival and advancement.[111]

Peyote represents a complicated area of the Drug War for two reasons: First, prohibition was piecemeal and at times exercised without clear legal jurisdiction; and second, the religious dimensions of peyote use created ideological conflict for some of those determining its fate, a conflict that never arose with opium or cocaine. Most analyses of the War on Drugs tend to privilege federal power—historians wish to explore congressional bills, the DEA, presidential decrees, and so on. Of course those are all self-evidently important and it's reasonable to inquire about how far Washington reached and regulated. But ignoring the small scale can omit significant parts of the picture.

The fact that Congress hadn't outlawed peyote often didn't matter for peyotists living in 1910 or 1920. In 1910, William Johnson had simply decided that his police power covered peyote even though the law hadn't mentioned it. American Indians practicing peyote religion suddenly found that Johnson had burned the entire stock of Laredo, that the vendors would no longer sell it, and that the mail companies would no longer transport it. Johnson was on shaky legal ground for sure, but that's an intellectual point irrelevant for how his interventions impacted peyotists, who suddenly found that the supply chain had vanished.

Peyote's price also doubled within ten years as it became very difficult to get; peyotists had to smuggle it while under greater surveillance. In cases where American Indians did manage to obtain peyote, it was also subject to confiscation from reservation officials. Through the collective efforts of missionaries, BIA agents, and Christian activist organizations, some states also prohibited peyote, producing new sets of challenges for acquisition and use.

Still, because some American Indians lobbied for peyote on religious grounds, would-be regulators sometimes found themselves in an ethical dilemma. US democracy was the gold standard for civilization as far as most white Americans were concerned. This democracy included religious freedom as a sacrosanct tenet, a tenet that colonized peoples often adopted and utilized for their own interests.[112] Although the Supreme Court determined in *Reynolds v. United States* that religious practice was not always protected if the practice was considered immoral (a decision that anti-peyotists sometimes explicitly brought up), it was still something around which one should tread lightly. By organizing peyote religion into the Native American Church, including Christian scripture in ritual practice, and offering pro-peyote testimonies, peyotists made many legislators uncomfortable with prohibition. In contrast, missionaries and the BIA argued that peyote was a new innovation, that it was not authentically Christian, and that peyote was merely vice masquerading as religion. In many places that argument never gained enough traction—a bit surprising given the various racial, religious, and prohibitionist ideologies that dominated American discourse in this era—and the end result was an institutionalized version of peyote religion that has survived into the present day.

Finally, both alcohol and peyote prohibitionism demonstrate the complex ways that power can operate. Many indigenous people converted to some form of Christianity after their colonization. Although there were undoubtedly colonialist pressures behind some of these conversions, one ought not assume that American Indians or Native Hawaiians were ersatz believers. Furthermore, when indigenous people accepted narratives about cultural evolution, civilization, or progress—narratives that typically placed them on a lower level of a racial hierarchy—we ought not assume that this was insincere, either. Racism was accepted science at the turn of the century and indigenous peoples had access to that discourse. It should be unsurprising then that some accepted the premise that alcohol or peyote threatened to destroy them. American colonialists didn't force them to participate in prohibition campaigns, but they certainly made use of native voices that validated colonial positions. Undoubtedly that came with some elevation of status or access within colonial hierarchies, but again, that itself is not evidence of insincerity. At the end of the day, some American Indians and Native Hawaiians were invested in Christianity, evangelism, and eschatological progress, and so joining forces with missionaries and the BIA to prohibit alcohol and peyote was an act of piety rather than colonial puppetry. Colonial substance use prohibition was therefore more complex than a one-way metropole/colony power relationship.

5

Protestants, Colonialism, and International Drug Reform

London (1923)

Although giddiness is rarely a trait found in missionary letters, which tend overall to be rather serious in tone, when H. L. Warnshuis wrote to the League of Nations' Advisory Committee on Traffic in Opium, his 1923 letter betrayed trace amounts of glee. Warnshuis wrote on behalf of the International Missionary Council (I.M.C.), a transnational group representing Protestant missionaries from Europe, North America, China, Japan, and portions of the British colonial sphere, which was headquartered in London's elite Belgravia neighborhood. One year prior Dame Rachel Crowdy had cabled a number of missionary organizations asking for help with the League's role in the fledgling global drug war. Crowdy wanted missionaries to provide the League with information: Had missionaries witnessed drug trafficking? Did they have information about where narcotics were manufactured? Was there any help that missionaries could provide for "spreading information in a propaganda form"? The League was careful in their approach; they expressed disinterest in turning missionaries into spies or asking them to do anything that would jeopardize their missional goals. They simply wanted a supply of information more trustworthy than what they were receiving through conventional channels. From the League's perspective, missionaries came with a ready-made global communications network, reform goals complimentary to those of the League, and the imprimatur of honesty, and so they wondered if perhaps these missionaries might be willing to do them such a favor.[1]

When Warnshuis wrote the League, he was happy to share that after receiving that request for help the I.M.C. had contacted every network from the United States to India asking for their cooperation. He also communicated that a related missionary group had published articles about substance abuse in both religious and secular periodicals. American missionaries had appealed to their federal government for restrictive legislation and support for the League's antidrug efforts. But Warnshuis's best news came from China. The League's request for help came in time to bring it to the attention of the National Christian Conference at their first ever meeting in Shanghai in 1922. The Conference—numbering in the thousands—was largely made up of Chinese Christians (all Protestants), who intended to meet annually. The Conference had resolved that "this great evil is regaining a foothold in the land" and that they must "call upon all the Churches and Missions in China to do whatever they can to help create a strong public sentiment against the selling, smoking or eating of this harmful drug," as well as the abolition of poppy cultivation. Warnshuis felt convinced that the "Christian forces in China" were poised to reform the narcotic landscape of Chinese society, and that this had been made possible "through the influence of the International Missionary Council."[2]

Warnshuis's self-congratulatory moment arrived at the confluence of multiple cultural forces. The League of Nations inherited control of the narcotic traffic in the bureaucratic aftermath of World War I, but the very idea of international control had deep roots in decades of prior missionary discourse. British and American missionaries—particularly those in China and other parts of the Far East—had expressed stern opposition to international opium traffic since the mid-nineteenth century.[3] China also served as a sigil for addiction; to mention opium smoking or opium traffic was to summon the imagery of stoned, Chinese addicts. This was often portrayed as a victim relationship with "Christian nations" profiting predatorily from "Pagan" ones. Drugs were often seen as a "demoralizing" force (in the sense that they sapped what moral vigor individuals or social groups might possess); this demoralization then obstructed Christian progress and the civilizing mission. Finally, as we will see, ideologues of the era proposed that such narcotic demoralization threatened other areas of the globe in multiple ways. Warnshuis's claims should be read through the lens of a divine cosmic battle, yet a battle that was becoming more frequently represented in secular idioms rather than explicit religious language.

The Spanish-American War and American Tutelage

Warnshuis may have been concerned with spiritual war, but conventional war played a significant role in the evolution of international drug control. In 1898, the United States battled Spain and won a relatively quick victory. The results of this were far more significant than American historical memory has typically afforded. As religious historian Matthew McCullough notes, "war always involves more than battlefields, bullets, and body-bags," since "it also inspires a conflict of meaning—the cause, the stakes, the identity of the combatants."[4] Although some sectors of public opinion and mass media interpreted the Spanish-American War as a tit-for-tat response to the sinking of the USS *Maine*, elite political discourse framed the war in terms of Christian morality and this represented a popular counternarrative. That Christian moral discourse proved important for Americans' understanding of their new insular colonies.

Americans often saw Spain as a brutal overlord. Prior to the *Maine*, Spain's General Weylar combatted Cuban insurgents with such cavalier disinterest for civilian welfare that his strategies bordered on genocide. Furthermore, the ongoing rebellion in the Philippines suggested that Spain's governmental failures were endemic, a notion commensurate with the long-standing Black Legend that interpreted Spain as an agent of Catholic tyranny rather than a legitimate colonial authority. When the United States fought Spain, it did so with a near universal backing of its Protestant clergy, who saw the war not as one of conquest but rather one of Christian duty. God had prepared Anglo-Saxon culture— and the United States specifically—to lead the world in Christianization. Furthermore, the suffering that innocent peoples experienced at the hands of a tyrannical and backwards metropole deserved better, and the United States was in a unique position to save them. The quick victory over Spain was widely understood to be the divine ratification of this position: America conquered Spain's insular empire not for self-interested glory but as a selfless act of charity.[5]

The Spanish-American War highlights American religious racial thinking particularly well. Although some argued that "tropical races" were presently unwelcome, unfit for self-government, or unassimilable into American culture, the logic of the civilizing mission dictated that white Anglo-Saxon Protestants had a special duty to assist other races with advancement.[6] WASPs' "civilized self-control," moral fortitude, and political know-how positioned them to teach other races how to catch up—or at least this was the story they told themselves.[7] Postcolonial theorist Julian Go notes that with regard to Puerto Rico and the Philippines, American colonialism was not just a project of economic or military advancement, but also one of cultural transformation, involving "exercises by colonial rulers to marginalize, manipulate, or control meanings while also imposing preferred cultural forms and practices."[8] Tutelage, the training of foreign cultures in civilizational practices, was the preferred term for this process of cultural transformation. Although a few especially advanced individuals might be capable of meeting the standards of civilization, American theories of democracy required that the general population of a given region must be capable of such standards in order to earn self-rule. American colonialists argued that Spain had failed to prepare Filipinos and Puerto Ricans for this. Even when some among the colonized affirmed American authority and precepts, colonizers often thought that these affirmations should in most cases be read as mimicry, not as authentic understanding.[9] This left American WASPs believing that the only path forward was for them to selflessly rule Filipinos and Puerto Ricans while training them for an eventual, far-off independence. If General James Rusling's account is to be believed, this is why President William McKinley authorized territorial annexation in the first place; McKinley believed God wanted and expected the United States to civilize Filipinos.[10] In sum, many Christian nationalists expected civilizing progress in their new, insular territories to unfold gradually over time, with God's hand guiding the process.

Charles Henry Brent and Colonial Eschatology

It was against this civilizing backdrop that Charles Henry Brent arrived in the Philippines. In 1902, Brent was dispatched to Manila as a missionary bishop on behalf of the Episcopalian Church. Brent went out of a sense of vocational obedience, not out of a personal desire to travel. On the contrary, he feared that he might die in the Philippines, thousands of miles from familiar customs and faces.[11] Missionaries today often understand their roles as primarily about bringing individuals into salvation. In Brent's day many missionaries saw themselves as agents of the civilizing mission, a role that made cultural evolution a primary focus. Individual salvations were good, but many missionaries considered structural, societal change over long periods of time more important. Brent fell into this category, believing colonialism to be part of God's plan. Brent once noted that "our responsibility is to put the Filipinos in the way of claiming as their own the very best in Government, science, education and religion, and not to mock them by feeding them with food that nauseates the palate of honest Americans."[12] Yet the extent to which he believed the American mission to the Philippines would lead to self-rule is questionable; only four years prior he privately wrote a friend that "the Filipinos are perennial children and will always have to be governed."[13] Whether he thought the mission accomplishable or not remains an open question, but at minimum he understood himself honor-bound to try.

For Brent, this cultural transformation was virtually coterminous with his postmillennial eschatology. He understood history as a progress narrative where God's work on earth continually advanced through positive social change, moral reform, education, science, and the arts. Eventually this divine progress would reach critical mass, culminating in the Kingdom of God on earth. Although Brent was postmillennialist from the beginning, his clearest expression of it came from late in his life. In 1924, Brent explained that "progress is determined by the measure of His reason, His way and His purpose, discoverable in human groups, the most important of which, after the family, is the nation."[14] Brent thought God did not distinguish between races or nations in terms of personal preference and that the "brotherhood of man" was legitimately egalitarian with regard to God's love. Equality of love did not mean that every race was equally civilized, though. In his view, nations' progress required good government, which itself required Christianity. Brent argued that nations stagnated without intentionally Christian leadership and that good statesmen were formed by good Christian morals.[15]

Brent felt Christian morality mattered for international leadership, but that hitherto Christian nations had failed to take seriously the biblical command to make disciples of all nations, a necessary step toward the Millennial Kingdom. Criticizing civilized nations, Brent wrote:

In none of them is the Christian motive the dominating motive, in none is politics controlled by Christian ethics. The Kingdom of God is not to national life the pearl of great price. [. . .] However laggard man has been in his search for the Kingdom, the Kingdom has not been laggard in its search for man. Slowly and relentlessly it makes its way in human affairs. Progress is not even all along the line. Progress is not evident at all in spots and through periods of time, for progress is not inevitable in that it is a co-operative affair contingent upon human effort just as truly upon divine.[16]

Even so, Brent considered that Christianity had embedded morality deeply within the cultural norms of "the West" and therefore any colonial rule by western powers was intrinsically capable of expanding the Kingdom. In his estimation only Christianity could produce true morality, but the overlay of Christian morals with western culture made colonialism beneficial even if western nations did not fully covet "the pearl of great price."[17] Since Christianity was embedded in every Western civic institution, training savage races to practice any form of Western culture was therefore tantamount to readying them for conversion.

Such claims have significant implications. Brent's explicit postmillennialism is one of the clearest examples of how the civilizing discourse sacralized all progress. It also illustrates a significant political theology often embedded in American colonialism, which is that while Christian morality ought to guide individuals' actions, it also ought to guide governments and international cooperation. For Brent, that meant privileging Christian morals as the guiding force of government and one that came with veto power over sin. Finally, since western civic life wrapped around a Christian essence, non-Christian populations benefitted from its lessons regardless of whether one announced it as religious or not.

Brent had no legacy of antidrug activity when he arrived in Manila, yet it soon became one of his lifelong moral concerns. In 1903—just a year into his time in the Philippines—the United States asked him to participate in what amounted to a fact-finding mission about opium use in the Far East.[18] Brent was one of three people chosen for this investigation, and his selection may have been connected with the lobbying he and other Protestant reformers had recently taken in opposition to the government's moves to create an opium monopoly in the Philippines.[19]

(Opium monopolies were a common approach at the time, wherein a government took sole control of the production and sale of opium.)[20] Indeed, it is possible that the whole fact-finding mission was itself a product of missionary intervention, since missionaries to China had written the Bureau of Insular Affairs only a few years earlier warning of substance abuse in the neighboring Philippines.[21] With regard to opium, missionaries had already been actively opposing non-medical use for decades before Brent targeted it.

Historical Context for Missionary Opposition

Although it is difficult to determine exactly when Protestant opposition to opium use began, it was on the table by at least the first years of the Christian Temperance Movement. In Britain, Christian opposition increased around the time of the First Opium War (1839–1842), with particular criticism of the British government's profit motives.[22] From this point onward religious objections to British opium policy only grew, drawing ire from across a range of denominational identities, including voices from within the Church of England.[23] American and British missionaries played a special role in generating religious discourse about opium use, which reformers back home drew upon. In missionaries' eyes, the opium problem stood in the way of Christian progress, representing colonial governments' unrighteous and predatory approach to global economics.

These missionaries made relatively similar claims to one another, and over the course of several decades established a standard set of talking points about the matter. At an 1877 anti-opium conference in Shanghai, a British missionary observed that opium, like all vices, "deadened the moral sense"; he also claimed that the Chinese dismissed missionaries' claims to righteous truth on the grounds that Christians had yet to end to the sale of ruinous British opium.[24] In 1892, an American Baptist missionary in Burma claimed that "the opium curse is the worst obstacle we have to meet," and that the Buddhists he wished to convert saw it as a degrading and damning substance.[25] Missionaries in the Far East sometimes also attributed slow conversion rates to opium addiction.[26] In China, these missionaries coordinated their efforts to oppose opium use, communicating across denominational lines through a periodical called *Chinese Recorder*.[27] Medical missionaries argued that opium wrecked health, wealth, and morality.[28] British and American missionaries also spoke to each other's cultural bases; for example, the 1894 book *Opium and Vice: Recent Personal Investigations* was authored primarily by the American medical missionary Dr. Kate Bushnell, but was printed in Britain and sold for British audiences.[29] Metropolitan Christian lobbying groups, such as Wilbur Crafts's International Reform Bureau in Washington, DC, or the Society for the Suppression of the Opium Trade in London, made use of such materials in their campaigns.[30]

Charles Henry Brent and the Shanghai Opium Commission

Charles Henry Brent did not arrive in the Philippines unaware of opium; as a well-educated churchman with an investment in Far East missions work, he must have been quite familiar with the Protestant ideology that preceded him. Brent became a much more vocal opponent of substance use after his 1903 study of foreign opium culture. He was also well connected to friends in high places, including such figures as the Archbishop of Canterbury and at least two American presidents. Brent wrote to his friend Theodore Roosevelt in 1906 about the matter, arguing that the only sure way to obstruct substance use was through international control. Roosevelt, who himself shared many of Brent's Protestant moral assumptions, replied that an international conference could do some "far-reaching good."[31] Roosevelt followed through: The United States and China cooperated to convene the Shanghai Opium Commission in early 1909. In short, Brent's Christian moralism spawned a rather important international meeting aimed at establishing international opium policy.

The primary concern at the start of the Shanghai Opium Commission was eradicating illicit opium traffic in China; however, by the end of the conference, international powers—including Britain, the Netherlands, Portugal, Japan, and the United States—agreed that any domestic or colonial drug control required some sort of international cooperation toward global control. The United States sent three delegates to the conference: Hamilton Wright, Charles Tenney, and Bishop Brent himself, who was then elected president of the Commission. China and the United States pushed for a prohibitionist approach, which other colonial powers hesitated to commit to. The Dutch maintained a relaxed approach to colonial opium control, opting for the monopoly system, and the British delegates were particularly skeptical of restrictions. Opium also represented a significant revenue source for many colonial powers, accounting for anywhere from 15 to 50 percent of income in some Asian colonies.[32] China and the United States framed many of their arguments in terms of moral duty, which the British delegation sidestepped, yet the British delegation also stonewalled attempts to evaluate opium through less self-evidently ideological lenses, such as its medical status.[33] But perhaps more to the point, they outright rejected the moral norms of their missionary critics. As Sir Cecil Clementi Smith put it, "to be entirely frank, the British Delegation is not able to accept the view that opium should be confined simply and solely to medical uses."[34] Nonetheless, by the end of the conference, the representative powers agreed to maintain regulations on opium (especially when it came to smuggling); encourage their governments to pursue scientific studies into opium; cooperate with China on its attempts to reduce opium use; and they agreed that each government would move toward greater stringency about allowing access to opium. These resolutions were so vaguely written that they committed the reluctant powers to no serious changes. As a symbol, however, the Shanghai Opium Commission galvanized Protestant reform movements and set the stage for the Hague Opium Convention of 1912, which was legally more consequential.

Christian Lobbyists and the 1912 Hague Opium Convention

American and British Protestant reformers were happy about Shanghai and they used it to campaign for substance use prohibition in other arenas. One example of such lobbying comes from Wilbur Fisk Crafts. Historian Ian Tyrell has noted that high-level American officials such as Elihu Root and William Taft considered Crafts cunning and competent.[35] They were correct: Crafts was ecstatic about the Shanghai Opium Commission and raised a ruckus about international next steps; he organized Christians to demand real, tangible results for narcotic suppression. Crafts used multiple methods to achieve his goals, but the most relevant two are that he published prolifically about the necessity of Christian moral intervention in law, and he also organized petitions and protest campaigns for specific aspects of this (e.g., drug prevention). Like many Christian lobbyists of the day, Crafts also worked across denominational lines, operating from within Methodist, Presbyterian, and Congregationalist milieus.[36]

A 1904 article penned for the WCTU's *Union Signal* offers a glimpse into how Crafts encouraged people to think about drug law. He referred to the idea that "you can't make men moral by law" as "the devil's proverb," arguing instead that "we can make morals by law precisely as we make health by law."[37] Vice and crime were like cesspools, he wrote, and just as removing a cesspool improves public health, removing vice and crime improves morality. He further claimed that the United States was Christian in essence and therefore US law should reflect Christian morals, especially since morals are "the supreme questions in politics." He went on to identify the cost of immorality: social collapse and dangerous conditions for Christian preservation. "In this age of cities the Church must save society if only to make a safe place for its saved souls," he wrote.[38] He finished the article by challenging readers to think of children's moral safety, insisting that churches and parents organize to "speak irresistibly to local, state, and national government." By this he meant that it was not enough just to believe in and vote for moral reforms, people must vocally demand it from their elected officials, giving no quarter to vice.

Crafts also extended this principle to colonialism. In his 1909 book, *Intoxicating Drinks & Drugs in All Lands and Times*, he identified the moral mantle placed around the neck of colonial powers, claiming that they had a duty toward "the removal of the greatest hindrance to missions, the greatest shame of Christian nations, the traffic in liquors and opium on the frontiers of civilization."[39] When Crafts wrote that "Our object, more profoundly viewed, is *to create a more favorable environment for the child races that civilised nations are essaying to civilize and Christianize*," what he meant was that prohibiting substance use was a prerequisite for completing the civilizing mission. Shanghai seemed like a small step in this direction.

The most important result of the 1909 Shanghai Opium Commission was the successive International Opium Convention (more commonly referred to as the Hague Opium Convention), which culminated in the first international drug control treaty in January 1912. The treaty has largely fallen out of popular memory today, yet its importance cannot be underestimated: It established the foundations for twentieth-century international drug law as well as US federal drug law. (The Harrison Narcotic Tax Act was passed partly to honor the United States' Hague Treaty obligations.)[40] Once again, the United States chose to send Bishop Brent and Hamilton Wright to the conference, along with the California pharmacist Henry J. Finger—this time with plenipotentiary power. The convention met with global narcotics control in mind. Representatives came from Britain, France, The Netherlands, China, Germany, Japan, Italy, Siam, Russia, and Portugal, which meant the bulk of the globe's colonial powers were present. Reprising Shanghai, Bishop Brent was again elected president of the meeting.[41]

Borrowing strategies from the Christian Temperance / Prohibition Movement, Christian reformers lobbied governments for change in advance of the Hague Convention. In the United States, Crafts launched a petitionary campaign to pressure various government agencies and politicians to support the Hague Convention and press for prohibitive policies. Crafts had a good track record with his lobbying efforts—these sometimes had real effects, and Tyrell grants Crafts some credit in shifting early federal approaches to opium in the Philippines.[42] The majority of these petitions used a standardized script, which Crafts distributed through the International Reform Bureau. He also encouraged people to send personalized letters, but the overwhelming number of surviving records from this petitionary effort used his form letter approach.[43] Many of these petitions survive in assorted archival collections and they demonstrate an important shift in reform strategies. Nearly all of the petitions come from Christian organizations: They are primarily from individual churches, but occasionally they come from other kinds of Christian organizations, such as parachurch organizations, ministerial associations, or one sent by Charles Blanchard on behalf of Wheaton College.[44] These petitions also demonstrate tactical shifts in how the Christian lobby approached legal interventions.

Despite having been authored by a Christian lobbyist and coming almost exclusively from Christian sources, these petitions are mostly silent about explicit religion. The sole reference lies in the opening line, where the petitioners express solidarity with the 1910 Edinburgh Missionary Conference, as well as with the people of Britain and China. Aside from that the petitions avoid religious reference, focusing instead on prohibitive legislation (both federal and international). The petitions also declare their distribution in the final paragraph, going out not only to the executive and legislative branches, but also the International Reform Bureau and "the press." (How one petitions an aggregate like "the press" is unclear.) In earlier petitions on similar topics, these same types of organizations often mentioned religious themes quite explicitly.[45] An 1892 petition circulated by the WCTU called on Congress to support efforts in Brussels to prohibit slavery and alcohol sales to "the heathens" in Africa, a Christian moral duty for a "Christian nation" (a phrase they used repeatedly).[46] An 1898 petition against alcohol in military canteens, for another example, demanded that the military protect "thousands of young men carefully nurtured in temperance principles in Christian homes and churches."[47] The early twentieth century saw a shift away from religious language to supposedly more neutral terms when it came to prohibiting alcohol, and this move is reflected in the antidrug movement as well.

One should not read these petitions as religiously neutral, however. On the contrary, they should be read as Protestant. Cleaning up the language might make the petitions more palatably useful for legislative purposes in an era where explicitly Christian legislation was becoming less popular. At the same time, the International Reform Bureau deliberately distributed these petitions to Protestant sources, and anyone receiving dozens of them must have noticed that a Christian constituency was pressing for drug prohibition. (This research did not turn up any caches of Hague Treaty petitions from other sorts of institutions, such as Chambers of Commerce or Parent-Teacher Associations; cases like those are rare and vastly outnumbered by the number of petitions coming from Christian institutions.) Furthermore, any petition arriving from a church must be read as a Christian plea, regardless of whether the petitionary language frames the request in secular language. Even if the petition contains no explicit reference to Christian tenets, biblical reasoning, or denominational positions, the petition came from an organization existing exclusively for religious purposes. By sending such declarations in the name of local churches, congregations identified the antidrug cause as part of their religious values.

It would be difficult to prove that President Taft consciously chose Christians to represent the United States at The Hague in response to these petitions, but at minimum two of the three representatives he chose would have been amenable to the Protestant petitioners. (The third may have been as well; Finger is something of a mystery, having left little mark on the historical record.) Bishop Brent strongly favored international and colonial legislation as part of God's plan for history. Wright also believed that God should be sovereign over both American law and international drug policy; he was also a friendly ally for Crafts.[48] Although it may be possible for Christians to draft and pass religiously neutral legislation, given Brent's and Wright's religious motivations for prohibiting substance use—a reform movement that was deeply indebted to normative Protestant morality—one should hesitate to read the successful passage of the Hague Convention as a religiously neutral act. If anything, we should read the general omission of religious language as a diplomatic concession to the Convention's international nature, where some representatives would have arrived with non-Protestant or non-Christian backgrounds. Some colonial powers—especially the British delegation—also had constituencies who held diverse opinions about opium, and it might have been politically imprudent to suggest that religious ideals should dictate economic policy. In other words, the Hague Treaty came about through a series of explicitly religious interventions yet culminated with religiously neutral language; it was the product of Protestant colonial eschatologies even if it omitted such justifications in its final text.

Cara Lea Burnidge's *A Peaceful Conquest* analyzes Woodrow Wilson's presidency and it offers helpful insights for understanding how Protestant ideals were able to quietly guide domestic and foreign policy. Burnidge has compellingly argued that Wilson held to a Presbyterian, postmillennial scheme to "Christianize America" and the world.[49] America could offer a "spiritual mediation" for the rest of the planet, who would eventually recognize God in Americans' moral example.[50] The League of Nations would benefit from American leadership, which Wilson considered to be Christian in its essential nature.[51] Most important, Wilson did not believe that this Christianity had to be verbally acknowledged for actions to count as Christian; a quiet Protestant morality that guided governmental affairs was still Christian in his estimation. (In assessing Americans' relationship to China, Wilson privately argued that regardless of whether it was "direct or indirect," "the Christian influence . . . ought to be kept there.")[52] In short, Wilson held that laws did not require religious language in order to be Christian. We should consider that this phenomenon was also in play with Crafts's petitions. Brent certainly held this same attitude, and given his visible, public approach to opium it seems likely that Hamilton Wright would have agreed with this, too.

As a signatory, the United States was obligated to find some way to implement the treaty after the Hague Convention was ratified and became international law. Given the separation of powers enumerated in the Constitution, Congress was unable to directly legislate substance use in individual states, but its taxation purview allowed for a loophole (a common route to federal moral reforms which sat alongside its equally exploited interstate commerce purview). Hamilton Wright helped Francis Burton Harrison devise what became the Harrison Narcotics Tax Act of 1914. Indeed, he was so influential in its creation that when the law passed, Harrison wrote Wright to congratulate him on it.[53] The Tax Act required two things: a tax on opium sales (thus creating a paper trail of how much was sold and who was buying it), as well as stipulations that certain substances could only be dispensed in the context of professional medical practices. This aimed to both monitor the traffic in certain substances as well as outlaw black market distribution. Vis-à-vis the Tax Act, the Supreme Court decided in 1919 that maintenance treatment was medically illegitimate, narrowing greatly the range of reasons doctors might prescribe narcotics and thus their use outside of very specific circumstances became de facto illegal.[54] (Maintenance treatment is when doctors prescribe narcotics to prevent addicts from experiencing traumatic and sometimes dangerous withdrawals.) The Harrison Act remained law until 1970 and served as a foundation for an evolving conglomeration of stricter federal controls.

The Hague Convention also expanded its reach beyond what it held in 1912. While some countries who were not initially present later ratified the treaty voluntarily, the Allied Powers of World War I—several of whom were original authors of the treaty—obligated all other powers suing for peace to accept it. Article 295 of the Treaty of Versailles, which ended World War I, required the signing powers to implement The Hague Opium Convention as part of the conditions for peace; Article 23 ceded authority over opium and drug treaties to the League of

Nations. (This appears to have been instigated partly by China, who may not have been a defining player in the war but who had enough clout to make demands if they were palatable to the allied victors.)[55] Similar obligations appeared for Turkey in the Treaty of Lausanne. Charles Henry Brent must have been ecstatic. Not only had his efforts to eradicate substance use paid off in the form of expansive international law, they were also being entrusted to a new institution that he personally considered part of God's plan for civilizational progress.

The League of Nations, Substance Use, and Missionary Societies

Although the Allied Powers chose to invest the League of Nations with guardianship over international drug control, the mechanisms by which they might do so remained unclear. One obstacle involved the original 1912 Hague treaty itself, which left the Netherlands in charge of managing the treaty and coordinating global antidrug efforts.[56] The Dutch government hesitated to cede this responsibility, not because they were eager for more administrative work, but because they were unconvinced that the fledgling League was yet organized enough to competently manage the job.[57] Although they handed over their duties by the end of 1920, they may not have been wrong to hesitate. The League was a fundamentally new organization that was still building its bureaucratic structures and methods.

Two developments seem particularly germane for this story: First, between December 1920 and February 1921, the League created and organized an Opium Advisory Committee to handle its new antidrug duties.[58] Second, the League also created the mandate system, which evaluated large swaths of the colonized world through a kind of civilizational etiology—colonized peoples were governed more or less strictly based on how culturally inferior the colonizers considered them to be.[59] The Opium Advisory Committee served largely as an informational, arbitrational, and investigative body that also occasionally dabbled in propaganda. It also served as a symbol; Protestant reformers and missionaries approached the Opium Advisory Committee as a promising ally and a mark of Christian progress. The mandate system proved relevant in that it obligated colonial powers to govern specific territories in line with the moral discourse of the civilizing mission, which they commonly used to justify imperial sovereignty. In other words, if colonizers were going to rest their right to rule the colonized upon a duty to improve inferior societies, the League expected them to implement policies that aligned with that argument. This included substance use regulations—colonial powers found it hard to argue that laissez-faire access to opiates and liquor improved their wards.

Based on the quantity of surviving League records, the Protestants most enamored with the League appear to have been the British-driven Anti-Opium Associations that popped up in assorted places, but which were linked to one another.[60] The Anti-Opium Associations had two goals with the League: first, to persuade them of the severity of the opium problem, and second, to impel them to intervene in British foreign policy. The International Anti-Opium Association, Peking (IAOAP) wrote the League in 1920 to describe the supply chain logistics for opium entering Yunnan Province through the British colony of Burma, and asked the League to handle it with Britain.[61] In 1923, the Edinburgh Anti-Opium Committee (EAOC) warned the League that China was considering an opium monopoly approach, a concept the EAOC considered to be "retrograde, and not fitted to check the illicit traffic or to diminish the opium vice itself"; they further implored the League to pressure China into a different course of action.[62] These bodies communicated with and supported one another. In London, the older Society for the Suppression of the Opium Trade published arguments from these other organizations and championed their cause. The IAOAP lamented though that Britons and Americans made up too great a portion of its membership, and went on to claim that "the masses of Chinese have not yet responded in the manner necessary" for wholescale change.[63] Overall the League was courteous to these organizations—and they voluntarily solicited information and input from them—but internal communications show that at least in its first years the League's opium bureaucracy considered some of their positions to be "extreme."[64]

As for the mandate system, the League divided much of the colonial world into three categories: "A" mandates, which were "semi-independent"; "B" mandates, which were former German colonies and which required stricter rule than the A mandates; and "C" mandates, which as one commentator put it were "the lowest class of territories under this sort of tutelage" and therefore required near total oversight.[65]

With regard to substance use controls, the League considered each category separately, but thought some degree of oversight was warranted
in all. Although the League regulated the A mandates too, they were
most concerned with B and C mandates. Each mandate was regulated
differently. In Nigeria (treated as a B mandate), for instance, the British only permitted narcotics for medical use, and "in practice, the only
dangerous drugs imported are those obtained by Government Medical
Officers from Lagos."[66] In Tanganyika (a B mandate), restrictions included agriculture with the prohibition of poppy and hemp cultivation,
as well as "the smoking of bhang" (cannabis indica).[67] In Western Samoa
(a C mandate), the British went further, actively directing the police to
monitor and punish opium smuggling, a vice they considered "almost
wholly confined, to the Chinese labourers, who use great cunning, cau-
tion and secrecy" to hide it.[68] Except for Iraq, the League did not consider A mandates to be under as serious a threat from opium as China
was, claiming in 1926 that "the situation in the mandated territories was
not of any particular gravity."[69] Although the League was limited in its
power, it endeavored to surveil global drug use and discourage cannabis,
opiate, and alcohol in colonized regions.

The League earned the attention of assorted reform movements as a
symbol of international moral control. For instance, the Fédération In-
ternationale pour la Protection des Races Indigènes contre l'Alcoolisme/
Native Races and the Liquor Traffic United Committee (headquartered
in a particularly posh part of Westminster) lobbied its prohibitionist positions with William Rappard, head of the Mandates Section.[70]
NRLTUC was chaired by the Lord Bishop of London, and included the
bishops of Chester, Croydon, Durham, Ely, Gloucester, Lagos, the Niger,
Rochester, and Willesden as some of its church-based vice presidents;
it also allied itself with missionaries and temperance groups from dis-
senting and foreign churches. One of their primary goals was to abolish
alcohol among white colonizers. They argued that "the social customs
of the Europeans in the Native Territories in the matter of spirits are
being copied by the natives, with the result that a section of the educated Africans liquor is looked upon as being a distinguishing mark of
civilisation, and that by the use of it they have come nearer to the plane
of the European."[71] Elsewhere they argued that "the natives' ignorance"
of the alcohol Europeans brought with them led to "a deep demoraliza-

tion for the negroes."[72] In other words, the Committee argued that any alcohol—even for civilized white administrators—countermanded the civilizing mission upon which the mandate system was predicated. This dovetailed a larger Protestant discourse about the relationship between colonialism, Christianity, and substance use, which had for decades seen moral reformers press various sovereign powers to protect "native races" from white vice.[73]

American Responses to International Control

From the American side, the two most significant lobbyists to engage the League on narcotics control were Elizabeth Washburn Wright—the widow of the late Hamilton Wright—and Richmond Pearson Hobson, of the International Narcotic Education Association and the World Narcotic Defense Association. Elizabeth Washburn Wright actually managed to embed herself within the League's infrastructure. In approaching the League in 1920, she told them "confidentially" that the US government would be pleased to have her assigned to the League as an observer.[74] That same year, Dr. Inazo Nitobe, the Japanese delegate to the League (and a Quaker convert) also suggested she could be useful, informing the Opium section that "she certainly is most deeply interested and equally well informed"; the Dutch ambassador to France also vouched for her to Sir Eric Drummond, who was then Secretary General.[75] What makes this especially interesting is that: (a) some of the information she provided the League at this point was wrong (such as that the Dutch were ready to hand over their management of the Hague Treaty), and (b) after she was appointed to the League, they found her rather unhelpful.[76] Nevertheless she maintained her role through much of the 1920s.

Wright moved among the upper echelons of international antidrug politics, and though she rarely (if ever) addressed her religion publicly, it motivated her private understanding of duty. Writing to a friend in the State Department, she claimed:

> Because I am a woman you may think it strange that I should want to do this work. You may also think that I greatly over-estimate my value. I know perfectly well that I have not half the mind my husband had or his driving-power. But I do not let myself think of these things—or of myself.

> I am a very small tool in the grasp of something behind me—outside of
> me—much bigger than myself. . . . I am a medium being used by some
> outside force—for some definite purpose. This is my value absolutely. . . .
> When I heard you had been brought home—I knew of course it was to
> help me with Opium!!!!!!!![77]

Although Elizabeth Washburn Wright may initially have come into her role by her connection to Hamilton Wright, by 1930 she was justifiably more confident in herself. As she put it in a letter to Admiral Mark Bristol, "there is not a soul in Europe or America who has been connected to this question [of opium] so long as I."[78] She also had access to high-level officials, both domestic and international. Charles Henry Brent even arranged a meeting for her with President Hoover, and she corresponded regularly with diplomats, newspapers, and other antidrug campaigners, many of whom she seems to have met while representing the United States in Geneva.[79] In any case, her motivation through this period seems to have been driven by the belief that a higher power had charged her with the mission. The language of "being a medium used by some outside force" suggests Spiritualist leanings, yet it could also reflect the evolving semantics of non-institutional Christianity. Given the absence of an explicit explanation it is difficult to pin down where her sympathies lay, other than to identify that she clearly felt her work was spiritually significant.

Wright was also not alone in her religious taciturnity; by the 1920s and 1930s, it had become fairly normal for religion to quietly motivate political reform in contrast to the open and explicit moralizing of the nineteenth century. Certainly there were exceptions to this, such as Bishop Brent, who expressed his religiosity quite openly. Up until his death in 1929, he maintained that religion and narcotic control went hand in hand, and he said as much to both the League and the general public. But Brent was also a clergyman, and the relationship between his personal religion and his politics was perhaps better insulated from social blowback than those who didn't hold ecclesiastical positions. What Wright represents is a second side to the religion/drug control equation: the submersion of religious positions beneath the diplomatic surface. It also mirrors the wider trends on this front—the WCTU launched its "non-sectarian" "scientific temperance" movement in the 1880s, Wilson elided his postmillennialist motivations in public speech, churches' petitions omitted Christian language by the 1910s, Hobson stopped speaking of his Christian motivations in the 1920s, etc. Wright's influence in the League—even if it was only slight—was guided by a sense of spiritual duty to improve the planet through the abolition of drugs, but like many others of her day she followed a trend of keeping quiet about it.

American Security and International Drug Control

American national security represented a voiced concern as it pertained to international substance use, sometimes framed in religious terms and sometimes not. Even the non-religious portrayals of international drug traffic contributed significantly to the construction of an American moral panic though, so this section does not focus exclusively on religious complaints but also works to lay important groundwork for the next part of this discussion.

The League of Nations's primary objective with substance use was to monitor and help regulate international traffic and production. For many American observers this was a helpful project, yet hardly the whole picture. The dominant antidrug narrative in the United States was one of predation. The narcotics that most concerned Americans in this era—cocaine and opiates—were mostly imported and were often portrayed as the product of nefarious foreign cabals taking advantage of US citizens. Many observers (both domestic and international) considered the United States unique when comparing its drug issues to other countries. "This is a distinctly American problem," wrote *Harper's Monthly Magazine*, "But it is an international problem as well. . . . We have discovered that the enactment of state and national laws, even if successfully enforced, is of little use when, day after day, quantities of the fiendish stuff are smuggled into our seaports and across our borders."[80] It was nice that the League of Nations monitored global narcotic traffic, but what many Americans wanted was a forceful intervention into international black markets.

In addition, many Americans saw international drug sales as a moral issue with domestic relevance. Reflecting in *The Christian Work* in 1924, Bishop Brent informed readers that "Moral questions have no boundaries. . . . If we exploit abroad where we defend at home, the downfall of the exploited will eventually become our downfall."[81] This dovetailed larger concerns about addiction as a contagious problem, but it also spoke to his concerns about the Kingdom of God. Postmillennial progress could not be sectioned off by nationality; the world rose and fell together, and shame on the United States if it failed its moral duty. These two themes worked together for many American interlocutors: international drug traffic posed a security threat to the United States, and the mythos of American exceptionalism necessitated US moral leadership in solving the world's drug problem.

International narcotic concerns also changed how people thought about particular regions. China remained the drug dystopia par excellence; it would not be until after World War II before people stopped thinking of it as a site for mass opium predation. However, during the early twentieth century, other areas became associated with drug problems, too. Egypt, for example, was treated as another site for opium and hashish addiction. In British circles (and to a lesser extent American), antidrug ideologues celebrated Russell Pasha, Egypt's top drug official. Indeed, in Baron Harry d'Erlanger's book, *The Last Plague of Egypt*, Pasha is portrayed in ways that make him seem a bit like James Bond. D'Erlanger was one of many at the time claiming that Egypt was suddenly overrun by narcotics, writing that Cairo and Alexandria now looked "like an Oriental version of Hogarth's Gin Alley."[82] In a curious turn in 1934, British officials grew agitated about Egyptians brewing black tea for too long. Rather than following "the proper process" that produces "a refreshing drink" in "the manner of the nations who are tea drinkers," instead the "criminal classes" were cooking their tea all day, brewing it into a narcotic that acted like hashish.[83] (Perhaps it doesn't need to be said, but tea cannot become narcotic regardless of cooking time.) More to the point, Egypt was viewed as such a den of drug addiction that even tea became suspicious and worth policing.

Egypt was not alone in this recasting—Yugoslavia, Switzerland, and Persia also gained more attention as sites for illicit drug traffic, but the most significant development was in Manchuria/Manchukuo. Egypt, Persia, and other places may or may not have had real spikes in drug use—substance use statistics from this era are rather untrustworthy. Manchuria though almost certainly experienced a real increase in opium use. What makes this particularly significant is that it occurred in conjunction with Japanese economic and territorial expansion during the 1930s, and therefore synced with pre–World War II concerns about Japan as a military threat to the United States. China already had a reputation as an unwilling victim of the narcotic trade, so for Manchuria to see increased traffic was itself no great shock to audiences. Japan invaded and conquered Manchuria in September 1931 on the pretense of security concerns for the Japanese-owned South Manchuria Railway Company, and thereafter established the colony of Manchukuo in 1932.[84] Even before the conquest, American observers were pointing to Japan as a culprit behind rising regional drug use in the 1920s, an accusation that only grew sharper and bolder after occupation.[85] American observers feared Japan was using addiction as a strategy for conquest.

Japanese pharmaceutical companies had been vending opium in Korea for decades, and when new markets in Manchukuo opened up profitable opportunities, this led to expansion in opium manufacture and export.[86] Japan sold opium under the auspices of maintenance treatment; its increased use in Manchukuo was explained as supporting those who were already addicts and could not be cured. This approach to addiction was unpopular with the American government and further exacerbated tensions between the two countries. Americans had been concerned about growing Japanese power for decades, and not without cause; at least as early as 1906, Japan was engaged in reconnaissance missions at US military installations.[87] Addressing Congress in 1911, Hobson himself had predicted that Japan would pose a serious threat to the United States if the American Navy were not better supported, since only Pearl Harbor stood as a defense between it and Japan.[88] The marriage of Japanese military conquest and opium addiction added a new dimension to the martial literalism of the Drug War. If foreign aggressors deployed addiction as a way to line war chests (as the Chinese ambassador to the United States implied in *Liberty Magazine*) as well as implementing it as a debilitating and therefore pacifying tool (as the *Washington Post* suggested), then addiction has military capabilities.[89] The Shanghai-based organization, the National Anti-Opium Association of China, complained to the League of Nations in 1932 that Japanese drug traffickers were active throughout the rest of the country as well.[90] Furthermore, after the Manchurian annexation, both official state documents as well as popular media reflected a concern that Japan was not yet finished with territorial expansion—when considered from the angle of narcotic policy, this would have meant that Japan was not finished spreading drug abuse, either.

For many Americans, foreign drug production, addiction, and smuggling represented threats to the United States, both martial and moral. When appealing to the Carnegie Corporation for funding, Richmond Hobson referred to his "war map," which "showed Eastern and South-Eastern Europe and the Near East as dangerous regions where the development of new bases might be formed," but went on to say that "the most dangerous sector in this far-reaching battlefront is now the Far East, with Manchukuo at the center."[91] This construction was ideologically consistent with how Americans were thinking about drugs in this era; Egypt, Persia, Yugoslavia, and Manchukuo were not just overseas problems to be ignored, but rather a serious threat to the United States. Harry Anslinger, the first head of the Federal Bureau of Narcotics, described America as a "victim nation," with foreign overproduction as the culprit.[92] The Washington congressman John Miller presumptuously claimed in 1930 to have "started the war on narcotics" since a bill he had introduced a few years prior was designed to strictly regulate when and how foreign drugs could be imported.[93] In 1934, Charles Kramer, a Congressional Representative from California, told the House that "syndicates" from "the Orient" were funneling drugs through Honolulu and from there onward into Seattle, San Francisco, Portland, Los Angeles, and San Diego. He also cried havoc over syndicates preying upon American youth, families, and military personnel, syndicates operated by an unnamed "master mind."[94] (His language also reveals close correlations and almost certainly direct quotes from Richmond Hobson.) For these antidrug officials it was a literal battle with the sinister forces of crime.

Domestically, many American legislators and academics treated narcotic addiction as a problem either imported by shifty foreigners or magnified by undesirable immigrants. In 1926, Congress considered deportation policies in connection with narcotics, which they saw as a multifaceted problem. On the one hand, addiction fit into the Progressive Era's construction of madness. Some members of Congress made claims such as "the alien insane" were costing New York $4.4 million in institutionalization expenses.[95] However, in line with 1920s nativism, they were more concerned with the foreigners who were *not* locked away.

The committee chairman Albert Johnson phrased it thus: "Do you think an alien narcotic peddler who puts in his time debauching children in schools should be deported at any time?"[96] It was a rhetorical question; Johnson meant to insinuate that predatory immigrants targeted children for drug addiction just to make some easy money. The chairman further explained that he wanted special legislation for foreign-born narcotic dealers so they could be more speedily deported.[97]

Additionally, some academics backed up these claims. Writing for the *Journal of the American Institute of Criminal Law and Criminology*, the criminology professor Ervin Hacker explained:

> It has long been accepted as an established fact in criminal-aetiology that all human aberrations such as prostitution, alcoholism, and addiction to narcotics, cocaine, etc., which are important from the standpoint of morality, have an influence on the magnitude and direction of criminality; and among immigrants we find many individuals who increase the sum of criminality under the influence of these indulgences.[98]

Not everyone shared this perspective, but many well-placed people did. Immigrants were often treated as more likely to be insane addicts or predatory drug pushers and therefore a burden upon American stability. Their degraded nature posed a contagious threat to American security: Through drug addiction they could destabilize the nation's moral core.

By 1930, popular understandings of the Drug War saw it as a war of foreign origins waged not just in Egypt and China but within the United States as well. This interpretation had consequences beyond the immediate realm of foreign affairs. It made the United States—widely understood to be a "Christian nation"—the victim of foreign, non-Christian nations, with Switzerland representing the only culprit who would have seemed "Christian" to American audiences. This gave Drug War rhetoric a nationalist tone, but one that played up particular religious differences, such as attaching hashish madness to Muslim customs or opium to Chinese "heathenism." The framework of security was easily translated into one of a religious culture war.

It may seem incongruous with the earlier discussions to say that Americans considered addiction a twentieth-century problem of foreign incursion, particularly given the widespread phenomenon of rehabilitation homes, mail-order addiction cures, and outrage over narcotics hidden in patent medicines. The fact of the matter is that "society" is never of one mind on anything, let alone with an issue so capacious as narcotics. People can also be inconsistent. Many blamed immigrants for drug addiction, but there were also many others who blamed unscrupulous American doctors. Additionally, not everyone speaking about these problems had the same base of knowledge and so some may have been unaware of addiction history. Finally, some may very well have been aware and either interpreted the earlier wave of concerns as being essentially the same thing (a foreign problem imported to the United States), or they may have seen the earlier wave as a product of medical ignorance that had since been fixed, reading the twentieth-century portion as the product of shifty drug syndicates and therefore wholly different. In any event, the presentation of drug addiction as a foreign problem was common rhetoric, regardless of whether it always aligned neatly with other discourses.

Conclusions

For both American and British audiences, the earliest and largest body of complaints about substance use came from Protestant voices. Missionaries especially played an important early role, offering antidrug narratives in which "the child races" were preyed upon by "Christian nations." These missionaries emphasized a colonial duty in which white Protestant societies needed to missionize and "uplift" these other races as part of the civilizing mission. For many of them, this was also a necessary step toward an eschatological end: The millennial Kingdom of God could not coexist with sin, nor could it progress in debased, demoralized, and degenerated opium-stoned societies.

Early criticism of substance use often appeared in explicitly Christian language, yet as time went on, cultural shifts muted much of this. Protestants with antidrug agendas did not abandon their religious rationales, they just held to them more quietly. Furthermore, Christian lobbyists could make their displeasure with drug use known without requiring the government to necessarily identify its own response in the same terms. Petition language—even from Christian sources—began eliding the explicit religious moralizing of earlier generations.

International antidrug cooperation might seem like a neutral, secular enterprise, yet its origins tell a different story. Some non-Protestant drug regulations and international treaties were in place before 1912, particularly in relation to China. Would the Hague treaty, however, have come into being without Bishop Brent? For him, the Drug War was a Christian endeavor and a step toward the promised Kingdom. The Hague Convention—which Brent presided over—was the logical next step after Shanghai, which he also presided over and which was his idea. Shanghai only came about because he asked Roosevelt to make it so. Brent's work with the 1903 Opium Commission was the catalyst for that request, but the commission itself was the product of earlier missionary arguments about Christian moral duty to Filipinos. Those missionary claims were themselves permutations of Christian Temperance that predated it by decades. It's Protestants all the way down.

The cession of international drug control to the League of Nations again seems like a religiously neutral move on the surface. Perhaps to some degree it was; certainly it was less self-evidently religious than postmillennialist celebrations of the move as a step closer to the Kingdom of God. This book argues that religion was a centrally important feature of the early Drug War and a necessary ingredient, but it does not attempt to claim that religion was the only force at work. The League of Nations was a legislative experiment at a time when many European and American politicians were self-consciously trying to step away from explicit religion as a motivation or engine for change, and some of the so-called Great Powers sent economic bureaucrats to the table rather than clergymen. At the same time, attempts to separate religion from other spheres of life—as though it were some easily segregated substance that could be boxed up and shelved—are always imperfect, and often more aspirational than anything else. People in this era often claimed that non-medical substance use was *scientifically* immoral and that cultural evolution in primitive societies could only advance if drugs were prohibited. If someone wishes to count biomorality as authentic science, then yes, preventing access to specific substances in order to protect morality is a secular maneuver. That's a pretty big "if," though. I am more inclined to think that Tisa Wenger is right when she assesses the colonial civilizing discourse as privileging Christianity (and particularly Protestantism) and elevating its transdenominational virtues to putatively secular universals.[99] The morality they wished to protect and teach to colonized populations was a Protestant extract. If all we mean by "religion" is "explicitly confessional statements of faith," then sure, the League's antidrug policies were not religious in nature. But if the boundaries of "religion" are blurrier than this, and if "religion" to any degree is more than just mere statements of belief, then we must recognize that religion bled into international drug policy.

The League also relied on missionary networks to supply them with information, a move that developed from within the League rather than from external pressure. These are the same missionaries who had been demanding drug prohibition out of Christian moral obligations for almost a century. Perhaps it is self-evident, but missionaries do not qualify as a religiously neutral source of information. The League's antidrug spy network (which is what it was whether they called it that or not) had an explicitly religious agenda for opposing non-medical substance use. They had been demanding international oversight for decades. Furthermore, when Rachel Crowdy asked them to promote antidrug propaganda, they were eager to do so. Missionaries' publications almost universally marked drug prohibition as a Protestant cause. Even the staunchest secularist must admit that this amounts to the League of Nations attempting to cultivate global antidrug culture through Protestantism. No wonder so many American Protestants thought of the League as a religious symbol of Christian progress. The League could claim religious neutrality all it wanted, but many of its reform efforts overlay postmillennialists' moral topographies and used Protestant missionaries as agents for its goals.

America never saw itself as the sole player in the war on drugs, and rightfully so—Europeans and China had been critical of opium for at least as long. The United States also considered its antidrug efforts at home to be contingent upon cooperative efforts with foreign powers. As such, the US promotion and cooperation with international players took on a kind of secular realpolitik, but just barely. The delegates it sent to Shanghai, to The Hague, and to the League represented Progressive Era Protestantism. Bishop Brent both presided over the design of international drug law and opened their meetings with prayer. Lobbyists campaigning for American antidrug policies restrained religious language in the petitions they distributed, but they distributed those petitions almost entirely to Protestant organizations. From a popular perspective these reforms were Christian.

Finally, for many Americans the international question was not just one of morality abroad but also one of morality at home. They argued that international drug traffic posed a security threat to the United States. This problem was sometimes constructed as a military threat, but also as a moral one. If the United States succumbed to drug abuse—a possibility that loomed in the stories about foreigners driving the domestic black market—then shared social morality would collapse. Wiley's future American supermen could never be born, and American civilization would slowly rot. This threat was central to the moral panic that popular media and Christian ideologues promoted to audiences.

6

The Products of a Moral Panic

New York (1931)

On February 22, 1931, Richmond Pearson Hobson addressed NBC's "Red Network" from New York City, an eastern chain of radio stations that stretched all the way to Kansas. Hobson was popular, charismatic, and by 1931, one of America's leading voices in the Drug War. Hobson launched into an impassioned jeremiad titled "The World War Upon the Dope Ring," begging listeners to take drugs as seriously as he did. He announced that the "rising tide of narcotic drug addiction menaces the very foundation of modern civilization, the future of mankind and the destiny of the human race," a position evidenced by "the unnumbered millions of the helpless tortured slaves." He claimed that opium, peyote, hashish, morphine, marijuana, and heroin permeated all nations and that synthetic drugs were the next up and coming wave of substance abuse. A "Commissioner of Health of a great American metropolis" also told him that the boys and girls there were getting hooked on drugs, which then compelled them to form criminal gangs, forget their personal hygiene and morals, and transformed them into spreaders of infectious diseases, including the "diseases of vice" (a euphemism for sexually transmitted diseases). He recounted stories of addicted youths tricking their families into addiction, robbing Detroit's Christmas shoppers, murdering widows, and creating an economic burden on the US economy equivalent to $16–80 billion in today's dollars. He posited that drug addicts made up the largest population of federal prisons and that scientists now called addiction "the living death." Addicts posed the greatest threat to American "public health, public morals and public safety." Hobson argued that this "World War" needed to be fought on several fronts. Three things could help wipe out substance abuse: education, laws (including laws his organizations were promoting with states), and policing (both domestic and international).[1]

Hobson had cut his teeth on Prohibition, which he supported as a full-time activist after losing his Alabaman congressional seat in 1914. Prohibition taught him the worth of public opinion, and after the 1920 passage of the Volstead Act, Hobson set his sights on anti-alcohol education as a way to maintain momentum against inebriety. He moved to Los Angeles to establish an organization devoted to educating people about the dangers of alcohol, and in 1922 he even tried to create a chaired professorship of "alcohol investigation" at Stanford University.[2] Hobson wanted to feel significant, though, and he soon realized that alcohol no longer felt as relevant to him as it once did. He repositioned himself as an antidrug activist, rebranding his "Alcohol Education Association" as "the International Narcotic Education Association" in 1923. Between 1923 and his death in 1937, Hobson transformed himself into an internationally recognized enemy of narcotics and the shadowy powers that produced them.

Public opinion mattered a great deal to him, and in fact, part of why he considered education valuable was that it could shape majoritarian outlooks. He argued,

> In order to carry out this program and maintain a permanent condition of adequate defense against this universal enemy, it is necessary to incorporate in the education systems of all lands organized and scientific narcotic instruction so that the individuals may have the motive of self-preservation always on guard and the people, duly informed through the press, pulpit, radio, screen, clubs, organizations etc. may understand the problem, whether in new forms or old, and may maintain a condition of public sentiment able to insure the effective application of all agencies devised for narcotic defense.[3]

In making such claims he laid out one premise of this chapter. With self-awareness, Hobson sought to cultivate and curate public opinions about substance use. He wanted the media to champion particular positions, he wanted churches to stand against drug use, and he wanted schools to teach children that substance use was the greatest danger to society. Hobson felt that if he could harness public opinion and steer it toward antidrug and anti-addict positions, then this would produce the necessary conditions for creating a militarized Drug War. He was right; the Drug War grew into the behemoth it did partly in response to public opinion.

That's not the whole story, though, since it relegates religion ("the pulpit") to merely one component among many. By 1931 Hobson was working with a moral panic that he himself helped to create, one he modeled after the Christian Temperance strategies of the 1870s–1880s. Christian Temperance—and in particular, the Woman's Christian Temperance Union—sought to reshape the United States into a fully sober nation. In the previous passage, Hobson demanded "scientific narcotic instruction." That word choice is telling. The WCTU grew aware that some Americans were uncomfortable about the explicitly religious motifs in their arguments. Embracing pragmatism over partisanship, the WCTU launched "Scientific Temperance" as a separate wing of their movement. Scientific Temperance avoided making explicitly religious claims. They instead took the WCTU's arguments and repackaged them as rational, scientific truths that anyone could accept. They soon gained national support for scientific temperance and despite its emergence from an explicitly Christian organization, their materials were often received as religiously neutral. All schools under federal jurisdiction, as well as many states, required that schools teach scientific temperance education, using the materials the WCTU recommended. The WCTU's endgame was to educate alcohol out of existence.

Hobson successfully reproduced this maneuver. Although he was privately devout and millennialism both motivated and informed his stance on drug control, Hobson subdued this religiosity in the public sphere. Instead, he presented his claims about addicts and addiction as merely scientific facts. By 1930, schools around the country were using his antidrug materials in classrooms, and media regularly looked to him as an expert. Harry Anslinger, the first head of the Federal Bureau of Narcotics, thought Hobson was performing a great service to the United States and the two men regularly supported one another.[4] Although Hobson wasn't the sole player in the drug panic, nor was religion the sole contributor, the end result of this era was a greatly expanded repertoire of state and federal drug laws, antidrug education, and a standardized depiction of substance use as a national security threat.

Moral Panics

The premise of a moral panic is this: People come to believe that some-one or something is posing a serious threat to them (or in some cases, to others) which may upset their way of life or perhaps even extinguish it. Good people are besieged by bad ones. In his interpretation of a British moral panic about mugging, Stuart Hall wrote

> When the official reaction to a person, groups of persons or series of events is out of all proportion to the actual threat offered, when "experts," in the form of police chiefs, the judiciary, politicians and editors perceive the threat in all but identical terms, and appear to talk "with one voice" of rates, diagnoses, prognoses and solutions, when the media represen-tations universally stress "sudden and dramatic" increases (in numbers involved or events) . . . then we believe it is appropriate to speak of the beginnings of a moral panic.[5]

Moral panics are driven by fear and the fear is authorized by people who are considered experts. In quoting Hall, I don't mean to suggest that moral panics are always "elite-engineered," as Erich Goode and Nachman Ben-Yehuda phrase it when describing Marxist approaches like his.[6] At the same time, Hall is right to note the centrality of expert discourse (editors, police, etc.) and its relationship to social regulation. Ordinary people respond and participate too (and certainly they have a relationship to who gets to count as "experts"), but narcotic moral panics are often incited through high-level ideologues demanding institution-alized controls.

The Christian Temperance folks of the nineteenth century were right that some people were getting drunk. They were also right that some people really were harmed by alcoholism. The antinarcotic activists in the 1920s were right that some people smuggled cocaine into the United States. They were also right that some youth became addicted and wound up in jail. What makes these moral panics are reformers' claims that addicts posed an existential threat to the United States. These are moral panics because experts launched campaigns against unidentified foreign cabals of drug peddlers and "the liquor interests." They're moral panics because the perceived threat of societal collapse and moral chaos produced new modes of regulatory control. Did drug addiction exist, sometimes even among prostitutes and thieves? Yes. Was cannabis actually capable of unraveling the very fabric of America, transforming teen girls into nymphomaniacal murderers? No. This is, as Hall noted, "all out of proportion to the actual threat offered."

Christian Temperance Morality and Goals

The Christian Temperance Movement considered substance use to be a serious threat to the United States, particularly alcohol abuse. That threat came from multiple quarters. One construction of this treated the United States as essentially a white Christian nation with core national values rooted in transdenominational Protestantism. Drinking caused people to behave immorally, and in biomoral constructions (particularly phrenological ones), it also degraded or dissolved their capacity to be religious. Because alcohol evaporated morality, drinking threatened to undermine the very essence of national Christian identity. For those inclined to accept the premise that God held special covenant with the United States, this alcoholic immorality threatened national security too, since if America defaulted on its end of the contract, God could and would withdraw his support, allowing the United States to collapse into oblivion like so many empires before it.

They also considered alcoholics dangerous people. Because alcohol degraded morality, people who drank were more likely to become criminals. They were more likely to harm their family members. They wasted their personal resources and failed to work as hard as they could, thereby depriving the United States of national wealth. A nation of drunkards was also less prepared for armed invasion, so alcohol was a security threat when it came to military readiness. Finally, because alcohol produced degeneracy, it also threatened to weaken and perhaps destroy white heredity. So far as Temperance activists were concerned, all of this was bereft of any religious sentiment—it was just factual, unobjectionable science.

Particularly in the early years of Christian Temperance, reformers wanted to keep their movement focused solely on gently persuading people to quit drinking, but Prohibitionism was becoming popular among Temperance activists even by the 1840s.[7] By the 1870s, Temperance activists concluded that alcoholics were in fact slaves of alcohol and therefore unable to quit drinking on their own; while alcoholism might involve sin, it was also a kind of prison. Much of this formed in conversation with new medical theories of addiction. Frances Willard was neither overly optimistic nor a pessimist when determining how much sobriety was achievable. She felt Prohibition was the only reasonable solution to fixing alcoholism in America, but she also recognized that this might not happen in her lifetime. By the 1870s, Temperance reformers had more than 50 years of activity behind them, yet drunkards continued to harm themselves, their communities, and the nation nonetheless. The Woman's Christian Temperance Union began rethinking how their goals might be achieved. By the late 1870s, the WCTU was teaming up with reform-minded politicians like Senator Henry Blair and had created their own "Legislative Department" to lobby for legal changes around the country.[8] But another solution stood out to both Blair and Willard, and that was "Temperance Education."

Public Education, Protestantism, and Alcohol

American schools have rarely been uncontested ground in the area of religious ideals. Historians have noted that a close relationship existed between public schools and Protestant values in the nineteenth century, with educators often imagining that Protestant virtue was essentially neutral and a fundamental component of secular republican patriotism.[9] At the same time, nineteenth-century Protestants often considered that religious liberty was a fundamental American principle and they did not see themselves as religious partisans. If they introduced classroom lessons from the King James Bible (a problematic translation for Catholics) or included a mediator between humans and God in their prayers (which Jews felt was a Christian innovation), Protestant educators did not see this as privileging any particular religion. To Protestants, if Methodists, Presbyterians, Baptists, and Quakers all felt comfortable reading the King James Bible, then clearly the book was not sectarian and Catholics were just being difficult when they complained about it. This sort of logic governed Protestant attitudes to public education:

As long as Protestants across varied denominations could accept some particular premise or moral precept, then schools were well within the boundaries of acceptable religious practice.

As education historian Jonathan Zimmerman notes, "*all* education contains an element of imposition, insofar as it seeks to refashion students in ways they might not endorse or even recognize."[10] Zimmerman is right, and by definition education requires this. Education is essentially an intervention in students' cognitive life. Even gym classes, which lack assigned readings, require students to keep moving when they are tired (thus training them to endure), or to recognize where a ball is going to be a few seconds from now (thus teaching them to strategize). Nineteenth-century educators saw school as a way to train children in moral discipline. Although that morality derived from transdenominational Protestantism, Protestant educators often considered that what they wanted kids to learn was not based in denominationally specific doctrines or rituals and therefore it was appropriate classroom material.

By the mid-nineteenth century, Horace Mann had introduced educational philosophies that would shape the future of American schooling and that were germane to Temperance education. Mann felt that all humans were born into the world with "appetites" for various things already built into their physiology (what psychologists would later call "drives"). All people hungered for food, all people desired sex, all people wanted to drink liquids. On their own, these appetites were neutral; they became moral terrain as people decided when and how to act on them. It was natural to feel thirsty. If someone quenched their thirst with water, that was a moral choice. To quench it with alcohol threatened to toss the drinker onto the pile of others "stretched upon the 'burning marle' of Intemperance." For Mann, if the appetites were "subordinated to conscience and the will of God," they became morally positive drives that could profit the individual and the world. Mann felt that people must be disciplined into this kind of moral fortitude, however, and public education was the best method for doing this.

> The world is to be rescued through physical, intellectual, moral, and religious action upon the young. I say, *upon the young*, for the number of grown men who ever change character for the better, is far too small to lay the foundation of any hope of a general reform. After the age of

twenty-five,—or even after that of twenty-one years,—few men commence a course of virtue or abandon one of vice;—and even when this is done, its cause almost invariably dates back to some early impression, which for many years has lain dormant in the mind.[11]

In other words, Mann felt that adults don't change once they've grown set in their ways, and such ossification happens between ages 21 and 25. Public education shouldn't teach kids to embrace some specific sect of Christianity, but rather should train them in the moral universals that would benefit them throughout their life and would produce the kind of generational character that could save the world from sin, vice, and evil.

Two decades after Mann made those claims, the WCTU, Henry Blair, and other reformers were eager to see education turned to the cause of Christian Temperance. The WCTU assumed many of the same principles as Mann. Many adults who drank hesitated to give it up just because Christian reformers told them to and they were also unlikely to support laws revoking their right to buy more alcohol. The WCTU held out hope that these adults would someday change their minds but they were also interested in long-term strategies. Children represented America's future. Teaching them the dangers of alcohol could shape their attitudes toward drinking as they matured and hopefully help engineer a future sober America. Although reformers considered transdenominational Protestant virtues to still be useful classroom material, those invested in Scientific Temperance felt that science—or perhaps more accurately, the authoritative narratives scientists offered—would validate what Christian Temperance activists had been saying all along. People could quibble with religious arguments but nobody could challenge science and still sound coherent.[12] Although that strategy predates the WCTU, it was the WCTU's "Department of Scientific Instruction" that would become its most successful champion, a department launched in 1879 by Mary Hunt.[13]

Mary Hunt was direct about why she thought Scientific Temperance mattered and how it could help to teach children about the dangers of drinking. In 1892, she explained:

Blot from the great mass of human ill-doing and suffering the consequences of the use of alcoholic liquors and other narcotics and something like the millennium would remain. But in a Republic such blotting must be voluntary with a majority of the people before it can be compulsory, because a government of the people cannot compel majorities. Majorities are the law-making power that must first be convinced that alcohol and kindred narcotics are by nature outlaws, before they will outlaw them.[14]

Hunt was essentially saying that Prohibition was the end goal but it remained out of reach so long as a majority of Americans were not ready to support it. "Something like the millennium" would emerge if America would only abolish "alcohol and kindred narcotics." The solution then was to somehow convince a majority. Hunt and others felt that training children to recognize the moral calamities of drinking would produce the majoritarian conditions necessary for legal prohibition.

Hunt may have been right about strategy. She spent much of the 1870s and 1880s lobbying for mandatory Temperance Education at state levels, often successfully, and often intentionally involving Christian constituencies.[15] These laws required that public schools instruct children about how they should react to substance use. In 1886, Senator Blair shepherded his "Temperance Education Bill" through Congress, which obligated the military academies, public schools in Washington, DC, and territorial public schools (which in 1886 included most of the American west) to instruct students about "intoxicating, narcotic, and poisonous substances."[16] When Blair's bill passed, 38 states had laws mandating temperance education, and every state had them by 1900.[17] The math is important here. The Volstead Act amended the US Constitution to prohibit alcohol in 1920, roughly 40 years after the first school systems implemented mandatory temperance education. Mary Hunt and Frances Willard played their long game well: The generation that passed Prohibition is the same generation that grew up under their mandatory Temperance curricula.

Temperance Curricula

Temperance legislation effected textbook changes in the 1880s. A few textbooks addressed Temperance topics even before Temperance Education laws were widely passed, but as more and more states began mandating such courses, publishing companies edited their content.

Textbooks are after all a commercial product. If a publisher's books do not explicitly address Temperance Education, yet many states have laws requiring that this be taught in classrooms (and perhaps even more states will do so in the near future), then to *not* address Temperance is to make one's textbooks unusable in large parts of the market. During the 1880s, textbook publishers released many new health books or revised existing ones to clearly identify their utility for Temperance Education, often highlighting that in the book title or preface. Mary Hunt even authored her own health book, which the WCTU promoted.[18]

When they approached topics about substance use, Scientific Temperance books uniformly came down against it and they often offered religious explanations as they did so. In 1883, for instance, doctors Chilion B. Allen and Mary A. Allen published a textbook written in an allegorical style, which they identified as the same didactic approach Jesus took with parables. In *The Man Wonderful in the House Beautiful*, the Allens identified the human body as merely a temporary home for an eternal self. It began by explaining that "the House Beautiful" was "built by a wise Architect, who has been building such houses ever since the human race existed." They also wrote that "maybe you have always thought that your body was you. But it is only the house that you live in."[19] The Allens identified various "friends" who came into this house to visit. Some of these friends, such as milk, fruit, or water, were beneficial to the house and honored the Great Creator. Other friends, such as coffee, "a Chinaman" named tea, habit-forming spices like pepper and mustard, and a black quack dentist named "tobacco," were bad guests. Alcohol was the worst, though, causing people to say vulgar things, loosing "the passions," making drinkers abandon kith and kin, and leading to "crime, indigence, insanity, incendiarism, fatal affrays, and degraded manhood." Women fared no better, since alcohol made them "no longer modest, pure, and delicate"; instead they become "filthy, homeless outcasts and wanderers, criminals themselves." *The Man Wonderful* also made the point that alcohol did *not* belong on "the sacramental table," as Reverend Talmadge had made so clear.[20] (Catholics would have found this claim sectarian.) In short, the Allens' health primer intended for public school use had explicitly Protestant content, drew on racist imagery to make its case, opposed dangerous substances ranging from opium to black pepper, and argued that alcohol led to extreme poverty, insanity, and degenerated gender performance.

It would be easy to dismiss *The Man Wonderful* as a sensationalist outlier, and some of its language choices are admittedly more heavy-handed than other examples of the day. However, other textbooks often reproduced the same themes. The 1885 grade school textbook, *How to Keep Well*, also identified the human body as "the house we live in," and argued that alcohol led to waste and ruin. "The most brutal crimes are often committed while a person is crazed with strong drink. . . . Self-respect, honor, conscience, common decency" disappear. Caffeine and tobacco are dangerous to children, and opium will lead people to "lie, cheat, or commit any crime, to get a dose of the fatal drug."[21] The 1887 textbook, *The House I Live In*, argued that "each body has its own living soul within." It also argued that alcohol makes it harder for people to work productively, and "persons who drink any kind of alcoholic liquor regularly become diseased, because such drinks do not make good blood as pure water and milk do." It also argued that the blood "cleans the brain" at night. If that blood were full of alcohol, it could lead to insanity, which "is the worst thing that can befall any one." *The House I Live In* implored readers to avoid tobacco and alcohol so that each can "use his mind rightly."[22] Although some might only refer to Protestantism obliquely, these textbooks and others like them made arguments about substance use as the source of social and economic downfall, as well as an inappropriate way to use one's mind, body, or soul.

Temperance Education came into being because reformers worried that America was degenerating into crime, madness, immorality, and national sin. Education was essentially a regulatory strategy. The curricula warned children of a wide range of awful consequences resulting from substance use, which educators hoped children would consider as they matured into their moral agency. Reformers had multiple reasons for this, but one of those was that they wanted each student to make choices that were beneficial for the kids themselves. These reformers had a political agenda to be sure, but it would be too callous to assume that these educators only had self-interested motives in mind. Looking back from the twenty-first century, the ideological tone and religious assumptions in these books are somewhat transparent, but that may be more obvious to us because we live and think with different cultural frameworks. From their end, Temperance educators were helping children understand the consequences of breaking God's laws of health. These were facts to them, not sectarian opinions. They also hoped to shape the moral outlook of the next generation in ways that would produce Prohibitionist legislation and that would cultivate a general antidrug outlook in which addicts were to be both pitied as well as considered dangerous.

Race and Moral Threat

If education represents one realm of the moral panic, the media represent another. Evaluating the media is challenging since they include a wide range of formats, political opinions, interventionist goals, commercial strategies, and moral assumptions. Scholars also theorize the relationship of media to audiences differently. At least when it comes to the news, this chapter treats the media/audience relationship as mutually constitutive. The media produce narratives which audiences receive. At the same time, reception isn't passive. Audiences think about what has been written or broadcast and decide what they make of it. They don't necessarily assume that everything they hear or read is true—widely held general trust in the news is something that has developed over time, and that trust waxes and wanes from era to era.[23] The media are also commercial products: They sell (and therefore speak) what people want to hear. In this way the media are themselves shaped by audiences. While the William Randolph Hearsts and Henry Luces may play important roles, the press can't sell a story that nobody wants to buy. Media can also play a central role in moral panics. Although moral panics can emerge from more than one source (and the substance use panics certainly did), news sources can lend credible authority to what are otherwise just personal impressions, opinions, and suspicions.[24]

Nineteenth-century media helped shape public perceptions of substance use. The United States experienced a resurgence of nativism in the late nineteenth century (especially in the 1880s), driven partly by hostility toward Asian immigrants in the west and Hawaii, as well as by European immigrants who were willing to work for poverty wages and whom some race scientists considered degenerate.[25] Although white people were regular consumers of assorted psychoactive substances, this wasn't especially newsworthy. White Americans sometimes worried about impoverished European immigrants taking their jobs or resources, but not with the same amplitude they worried about African Americans, Chinese immigrants, or Mexican border labor. They frequently also assumed that racial others were biologically/biomorally inferior and so were therefore more dangerous when they used drugs. The dominant media, whose white authors wrote narratives for white audiences, were more likely to report on racialized drug use because it fed their audiences' interests.

Media about Chinese immigrants particularly emphasized them as "heathens" with a penchant for substance-based immorality. Nationally, newspapers identified San Francisco as a particular site of opium infestation. For one example, in 1877 the *Milwaukee Daily Sentinel* ran an article titled "Devil's Heaven," which was itself reprinted from the *San Francisco Post.* According to the story, adjacent to St. Ignatius College, a plainclothes police officer discovered an opium den in the back of a Chinese washhouse. In the center of the den was a "luxurious" and "curiously shaped" bed on which two white American men lay smoking opium. The Chinese immigrant who ran the place told the officer that women were not permitted into the establishment *before* 11 p.m.[26] The implications of white women frequenting a Chinese opium den after 11 p.m., a place where the opium was served in the middle of a fancy, unusual bed, was meant to imply the worst sins imaginable to readers. Other articles around the country ran similar tales: children finding Chinese corpses under piers, their face and hands eaten by rats; Chinese shippers smuggling opium into the United States by hiding it in their shoes; stories of the opium-faded Chinese in turn eating the rats themselves as slum residents living among New York's Jews and Italians; incredulity over the Chicago police's claims to have cleaned up opium, when clearly the Chinese were still smoking it; and so on.[27] Papers also sometimes emphasized the difference between the Chinese and African Americans. In 1877, the *Boston Daily Advertiser* ran an article about Blanche Bruce, a Black senator elected from Mississippi during Reconstruction, touring San Francisco's Chinatown with Pinckney Pinchback, the Black former governor of Louisiana. Bruce told the paper that he assumed tales about Chinese unassimilability were exaggerated prejudice, but now having seen the squalor and opium for himself, he found he agreed—the "peculiar repellant qualities and disinclination of the Chinese to mingle with or adopt European customs" made them fundamentally un-American.[28] These sorts of stories increased throughout the 1880s and reached their apex around 1900; however, the premise of drug-addled Chinese immigrants debauching white Americans was ubiquitous, and remained newsworthy until the 1920s when the stories declined.

If the Chinese were feared as heathenish narcotic threats they were hardly the only racial others that white Americans worried about. In the 1880s, cocaine became a topic of fascination as German medical researchers discovered its anesthetic properties.[29] Americans soon recognized that it could also take the edge off taxing labor and began employing it to these ends. By the 1890s, Black dockhands were using it to get through hard shifts in New Orleans and elsewhere along the Mississippi, often with the blessing of their employers. Some plantation owners even distributed it to Black laborers as a strategy for increased productivity. But by the 1900s, cocaine was getting a reputation for instigating an increase in crime, appearing in the underworlds of New Orleans, Pittsburgh, Chicago, New York, Kansas City, and Dallas.[30] People suspected that cocaine was producing criminal behavior and exacerbating the innate wild nature they thought all Africans had. The press played off this. A 1906 edition of *The Baltimore Sun* ran a lengthy news story entitled "Baltimore Negroes Are in the Thrall of Cocaine: Amazing and Dangerous Growth of a Habit Unknown a Decade Ago," which averred that "the practice of cocaine using is confined at present almost exclusively to the colored population and to degraded white women," and argued that cocaine's greatest menace was its "faculty of destroying the moral sense." The *Sun* also cited a judge who claimed that 90 percent of Black defendants were addicted to cocaine, which he considered a "conservative estimate."[31] In July 1910, the *Harrisburg Telegraph* reported that a Black addict in Tampa had become "crazed" with cocaine and shot up a church before going home to commit suicide.[32] In 1914, the *Austin American* reported that a Black "cocaine fiend" had murdered a police chief in Shoshone, Idaho; the white folks had ordered every Black resident to leave town and the paper warned that the threat of mass lynchings ran high.[33] These are only examples of a much wider phenomenon; there is no shortage of articles about cocaine transforming Black men into crazed, murderous villains.

Chinese opium fiends and coked out Black berserkers are only two categories of racialized substance use; much could be said about associations of Mexican immigrants with cannabis or of American Indians with alcohol and peyote. There was also overlap among these categories. For instance, while media tended to run more stories about Black cocaine abuse, there were also plenty of articles about Black men abusing other drugs, too. A 1907 article in the *St. Louis Post-Dispatch* described how four white women in their early twenties were caught in a Black opium den, and how the police were forced to beat the "gigantic negro" peddler into submission.[34] Not just newspapers, but popular media in general generated such stories—books, silent films, magazines, radio. We shouldn't assume that American audiences passively absorbed everything at face value, but we also shouldn't assume that they challenged and dissected every article, either, particularly when these media repeated stories of racial threat ad nauseam. Additionally, many of these articles weren't so different from what scientific experts were saying.

Race scientists had been arguing for decades that races were different by nature, not just physically, but intellectually, emotionally, and spiritually too. Criminologists, anthropologists, court officials, police chiefs, missionaries, and medical experts also attested to the validity of racial difference as fact. This position created a police cycle as well. Around the turn of the century, criminologists examined statistics which showed African Americans were being arrested and convicted of crimes at disproportionately high rates. Many assumed that policing was racially neutral and that the statistics therefore demonstrated that Africans were preternaturally prone to crime, perhaps even morally unsalvageable.[35] Such statistical arguments fed white supremacist narratives. The reaction to assumed Black criminality was to police Black neighborhoods with greater zeal. Increased policing—paired with the suspicion of endemic criminality—likely led to greater arrests, feeding the cycle further. Experts also suggested that some races were naturally more driven to substance use than others. If day after day, year after year, American newspapers ran articles about drugged out racial others debauching white women and committing acts of violence, they were operating within plausible scientific frameworks and confirming white fears.

With the exception of calling the Chinese immigrants "heathens," there is little about this line of racialized discourse that is *explicitly* religious. However, it doesn't need to be explicitly religious in order to matter for this story, and furthermore the lack of explicit religiosity is hardly evidence of neutrality. The WCTU offers an analogous example that may be helpful here. They felt the need to embrace "Scientific Temperance" in the 1880s in deference to shifting attitudes about religion in the public sphere, a strategy that only expanded during the twentieth century. During Prohibition, Protestants often rallied for prayer, lobbied legislatures on church stationery, and demanded that Christians lead the nation toward its moral future. The laws they fought for, wrote, and passed almost never mentioned religion. The absence of explicit religious reference didn't magically make Prohibition secular, though. Religion is much more than just the language someone uses to frame their arguments. It can also include worldviews, eschatological expectations, epistemologies, emotions, moral practice, and lived social hierarchies (among other things). People bring all of that and more with them when they interact and engage with their worlds, including when they draft new laws or report/read news of current events. Newspapers and other media might not explicitly emphasize religion when they publish articles about racialized drug abuse, but that omission doesn't mean that Protestants therefore read such stories without considering the Kingdom implications. Postmillennialists had been trying to reshape America into the Kingdom of God since at least the Revolution. Even if the *Baltimore Sun* said nothing about the Kingdom, Protestants invested in postmillennialism would have understood the implications of cocaine madness for their eschatological goals. In short, when Protestant audiences interpreted media, they understood those narratives through religious frameworks.

Many people also considered the United States to be a fundamentally white Protestant nation in which racial others were either guests or students. Some histories of the Drug War have emphasized how racist the early laws and discourse were and approached its manifestations as essentially about punishing racial minorities. They're not wrong. At the same time, a slight modification can bring into sharper focus that this was not solely about punishing racial others, it was also about building whiteness. Some race scientists who claimed that Black criminality was a racial truth argued that African Americans were a dying race who should be allowed to perish; those same race scientists in turn acknowledged that white crime and vice also existed, but insisted this was symptomatic of a sick society and no expense should be spared in redeeming it.[36] White Protestants often felt America was destined to be a paragon of white Christian virtue that would demonstrate to the rest of the world the value of liberal democracy. Eugenicists wanted to edit heredity in order to build "the Future American." For them, white civilized leadership, vested in American Anglo-Saxon institutions and values, would be what led to the Kingdom of God. If other races were now using drugs that upset their innately inferior nature, causing them to commit acts of violence against white Americans and debauch young white women, this jeopardized what was essentially a religious-racial project. Media representations of dangerous racialized substance use didn't exist in a vacuum independent of this outlook, they served as warning signals that white Protestant utopianism was imperiled.

White Protestant Panic and Narcotics

There's good evidence for interpreting the racial panic about narcotic use as coterminous with a Protestant one based in white Christian nationalism. Richmond Pearson Hobson serves as a model example of this, but there were plenty of others who produced comparable positions— Hobson just happens to be among the most influential of those who held such ideas. He is also useful for demonstrating that the religious elements of the early Drug War were sublimated. During his Prohibition years, Hobson made his Protestant ethos explicit. During his antinarcotic years, he still championed those positions in very specific settings, but generally omitted them from his reform work. His motivations were religious but he aimed to create a secular argument.

The "Men and Religion Forward Movement" took place between 1911 and 1912 and sought "the enlistment of men and boys in the work of the kingdom of our God," which they hoped would result in "the winning of North America to an enlistment in an aggressively active campaign which will bring the Church as a mighty army to the feet of Christ."[37] Many famous men spoke at the concluding "Conservation Congress" that took place in New York City. On a Sunday afternoon in April, Hobson shared the Broadway Tabernacle stage with Booker T. Washington as he delivered his speech, "The Church in Relation to Temperance."

Hobson declared that his approach was "purely scientific" as he recited text that reproduced arguments he'd made in the House of Representatives only 14 months earlier. Hobson explained:

> You have the red man on the reservation; let him get drink and it is not long before he wants to turn savage again. Take the black man, and let him indulge in excesses, and it will not be long before he is a cannibal again. The result of my observations, is that the black race in its destiny will largely be determined by whether or not you eliminate this great destroyer. If you do, the future will give beautiful and glorious results; if you do not, we will see a multitude of instances of the lapses which now unfortunately occur to startle the nation. You take a white man, of any type, an evolution of the highest kind, a tender-hearted man, and let him come under this toxin, and it will not be long before he will pass from the high type to semi-civilization. The noblest man that ever lived can be dragged down to the lowest level by this destroyer.[38]

Hobson proceeded to explain that alcohol causes the human species to degenerate, and that children born to alcoholic parents who drink are less likely to survive, have more deformities, more cases of epilepsy, and that 20 percent of them grow up to be insane. He argued that it also led to waste and crime. According to Hobson, American Christians had a special duty to their nation and to the world to solve this problem. He argued that "the church, humanly speaking—is the greatest agency to bring about the evolution of mankind, and to uplift the race. The attitude of the church must be that of endless, undying warfare against this great evil."[39] For Hobson, alcohol was a degenerative race poison that reduced nations to charnel, reducing white people to "semi-civilization," but Black people to outright cannibalism. Defeating "the great destroyer" though would mean a future of "glorious results." It was racial doom if alcohol stayed and Kingdom advancement were it abolished.

Hobson also saw the roles of government and Christianity as related. During his unsuccessful 1914 reelection bid, Hobson stopped in Tuscaloosa to give a campaign speech, where he explained:

> I desire to report to you that for my part, my campaign has been on a high plane; that I have recognized throughout it all that great moral and

spiritual forces are paramount; that every speech I have ever made and every word I have ever uttered had only for the hearers an effect of uplift. I believe that God's rules in this universe and that in the affairs of nations and in the great questions of government, that there are great principles which should be paramount. . . . I have felt that in a self-governing country where the great body of our people have undertaken to guide a mighty nation down its career of destiny, that our people should realize and we should all realize that a nation is a great living thing; we should comply with the great fundamental laws of life and above all, the law of improvement, the evolution of the building principle in all life, and that the great object of governmental policies should be to insure that the rising generation shall always improve over the previous.[40]

This is relevant because it provides some sense of how Hobson thought about reform: the nation was itself a Christian entity and Christian principles must guide it. The role of government was to shape conditions that allowed for God's plans to progress. It's clear from his statements in this speech and elsewhere that he believed fully in free will; God had plans for America, but that destiny could be thwarted if people refused to cooperate. Ultimately what he wanted from both government and American culture was an ever-growing improvement of racial heredity, civilizational progress, and moral uplift; law and education were two means by which to accomplish this.

Prohibition went into effect in January 1920. Hobson tried to remain enthusiastic about alcohol education and law enforcement, but his heart wasn't in it—the fight had been won and booze was now illegal nationwide. By 1923, he had found what was for him a new cause: narcotics. Alcohol and other substances were allied problems in the minds of Temperance reformers since the early nineteenth century, but Hobson himself had rarely mentioned any substance besides alcohol prior to the 1920s. It is unsurprising that he made this move, though. Hobson desperately wanted to have a visible leadership position and there were none available for a finished cause. In 1921 Hobson was making plans to establish the Alcohol Education Association in California, but by 1923 he had rebranded it as the International Narcotics Education Association (INEA), incorporated in Los Angeles. Creating an antinarcotic crusade was a logical step and he understood himself to be forging new terrain.

Antidrug discourse had been around for some time, but Hobson brought it to a fever pitch in the late 1920s. The INEA was only the first of his organizations; he also created the World Conference on Narcotic Education (WCNE) in 1925 (with its first meeting in Philadelphia in 1926), of which he styled himself the "secretary-general," and the World Narcotic Defense Association (WNDA) in 1927, based in New York. Initially many people did not take him seriously. Malcolm Delevigne and Rachel Crowdy at the League of Nations made jokes about his WNCE invitations.[41] The State Department had to repeatedly ask him to stop meddling in international diplomacy. Even some of his allies thought him unsuited for the work. David Starr Jordan, the eugenicist, Stanford president, and close personal friend to Richmond and Grizelda Hobson, resigned from the INEA in 1923 and asked him to remove his name from the stationery because the American Medical Association was hassling him about its sensationalist, unscientific rhetoric.[42] In January 1926, General John Pershing of WWI fame agreed to be on Hobson's WCNE conference committee, mostly as a way to lend his name to the antinarcotic cause. Pershing resigned in December after a letter from a third party accused Hobson of financial duplicity and he politely insisted that Hobson remove his name from the stationery despite its cost and inconvenience.[43] By the 1930s, though, Hobson was respected enough that the head of the Federal Bureau of Narcotics took his calls, world leaders praised his drug education programs, and the League of Nations welcomed him to speak in Geneva.

While Delevigne may have disdained Hobson, the popular press did not. Within a month of the INEA's founding, the *Los Angeles Times* ran a headline reading, "Pastors Laud War on Drugs." The article praised Hobson's work, which the Los Angeles Ministerial Union supported. Drug addicts now "numbered in the millions," but the INEA would educate schoolchildren about how dangerous habit-forming substances were.[44] In 1924, the *Washington Post* ran a feature story about Hobson's work, placing a picture of him in the middle of a full-page cover story in their Sunday magazine which presented him as an expert. The article (titled "Snatched by Dealers in Human Souls!") also featured an illustration of a gigantic, black bony hand abducting a teenaged white girl in front of a school. The article accepted Hobson's explanations uncritically, explaining that narcotics caused "a very swift degeneration of the upper brain," which in phrenological terms was the seat of religion and morality. It also caused physical degeneration; the *Times* claimed that "children of addicts in the early stages are always subnormal" and that in later stages, addicts become permanently sterile, which the paper linked to race suicide. It claimed that "school boys and girls" worship "the god 'pep'" and use drugs "to keep up with the jazz pace of the day." Drugs were also of foreign origin, and these pushers were deliberately targeting America's youth. The *Times* repeated Hobson's arguments that addiction produces a mania in which addicts sought to convert others—even their own children—and lost all sense of morality. "Every addict is a potential murderer and always a public enemy," it read, predicting that the United States could soon have as many as eight million addicts.[45] Newspapers and magazines throughout the country ran comparable stories; they took Hobson's antidrug claims and presented them as factual truth until his death in 1937.

Perhaps it's natural that the media took Hobson seriously. He headed three antinarcotic organizations and one might assume that someone in that position would know what they were talking about. Hobson's reliance on statistics also gave him the aura of credibility. These statistics were often bogus, though, enough so that in 1929 the Department of State asked him to stop using them.[46] In 2005, comedian Stephen Colbert offered the term "truthiness" to describe something that *feels* true, even if one can't credibly demonstrate it. Hobson lived in truthiness. He was fully convinced that narcotics posed a serious threat to the United States and that the problem was worse than some other people were making it out to be. In his authoritative 1,000-page book *The Opium Problem* (1928), the Jacksonville-based medical researcher Charles Terry dryly quipped that "certainly, our news agencies have not minimized the importance of the problem or lessened the public's interest in it," but went on to observe that drug statistics were wildly unreliable, with addiction estimates ranging from a few thousand to millions upon millions.[47] Because Hobson's gut told him that the problem was worse than the government reported it to be, the most dramatic numbers were nearly always the ones he shared with the press. William Randolph Hearst was also convinced that drugs were a serious problem and used his massive media empire to push that argument, too, sometimes supporting Hobson's efforts in the process.[48] Hobson received support from other papers as well. The end result was a news landscape that informed Americans that addicts were dangerous, ubiquitous, secretive, and conspiratorial.

This media cycle worked to antinarcotic activists' advantage, and the 1920s saw a wave of new antidrug regulation. The 1914 Harrison Narcotic Tax Act had been an American response to the missionary-driven 1912 Hague Convention. Initially this law had only regulated who could buy, sell, import, or export certain substances, and it required pharmacists to keep records. The law's purview for controlling specific medical approaches (particularly maintenance treatment) was initially unclear. The Department of Treasury, which oversaw the law's implementation, had insisted abstinence was the only legitimate medical treatment since 1915. That position was at first hard to enforce, but a Supreme Court decision in 1919 made the policy legally binding and physicians and pharmacists found themselves on shaky legal ground if they prescribed for maintenance.[49] Additional new legislation soon popped up. In 1922, the Jones-Miller Narcotic Drug Import and Export Act established stricter rules for drug traffic; created a Federal Narcotics Control Board within Treasury to police drugs; prescribed punishments of up to $5,000 fines and 10 years in prison for violations; and made possession of cocaine or opium sufficient enough evidence for conviction.[50] By 1931, 36 states had reproduced the possession-as-guilt proviso, and eight counted possession of syringes as convictable evidence, too.[51] In 1924, Stephen Porter led the House of Representatives in combatting heroin, arguing that addiction "sprang from sin and crime." Experts testified that heroin destroys people's sense of moral obligation "to the herd" and that most addicts were 17–25 years old.[52] In 1926, the House of Representatives debated whether stricter policies were needed for foreigners, whom Chairman of the Committee on Immigration and Naturalization Albert Johnson suspected of peddling drugs to children.[53] In 1930, Representative John Miller (of the Jones-Miller Act) claimed to have "started the war on narcotics" in his reelection materials, which illustrates an important point: by the end of the 1920s it was politically marketable to be an enemy of drugs.[54]

One should be cautious to not reduce drug opposition solely down to its political usefulness. It is true that politicians found antidrug positions to be useful. It cost them nothing to say "I'm against drug addiction" since nobody was actually *in favor* of addiction, and since plenty of their constituents worried about it. At worst, opposing drug addiction had no effect on their electability, but potentially it earned them points with those who viewed drugs as an existential threat. However, by 1930 politicians were speaking to a populace that had been reading for years about the dangers addicts posed to them, how pushers invaded schools and peddled to children, and how narcotics transformed racial others into dangerous debauchers of white girls. These articles rested on nearly a century of cultural discourse about substance use and had statistics and science to back up their claims, but now the frequency and intensity of such arguments had increased. Politicians and legislators may sometimes have opposed drugs because it was politically expedient, but it is just as likely that some of them felt a duty to represent their constituents' concerns, and what their electors were concerned about was drugs. Furthermore, legislators are neither aliens nor robots, but are themselves humans socialized into their culture. They may have read the same papers as their constituents and arrived at sincere convictions that drugs and addicts were sinister evils in need of address.

Hobson wasn't solely responsible for that phenomenon but he was an important cultivator. Early in his antidrug career he considered manipulating public opinion to be part of his mission. In 1925 he informed Pershing that the League of Nations had recently called upon the world's governments to disseminate antidrug literature through their schools, and that they had also suggested that antidrug "propaganda should come from some special organization." He identified the INEA as meeting this need, having already anticipated the importance of such materials.[55] His sensationalist interventions in the press were intentional and Hobson had the skill set to do it well, treating education and media intervention as twin strategies.

Cultivating a Moral Panic

Hobson may have valued ecumenicalism and moderate-for-the-era approaches to race, but his outlook was very much one of white Protestant nationalism. A few months before his death, Hobson addressed St. Thomas Church (Episcopal) in midtown Manhattan as part of a Sunday evening service in honor of Armistice Day. Hobson marveled over the sacrificiality Americans displayed during the Spanish-American War, assuming the financial burden of liberating Spain's oppressed Filipino, Puerto Rican, and Cuban wards, and then devoting themselves to civilizing these foreign peoples. He lauded American humanitarian missions to Japan, Martinique, Armenia, and held up the United States as a safe haven for oppressed minorities everywhere. To Hobson, America was both sacred and unprecedented. He explained:

> as I contemplate America as a living thing, its heredity, its gestation and birth, its rugged childhood, its mighty youth, I realize that nature, and nature's God, have brought forth a "Variation," a precious variation of surpassing beauty. Each day that I look out upon the troubled world, so messed up by hate, and fear, and anger, and intolerance, I realize more and more the boundless destiny of service to which America is called.[56]

Hobson went on to suggest that as "dean of the New World" the United States was responsible for ensuring that freedom survived, and for "bringing in a new Golden Age"—none of which was guaranteed, but all of which was possible if the United States adhered to God's plans and defended itself and others from destruction. In other words, Hobson considered America to be God's chosen instrument for advancing the Kingdom, the locus of a new racial "variation," and the heart of the free world, but only a secure and a morally sound nation could make this real.

Hobson's take on security was holistic; it included military readiness, for which he was an outspoken advocate, but it also included the belief that the American people were healthy in mind, body, and spirit. Decades earlier, Mary Hunt and Frances Willard had promoted education as a potential means for changing public opinions about alcohol, which threatened to destroy the nation. Education would help disseminate particular viewpoints as children brought "Scientific Temperance" home with them and discussed its content with their parents. It would also shape future generations of Americans by socializing them into sober moralities as they grew up. Hobson's approach to public opinion was nearly identical to the WCTU's. He intervened regularly in legislative affairs, sometimes successfully; both the Democratic and Republican Conventions of 1924 included his phrenologically driven antidrug materials in their official platforms. Hobson also followed the WCTU's position that good education could produce good legislation, as well as alter public opinion—this was where he would leave his most lasting effect.[57]

Narcotic Education

When Hobson lobbied the media to reproduce his antidrug narrative, he often emphasized education as the central remedy for the crisis. The most successful of his interventions was "Narcotic Education Week," which occurred annually from 1926 until roughly 1937 (usually in February) and which public, private, and religious schools around the country theoretically observed for a week.[58] Decades earlier the WCTU's Scientific Temperance wing had observed "Alcohol Education Week," "Anti-Cigaret Day," and "White Ribbon Day" as part of their temperance education strategies; Hobson was almost certainly using these as his template.[59] Sometimes the INEA's access to schools came through the support of a particular school system or superintendent. At other times, it came through the support of politicians, such as when New Jersey Governor Harold Hoffman issued an official proclamation for the observance of Narcotic Education Week, insisting on its importance for defending individual morals, maintaining a healthy economy, defending society from the dangers of drug-based crime, and sparing children from "Marihuana cigarettes, which are especially deadly to youth."[60] Many governors issued such proclamations, often using Hobson's suggested language; these frequently committed state schools to its observance. But highly visible politics aren't the only place one should look for these since smaller venues can matter just as much. It was just as common for politicians with smaller stages to make such declarations, when for example the mayor of Hearne, Texas (population 3,000) called for the town's "clergymen, educators, and all persons in positions of influence" to observe Narcotic Education Week by teaching kids about drugs.[61] Individual teachers also sometimes made their own decisions about it, such as when F. Harris Leavitt, a high school science teacher from Rutland, Vermont, chose to observe Narcotic Education Week.[62] City or statewide decisions to implement Narcotic Education Week meant that large numbers of schoolchildren went through the programs, but individual teachers electing to do this work on their own can also add up quickly.

School systems, universities, and religious organizations nearly always responded positively to Narcotic Education Week. Records for its tenth observance in 1936 (a year in which Hobson was particularly worried about cannabis) offer a good snapshot of this. Many school systems such as Boston's expressed a vague but affirmative plan to cooperate with Hobson's goals.[63] Others, such as Lansing, purchased his brochures for distribution to teachers (one brochure was about marijuana and another identified the scheduled arguments of Narcotic Education Week).[64] Religious organizations, both local and national, also purchased these in order to distribute them; examples include the Knights of Columbus and the Youth's Temperance Council of the WCTU.[65] The bishop presiding over the Protestant Episcopal Church in the United States of America went so far as to say that Episcopalians had "a duty" to cooperate.[66] Universities also observed Narcotic Education Week. Purdue University charged its College of Pharmacy with implementation; they achieved this by giving four radio talks, speeches before PTAs, luncheon clubs, local medical associations, and the League of Women Voters, all of which emphasized the new dangers posed by marijuana and the need for better education and legislation.[67] Hobson's efforts to conscript religious and educational institutions into his antidrug campaign were effective.

The materials for the 1936 Narcotic Education Week did not differ radically in content from any other year except that the cannabis fixation was still relatively new. These materials emphasized substance use as an enormous danger to American welfare, they called for specific laws and regulations, and they championed the INEA, WNDA, and the Federal Bureau of Narcotics as the antidrug vanguard. "Marihuana or Indian Hemp and its Preparations"—the pamphlet that so many schools were asking for—identified cannabis as an insidious new problem that even most well-educated Americans didn't yet know about. It claimed that while smuggling other drugs might present challenges, cannabis could be grown in the United States, and peddlers were cultivating thousands of dollars worth of it in abandoned Brooklyn lots and California orange groves for sale to "Mexican addicts." These materials called for all states to embrace strict new legislation and encouraged readers to lobby for this.[68]

Many states wanted to work with the WNDA on such legislation, who advocated in particular for the "Uniform State Narcotic Law." Since Congress did not have a clear purview to prohibit substance use, state laws were the highest level through which reformers hoped to achieve total prohibition. Ensuring states held matching narcotic laws would ensure that someone couldn't make use of lax laws in one state for trafficking in another. In 1929, state representative Milton R. Palmer told the WNDA that Michigan had modeled their new narcotics law based on the Uniform Law that the WNDA had shared with them, making special note that marijuana was becoming a problem in Michigan because of "Mexican laborers."[69] New York assemblyman Howard Dickey invited Hobson to Buffalo in 1933 to join him and Harry Anslinger in celebrating New York's passage of narcotic legislation.[70] Many state legislators were happy to affirm Hobson and his mission and made use of his uniform model.

Narcotic Education Week has largely been forgotten today, but it was well-known in the 1930s and transformative for the antidrug landscape. Hobson had more than one organization, and while it began in the INEA, the WNDA also pushed for its success. Turkish president Gazi Mustafa Kemal (better known as "Ataturk") personally wrote Hobson to praise it.[71] Narcotic Education Week also received praise from Franklin Delano Roosevelt, Benito Mussolini, the Vatican, Francis McConnell (president of the Federal Council of Churches), and world-famous author Rabindranath Tagore (among others).[72] The WCTU's *Union Signal* devoted a special issue to it.[73] Hobson frequently used Narcotic Education Week to gain access to the radio waves. Given its high visibility, NBC and CBS had good reason to permit Hobson to broadcast special Narcotic Education Week messages over their stations.

These broadcasts usually came from Hobson, other members of the INEA or WNDA, or allies of the organizations, such as Ida B. Smith (president of the WCTU), or Harry Anslinger (commissioner of the Federal Bureau of Narcotics). As part of Narcotic Education Week, these broadcasts aimed to teach Americans about narcotic peril. Much of it was sensationalist. In 1932, for instance, Navy Captain Lawrence Adams (WNDA) warned NBC's Blue Network that "the illicit international Drug Ring" posed "a real threat to civilization," since customs officials were now seizing tons of drugs in contrast to the ounces they seized in previous years. He also claimed that these seized tons only represented 5 percent of illicit imports and that smugglers were murdering government officials in order to achieve their goals. He further claimed that hashish was no longer an Egyptian problem, but was being smuggled into the United States from Mexico as "marihuana," a maddening drug that came in the form of cigarettes called "muggles." This was also leading to burglary spikes in New Orleans, where cannabis turned people into criminals.[74] In her 1935 Narcotic Education Week address, Ida B. Wise Smith also argued that marijuana (spelled out phonetically in the script since the word was unfamiliar to her) was threatening America's youth in horrifying ways. Smith cited newspapers as her evidence, noting that Chicago was facing an untold onslaught of cannabis crime, choir boys were falling prey to paregoric (opium), customs officials had deported dozens of weed dealers back to Mexico, and peddlers were having hundreds of girls over to their apartments for "dope jamborees."[75] She echoed Adams and Hobson in identifying education and new laws as the right solution to the problem.

The WNDA and INEA also sought to reshape school curricula in the same manner that the WCTU had done. Gertrude Robinson created evaluative lists that these organizations circulated to educators of which textbooks could be used for narcotic education. Her 1928 *Treatment of Narcotic Education in School Textbooks* was mostly evaluative, insisting that children needed rational scientific education that instilled in them a real knowledge of substance dangers rather than just a fleeting emotional distrust of drugs. It particularly rejected the earlier generations' fearmongering over caffeine, arguing that children could see very well that tea wasn't hurting anyone and insisted that opposing caffeine undercut credibility for their other, valid claims. Her 1930 *Revised Syllabus in Narcotic Education* went further, and this was something Hobson frequently distributed to schools. *Revised Syllabus* offered specific plans for what information children should learn in which grades. It also told educators that they needed to be discerning about what information to share; not all knowledge was good and children with "unnatural questions" should be denied answers. The educational model had eugenic undertones in general, but these were sometimes explicit. In contrast to her previous arguments about reason over emotion, Robinson suggested that educators might have to rely on fear for eugenically inferior students:

> In case no motivation of a constructive sort is likely to appeal to the lower group of sub-normal children there can at least be a habit or attitude

crutch built from the conviction that any indulgence in narcotic drugs of any kind means FAILURE plus SUFFERING.[76]

Archival evidence suggests that some schools wanted this document, but it is hard to evaluate how extensively it was actually used. At any rate, Robinson's *Revised Syllabus* offered supplemental classroom material and advice for constructing narcotic education plans overall.

The moral panic Hobson helped shape also coincided with shifts in how health textbooks discussed narcotics. Books from the 1880s often identified narcotics negatively, but by the 1910s–1920s, discussions had diminished. The 1920s–1930s witnessed revived interest in earlier tropes. These books usually stayed away from explicit language about God, but they maintained the attendant language that had accompanied those earlier arguments. The 1936 junior high textbook, *Hygiene: A Way to Happiness*, identified itself as teaching the "fundamental laws of physical, mental and social well-being." Health was holistic.

> If one's bodily health is not good, he will find the learning of facts and the agreeable treatment of people more difficult for him than if he is strong and feels well. If his mental health is poor, he may learn queer and useless things. His bodily health may not be normal because his ideas are so warped.

This included "spiritual health," and according to *Hygiene: A Way to Happiness*, substance use disrupted the entire system. The book also adopted Hobson's language and arguments. It posited that physicians call addicts "the living dead," and that addicts sacrifice all morals in pursuit of the drug, going so far as to "blackmail other people, even their own fathers or brothers or sisters." These substances also turned addicts into monsters bent on converting everyone around them into addiction, too.[77] West Virginia's state-level booklet, *A Guide for Teachers Concerning Alcoholic Drinks and Narcotics* (1936), took a similar tone, arguing that girls who drank were likely to be assaulted, boys who drank would be bad athletes, and both would decline morally. Worse than alcohol, narcotics posed an existential threat to the United States, and students must support antidrug legislation. West Virginian students who avoided substances though would enjoy "greater mental ability" and "higher moral and religious ideals."[78] Most of these new health books did not take Hobson's full argument and package it as science, but they did tend to emphasize that substance use turned people into immoral, uncivilized beings.

Conclusions

Christian Temperance reformers saw themselves as agents of change, charged by God with putting an end to drinking. For many, this was an important step toward the Millennial Kingdom. They were frustrated that dry laws floundered in the United States for most of the nineteenth century and that their attempts to convince drinkers to quit went unheeded. They were also coming to terms with the idea that even people who wanted to quit sometimes found it impossible. In response, women like Frances Willard and Mary Hunt innovated. If drunk adults would not or could not make the moral choices necessary to save the nation, well the Kingdom was a long process—maybe intervening in children's morality could get them where they wanted to go.

Temperance Education assumed the dominant educational norms that approached schooling to be at least partly about character formation. Prescribing specific religious tenets or ritual practices might be off-limits, but the ideals and virtues that every Protestant could agree on were an important function of public education. The WCTU, aware of the discomfort some Jews and Catholics felt about their Protestant moralism, chose to insert their alcohol positions in public schools through "Scientific Temperance." Their lobbying was successful, and they got municipalities, states, and even Congress to mandate that children learn from WCTU-approved materials. Textbook companies adapted their texts to meet the WCTU's standards for what passed muster as proper Temperance Education, uniformly taking positions that marked alcohol, opiates, and tobacco as damaging and demoralizing substances, and sometimes taking shots at caffeine and spices, too. The WCTU wanted two things from this: to reshape children's morality so that they would abstain from drinking as adults, and to shift the public opinion of the next generation to one that supported Prohibition. Although it is impossible to judge the specific measure of their responsibility for it, the kids they taught to be anti-alcohol were indeed the generation that ended legal beverage alcohol.

Temperance Education and a rising moral panic about narcotics contributed to new antidrug regulations. Alcohol may have been the WCTU's primary enemy, but the changing ideas about addiction and how it worked began merging with 1880s racial fears in new ways. Chinese immigrants in particular were suspected of opiated lechery, luring white women to their dens in exchange for narcotic slavery. By the turn of the century, white Americans were also beginning to fear Black cocaine use. Some southern police departments went so far as to upgrade their bullet caliber from .32 to .38 in response to fears that Black men on cocaine couldn't be stopped with anything smaller.[79] Many of these narratives were pushed by news media, who repeated story after story after story about Black or Asian men debauching naïve white teenage girls. What emerged from this was a racial-religious threat. The dominant narrative in this era treated the United States as a white Protestant nation and God's chosen instrument for bringing about the Millennial Kingdom, but racial others threatened that destiny with iniquity, degeneracy, and crime.

The media rarely made such explicitly religious claims, though, and it's likely that many journalists weren't preoccupied with the Kingdom. Many of those writing about Black men and immigrants debauching white women may have understood themselves to only be telling what they thought was an interesting and true story. It would also be remarkable if many of them zoomed out to recognize their articles as one more derivative piece of racist dogma. But what individual journalists understood their work to be and what that work meant to readers are different things. Race can't be sectioned off from the rest of culture any more than religion can. To readers coming from a Protestant, Kingdom-oriented outlook—which in this period would have been the hegemonic position—racialized drug use was an obstacle or perhaps even existential threat to their utopian dreams regardless of whether or not newspapers wrote that.

Hobson's antidrug campaigns were motivated by such an outlook. Although he considered America to be authentically welcoming for people of other races or religions, that welcome was an extension of Christian charity from a Christian nation. God was forging a new white race out of the United States, which was destined to lead the world toward the promised Kingdom. American destiny was not a sure thing—it was God's offer, not his guarantee. Substance use of any kind degraded and degenerated biomorality in catastrophic ways. Alcohol, opium, cocaine, peyote, and cannabis took otherwise good people and made monsters of them. Addicts stole, murdered, and "converted" others into addiction, including schoolchildren. Yet Hobson maintained faith that most people would accept truth when they encountered it.

After Prohibition, Hobson challenged narcotics as the next contagion to clear from America. In considering how alcohol prohibition had been achieved, he looked back to the earlier models of the WCTU and reproduced them. He saw substance use as a threat to Christian progress and the American people, but public opinion and education were its solution. He established multiple antidrug organizations and placed himself at their helms. From this position he lobbied media to publish his claims, launched public demonstrations, worked with legislators to craft and pass new antidrug laws, and successfully pushed for antidrug models of education.

Hobson left a legacy. Narcotic laws are easier to create than they are to revoke. Today, drug offenses are by far the largest conviction category for federal prisoners, more than double that of the second-highest category (violent crimes). The first waves of truly punitive drug laws emerged in the 1920s and 1930s during the moral panic that Hobson was quite intentionally trying to produce. He considered addicts pitiable slaves, but he also thought they were extraordinarily dangerous. Many of the meaningful early laws—the ones with prison teeth—were enacted at state levels in this era. Yet the Drug War has historically been something that expanded rather than shrank. New laws build off the old ones or somehow reshape them; repeal is rare enough to be noteworthy. Hobson helped legislators draft many of these first laws upon which the future ones were founded.

He also helped propel the moral discourse that would come to characterize the later stages of the War on Drugs. Other historians have often attributed this to Harry Anslinger, who was admittedly important, openly racist, and avowedly punitive in outlook. Anslinger wasn't charismatic, though, he was a crotchety bureaucrat working for the Department of Treasury. It's impossible to say how things would have progressed had circumstances been different; perhaps Anslinger *would* have gotten the national conversation about drugs and addicts to go the direction it did. Yet when Anslinger came to hold his position at the Federal Bureau of Narcotics, Hobson had already been working the press, the schools, and the reform movements for nearly a decade, using his fame and charisma to lobby Americans to recognize drugs as a crisis. Once Anslinger came into power, both he and Hobson teamed up to repeat the same mantra: Addicts threatened to destroy America's entire social reality.

Education may have been Hobson's most important intervention. Millions of American schoolkids grew up in the 1920s and 1930s with Narcotic Education Week, using textbooks that emphasized how bad drugs could be for destroying morals, health, and respectability. A widespread narcotic panic in the media, the political realm, and churches would have accompanied schools' antidrug messaging. To an extent, Horace Mann and Mary Hunt were right about the relevance of children's moral formation. Personalities and worldviews may not be as permanently cemented as Hunt and Mann imagined them to be, but they were right that childhood and adolescence are important periods in which children learn how to interpret and live within the moral frameworks of their world. If the generation that grew up with Temperance Education (at its height between 1883 and 1906) went on to pass Prohibition in 1920, we might pause to question what the Narcotic Education Week generation (1923–1937) went on to do 30–40 years later.[80]

The 1960s and 1970s brought a wave of new antidrug measures, many of which were stricter than what already existed, including the Controlled Substances Act of 1970. The 1960s media and legislative discourse repeated many of the Narcotic Education Week tropes: Substance use (which now included LSD) led to immorality, crime, and social disruptions; better education was needed; and fools sought drugs pursuing the "illusory" goal of happiness.[81] It may surprise no one to learn that Richard Nixon (who many have erroneously credited with creating the War on Drugs) grew up with Narcotic Education Week. Nixon went to grade school and high school in Whittier and Fullerton, both of which are in the Los Angeles metro area. He graduated high school in spring of 1930. Los Angeles was the heart of Narcotic Education Week and home of its earliest iteration; it would be shocking if Nixon never encountered it. Nixon amplified existing antidrug structures and reshaped national narratives, yet it seems highly likely that he himself was influenced by Hobson's work.

There's more: 1920s–1930s Los Angeles was also home to Daryl Gates, perhaps best remembered for his role as police chief during the 1992 unrest over police violence against Rodney King. Gates was born in Los Angeles in 1926 and would have grown up with Narcotic Education Week, which some parts of California were still observing even as late as 1939. Gates was also the creator of Drug Abuse Resistance Education, better known to many Americans as D.A.R.E. The D.A.R.E. program began in Los Angeles in 1983 and placed uniformed police officers in classrooms to teach children about substance use, eventually evolving into a national program. (Remarkably little critical scholarship has been published about D.A.R.E.) Growing up in Indiana, I remember officers coming to my elementary school classrooms in the early 1990s to explain the horrors of drug use. We watched videos of teens jumping to their deaths through skyscraper windows. Officers described the moral tragedies attendant to marijuana and let us know that if anyone we knew used it, including our parents, we should turn them in. More than 30 years later I still recall those lessons; they are etched into my long-term memory forever. That enculturation has a genealogy, though. My D.A.R.E. officers were part of a national program designed by Gates and the Los Angeles school system, but Gates himself would have participated in Hobson's version when he himself was of D.A.R.E. age. Hobson's program was the resurrection of Christian Temperance. At the end of the day, we're still living in the shadow of our forebears' morality.

Conclusion

The Long Arm of Protestant Hegemony

Atlanta (2010)

In April 2010, Barbara Harris and Lynn Paltrow joined CNN's Campbell Brown to debate the merits of Harris's non-profit organization "Project Prevention," which pays addicts to use long-term birth control, including permanent sterilization. Paltrow represented her organization, National Advocates for Pregnant Women, and took exception to Project Prevention's policies. CNN's graphics at the bottom of the screen juxtaposed three pictures for viewers at home: a pot leaf, a teddy bear, and a razor blade between lines of cocaine. Campbell Brown invited Harris to respond to critics who called her efforts "Nazi-style social engineering" and "morally reprehensible." Harris made her position clear, saying,

> I mean, I don't think there's anything moral about a woman giving birth to 8, 10, 12, 21 children that end up in the foster care system. I know that I'm doing it from my heart, I adopted four of eight children, born from a drug addict in Los Angeles, and watched how they suffered. And those who object to what we're doing, they're not usually willing to adopt any of these children, nor have they, yet they campaign for the right of these women to procreate. . . . Responsibility has to come along with every right. They believe these women have a right to procreate, but they're irresponsible.

Brown asked Paltrow to respond. Paltrow began by applauding the parts of Harris's program she could agree with: It was great to help people access birth control and sex education, and she further noted that addicts faced serious obstacles to getting treatment, arguing that 48 percent of them can't access a program. She took exception to Harris's discourse, however, arguing that Harris stereotyped drug addicts as an entire class of people who ought not procreate; that she portrayed all children of addicts as damaged; and that this rhetoric supported and perpetuated a system that frequently took children away from loving parents who hadn't yet conquered their addiction and dumped them into a broken foster care system. Brown was unimpressed with Paltrow's answer, demanding that she instead "deal with reality," further arguing that Harris had more credibility than Paltrow since she worked with addicts regularly and had indeed adopted their children herself.[1]

The positions that Project Prevention take are not wholly identical to the eugenics discourse of a century earlier but neither are they fully separate. They pay addicts to use long-term birth control, of which sterilization is one form. As of May 2021, Project Prevention had paid for 401 vasectomies and 2,444 tubal ligations out of a total of 7,695 alcoholics and addicts paid, meaning 37 percent of the addicts were sterilized.[2] Project Prevention's arguments are less about biomoral heredity per se and more akin to eugenicists' arguments about the morality of American economics and children's welfare. The general arguments are: (1) that alcoholics and addicts produce children who are often born with addictions formed in utero, or with disabilities that produce suffering in the lives of those children; (2) that addicts are unequipped to care for children, who suffer neglect or abuse if left with the addicts, or transience (and possibly still neglect and abuse) if placed in foster care; (3) the abuse and suffering that addicts cause for children taxes the addicts' well-being too, leading them further into addiction; and (4) that addicts' children place an economic burden on society, with each foster child costing $150,000 annually, or every 4,000 children born to addicts costing society $561 million to $1.29 billion from birth to age 18.[3] Project Prevention argues that paying addicts $300 to not procreate is better "than paying millions after it happens in cost to care for a potentially damaged child."[4] In short, Project Prevention predicates its existence on the morality of taxes (how much are these kids going to cost responsible people?) and the morality of child protection (addicts' children may be born disabled or as addicts themselves, which causes suffering, so we should prevent those children from being born).

Where the official and the informal narratives deviate is in the representation of addicts' voices. Project Prevention offers addicts' testimonies in varied formats, but a curated collection posted to their Facebook page on May 25, 2021, serves as one example and illustrates the longevity of moral discourse about addiction. Project Prevention asked addicts to explain why Project Prevention should "do everything possible to get addicts long-term birth control," and addicts' responses included the following:

- addiction is hereditary and a child born to an addict does not have much of a chance for a normal life
- to prevent the cycle of having more addicts. To protect both babies and mothers.
- Because we are just spreading the addictive gene until we are clean and sober we cannot love and care for a child in the manner they deserve. And to me most of all a child does not deserve to be brought into the world with strikes already against them its like the unborn isn't even giving the chance to live the tax payer is also getting slammed with the hospital bills of the babies who need expensive medical treatment

These positions reproduce the idea that addiction is hereditary, which isn't necessarily wrong: Contemporary psychological and psychiatric literature supports the position that genetics can be one factor for addiction. Where Project Prevention becomes eugenicist is in reproducing the claims that sterilization will break the addiction cycle by ending the genetic line that causes it. Some addicts themselves argue this, and Project Prevention has collated their voices to create an informal, contemporary eugenic argument. Structurally there is little difference between this kind of curation and that of BIA officials gathering anti-peyote testimonies against the Native American Church. Project Prevention has found voices to echo their own sentiments and created discursive instruments from them, offering a message that addicts themselves want to be sterilized because it will help taxpayers and future generations.

Project Prevention is ethically complicated. On one hand, many children born into situations of severe addiction undeniably suffer because of it, and while Harris tends to market the worst-case scenarios (i.e., infanticide), the more ordinary cases aren't necessarily rosy either. Addiction can and frequently does produce conditions detrimental to children's welfare. Barbara Harris seems genuine: There's no real reason to doubt that her primary motivation is a desire to see fewer children suffer. Pretending that she has a sinister malevolent intent misrepresents the nature of her interest. Although the presentation of addicts' voices is curated, there's no reason to doubt their sincerity either. Some of those represented in Project Prevention's literature almost certainly do want sterilization.

One of the many contestable features of Project Prevention emerges from their practice of offering addicts money to embrace long-term birth control, including sterilization (which more than a third of them choose). Two issues arise from this. One issue is that offering money to addicts who may find themselves in financial need is coercive. Project Prevention could save money by paying *only* for the birth control and nothing else. Instead, they are offering addicts a $300 incentive in order to convince people to accept these procedures who would not otherwise choose them. Additionally, people who refer cases to Project Prevention are also entitled to $50. One source for such referrals is addicts themselves, who can refer other addicts. Another source is jailors and probation officers.[5] Being arrested is expensive in both direct and indirect ways, and addicts in such situations may find that accepting IUDs or permanent sterilization can defray their legal costs. When they are referred by jailors or probation officers it necessarily means Project Prevention is offering addicts $300 at a time when they badly need money.

The other significant ethical complication arises when we consider the moralities governing why some addicts choose sterilization as their option. Choosing sterilization "to prevent the cycle of having more addicts" assumes that heredity is the dominant and perhaps even the only reason for addiction. Under this logic, ending the family tree through sterilization helps end addiction for future generations. This is also positioned within a national moral framework that identifies addicts as inferior, broken, debased, or awful people, ideas that come out in the accusatory language by which addicts self-identify in Project Prevention's posts. Many of them express deep shame and regret over who they are, shame that leads them to conclude that something they may want very much (children) is something they should never have. One addict explained for instance that "babies deserve sober parents and if you can't be sober you don't deserve children, they are a gift." Another attested, "nobody would want to go through what I went through. I have seven beautiful children, 6 in foster care. I have a slim chance of ever getting them back." These are not the voices of people who do not want children, they are the voices of people who wish they were good enough to have them. They are also voices of resignation. They do not expect to beat addiction and cannot imagine a situation where they will have the families that they desire; it is better for them to give up on this dream and accept sterilization for the benefit of other people. Project Prevention agrees with them.

Project Prevention demonstrates how much of the Drug War's past remains the Drug War's present. It also shows that the War on Drugs isn't bound up solely in laws, but instead illustrates that the Drug War is waged across multiple fronts. It also highlights how irremovable morality is. Harris's position is that individuals and society at large have an obligation to future generations to see that they are raised in the best circumstances possible, a moral precept that on its own is hard to refuse. Lynn Paltrow's argument, which Campbell Brown didn't quite understand, was also moral in nature. Paltrow was essentially arguing that discourse bears relation to the operations of power, and that the consistent language describing addicts as immoral people who should not reproduce contributes to a matrix of social norms that punish and regulate a certain class of people. Paltrow wasn't arguing in favor of child abuse, she was arguing that Harris's language and project represent addicts as social contagions, and that such discursive strategies cultivate harsh and harmful reactions to substance users. Harris's moral concern was that we owe it to children to see that they are born into wholesome, heathy circumstances; Paltrow's moral argument was that we owe it to addicts to discuss them in humane language that leads to better healthcare and recovery access without contributing to the moralistic discourse already foundational to a draconian prison system.

Project Prevention represents a contemporary variation on a much older theme. Barbara Harris didn't pull her ideas from the sky, she formed them in conversation with the normative demands of moral citizenship, Drug War discourse, and biomoral knowledge. This is not to suggest that sterilization remains the *most* central part of the Drug

War, which would be a hard case to make. Eugenics's most lasting effects are more likely to be found in attitudes—attitudes about what ethnic backgrounds make acceptable immigrants, attitudes about what kinds of disabilities warrant interventions in utero, attitudes about criminal parents, and so on.[6] The widespread government sterilization program that eugenics birthed are a dead letter. Eugenicists' moral revulsion to addiction though is alive and well—changed, yes, but alive. Attitudes toward reformed addicts—those who repent of it—have softened somewhat. Those who use the substances we categorize as "drugs" remain morally unfit.

The War on Drugs has been so named for at least a century and has been going for roughly two. Looking beyond Project Prevention to the wider American landscape, the racialized character of the contemporary Drug War continues too, impacting people of color at grossly disproportional rates. How did we get here? Colonialism, white supremacy, and Protestant morality gave birth to the Drug War and their fingerprints remain all over it. Understanding how religion shaped its genesis is important for recognizing how it continues to matter in the world today.

A Moral Kingdom

Postmillennialism dominated nineteenth-century American Protestantism and came with certain moral norms. Their postmillennialist story was one of growth: The early apostles learned their Christian truth from Jesus first, then gradually spread it through the Roman world and among the Germans. Some parts stagnated into Roman Catholicism, but in greater wisdom, the freedom-loving peoples of Europe overthrew that tyranny with the Reformation. America was the greatest scion of this cause. As a Christian nation built on freedom, generosity, and moral covenant, the United States was thus poised to lead the rest of humanity into a greater future. The Millennial Kingdom was cooperative in nature; most imagined Christians had a moral duty to work alongside God to build it. Science, health, art, morals, law, language, industry— every part of human existence needed to be reshaped into final forms for the Millennial Kingdom to commence. All human progress was therefore sacred and people contributed to the Kingdom's advance in their own ways, each with their own vocation.

White postmillennialists were uncertain how much they could expect from other races. As far as postmillennialists (and others) were concerned, anthropology and race science proved that different people groups had different abilities and that some people were more civilized than others. Some might be dying off (American Indians, African Americans, and perhaps also Hawaiians), and some were biologically inferior in terms of the moral and mental aptitude necessary to comprehend full truth. If natives lacked genuine comprehension, then any demonstrations of cultural change were merely imitation. Furthermore, it was possible that human evolution had favored white people to advance in ways that were impossible for others. If morality was indeed a biological function, then biological differences could account for other races' immorality. Anthropometrists and phrenologists seemed to think this was the case, arguing that Africans and Asian physiognomies evidenced their cognitive inferiority. At the same time, the fact that some races might be incapable of true morality or true self-government did not excuse Christians from attempting to help them. In a worst-case scenario they would simply become colonial wards of the state who were cared for rather than emancipated into certain self-destruction.

Early addiction theorists suggested a range of options for why some people got hooked on substances, but most agreed that addiction was a kind of slavery. Whether alcohol, caffeine, cocaine, peyote, or heroin, they also agreed that substance use damaged the mind and therefore the morals. Such damage might even be permanent. Yet to repeat the words of Reverend Vruwink, "the Indian is essentially religious; he must drink from the supernatural spring, be that spring bitter or sweet, wholesome or poison." Race scientists made similar comments about the character of Africans or Asians; some thought they were intrinsically in need of superficial, illicit entertainment. If such peoples were permitted unrestricted access to damaging substances, then the civilized world would watch their wards degenerate into oblivion and ruin. For American postmillennialists especially, God expected the United States to fulfill its moral duty to civilize the uncivilized in ways that Europe had forsook. If inferior races were unable to abandon substance use (or understand why they should even try), then Christians must make those choices for them.

Much of that regulation took place on small stages, such as when William Johnson burned the peyote stocks of Laredo or when British officials shook down Chinese migrants for opium in Western Samoa. It also made use of authorizing indigenous voices who found the colonizers' discourse useful or even amenable, such as Jonah Kuhio Kalanianaole, who used civilizational discourse to call for alcohol prohibition by decree, or Chinese folks who complained to missionaries that Christian nations' passively destructive, laissez-faire attitude about opium sales showed that they operated in bad faith. It also happened on big stages. The first national laws about substance use in the United States were those that prohibited selling alcohol to American Indians, a regulation derived from the discourses of both civilization and national security. The first serious international drug law, signed at The Hague in 1912, evolved out of missionaries' urgent desire to protect China and racial others from opium addiction.

Postmillennialists didn't always identify their eschatologically derived moralities as they lobbied for substance use regulations. Sometimes they didn't even consider them relevant. Woodrow Wilson didn't feel that he needed to identify his goals as Christian; if the end result of his policies represented Christian progress, what difference did it make if he said so out loud? Sometimes reformers intentionally masked them, as Mary Hunt and Richmond Hobson did. And sometimes they kept them front and center, as Wilbur Crafts, Charles Henry Brent, and Frances Willard did. Either way, postmillennialists made meaningful contributions to the creation of a Drug War. They took scientific racism and addiction theories and incorporated them into an eschatological framework that gave them religious significance. Addiction wasn't a private matter or a neutral non-issue, it was a moral crisis. Drugs degenerated individuals and societies and they transformed addicts' essential nature into one of metastasizing immorality. Christian nationalists felt they had been born at a dynamic point in history and entrusted with leading the world toward a promised utopia, yet the challenge drug use posed to their progress demanded war.

The Long Reach of Eugenics

Eugenics was a logical extension of nineteenth-century American postmillennialism. American postmillennialists in the nineteenth century were overwhelmingly interventionist, which makes sense since they were convinced that the Kingdom advanced only through human coop-eration. If human cooperation is a fundamental part of the equation, then reforming those social structures and systems that fall below God's standards becomes a natural response. Postmillennialists were also fre-quently convinced that science was a kind of revelatory truth in its own right. As far as they were concerned, addiction either produced bad off-spring or was itself indicative of a deeper, blood-level degeneracy.

If degeneracy theory was pessimistic then eugenics was its optimistic partner. Humans didn't have to fatalistically accept degeneracy. Postmil-lennialism was a story about things getting better, with science repre-senting a major contributor to that progress. The compass had allowed sea travel, steam physics—the locomotive, pasteurization—a safer food supply, the vaccine—an end to smallpox. Each discovery had its applica-tions and each was a step toward the Kingdom. Now that scientists had uncovered the secrets of racial biology, eugenicists felt sure they could apply it toward building a perfect race.

Although eugenics could hypothetically apply to any race (and certainly sterilization programs affected people of color disproportionately—severely in the case of Puerto Rico, where at one time sterilization rates may have reached as high as 35 percent), eugeni-cists overwhelmingly cared about building and preserving whiteness.[7] Few imagined "the American Race" would be anything other than white and biomorality represented an important racial concern. Since addic-tion was seen either as the precursor to immorality or itself evidence of defective biomoral heredity, those who got hooked on substances were considered a threat to American genetic integrity. Eugenicists (some confessional Christians, some not) wanted a perfect future for the United States, in which people were smarter, stronger, healthier, and more moral. Addicts had no place in such a world.

Eugenics served as an important bridge for translating religious moral norms into secular language, which is perhaps best illustrated by the work of Harvey Washington Wiley. He abandoned the Christianity of his youth; his interventions into American drug policy and discourse occurred at a faithless stage of his life. Yet Wiley's postmillennialist ex-pectations for America continued long after he gave up on explicit reli-gion. He believed that "the Future American" deserved to be born with good heredity and environment and that substances like caffeine, tobacco, and opium threatened that racial future. Eugenics can be thought of as a canvas upon which one could paint their ideal society. The continuity between Wiley's biblical millennium and his eugenic one helps underscore the significance of public Protestantism. Postmillennialists were setting the discursive terms for shared cultural norms, and that kind of hegemony helped translate contingent religious expectations into moral universals.[8] Eugenics took Protestant morality, rebranded it as science, and then deployed it as a multilayered strategy for social regulation. Eugenics also altered the preexisting antidrug discourse by marking substance use as a symptom of moral degeneracy as well as a cause of it.

Secular Morality and Cultural Hegemony

Although "secularism" can mean many things, one of its definitional uses is in dividing human activity into "religious" and "religiously neutral" categories. If one assumes that "religion" only refers to very specific things like styles of baptism, denominational doctrines, or beliefs about the afterlife, there's no reason that "religion" can't be segregated from public spheres. That's a very limited definition of "religion," though, one that few religious studies scholars would still accept today. Wherever scholars might choose to draw their boundaries on "religion," definitions typically include norms about what people should expect from one another, how social roles get divided up, how humans should relate to supernatural beings (if such beings are part of that religion), and ideas about what counts as "good" or "bad." In other words, religions include morals. Yet morality is a protean concept that allows—perhaps even necessitates—that religion intermingles with everything else. Concepts like "industriousness," "civility," or "rationality" stand with one foot in both categories—they are "religious" and "secular" at the same time.

This kind of moral bleeding was central to the early history of the Drug War, except the specific points of morality were far more varied than just industriousness or rationality. The Drug War amalgamated from the moralities of white supremacy, colonialism, millennial progress, cognitive normativities, and Christian nationalism (among others). Each of those categories also imbricates the others, and as this book has argued, they each have explicitly religious roots. Except perhaps for

Christian nationalism it was also possible to present and campaign for each of these without making explicit reference to religion. Postmillennialists can champion progress toward the Kingdom by just calling it "progress," people can argue for colonialism not on grounds of Christian missions but from the pulpits of "civilization." These were moral projects that sought to reform how other people lived. They were Protestant projects, born from transdenominational norms and expectations of what individuals were accountable for to one another. There were different reasons why Protestants chose to omit, reframe, or finesse the religious rationales for their public arguments, but by the 1920s, the discourse had evolved in ways that made these moral projects linguistically secular.

Substance use stood in the way of these moral projects. Medical experts agreed that substance use ruined people's capacity to be moral, which was tied to their cognitive performance. If addicts posed existential dangers to American security and white eugenic progress, then drugs required serious oversight and policing. If alcohol, peyote, and opium held back Kingdom progress by distracting and seducing weaker races, then colonial powers must take them away. The rebranding of these religious projects as secular and neutral allowed two significant developments for the Drug War: First, it made it a more natural area for governmental regulation in an era when Americans were beginning to feel discomfort about self-evidently religious legislation; and second, it greased the rails for non-Protestants to join in with the reforms.

The secularizing of the early Drug War produces an interpretive problem: Is the War on Drugs still religious today? Brent, Hobson, Crafts, the BIA missionaries, the missionaries in China, and a host of other reformers were driven by explicitly religious motivations. I have argued (and continue to argue) that changing the language doesn't change the nature of the project. The Drug War was still religious well after people stopped predicating it on religious language. However, do we want to say that because the Drug War *began* as a religious project it is therefore *always* religious? That argument seems tenuous; it would mean that religion has a kind of social essence that can never be erased, and anything that began as religion (universities, hospitals, astronomy, etc.) can never be otherwise. Under some looser approaches to religion, that might not be a problem. Yet if we assume that religion has *some* boundaries (wherever exactly those may be) then taking a "once religious, always religious" position requires an unwieldy kind of essentialism to make its case. Beyond the academy such claims are also sure to be met with incredulity.

Just as covering a leopard's spots doesn't make it a lion, rebranding the early Drug War as religiously neutral didn't make it so. These reformers sometimes deliberately masked their language in order to present it as religiously neutral. At other times they thought that by removing religious language it in fact *was* a secular argument; word choice and argumentative approach were to them the features that divided those. (Mary Hunt's approach is a good example of this.) The language of universal morality offered leeway for taking religious arguments and understanding them as secular, particularly when the principle being considered appeared in multiple traditions. That multiple styles of Christianity, Islam, and Buddhism reject drunkenness as bad gave reformers grounds to interpret opposition to something like peyote as secular even when organizations like the Native American Church claimed it as a sacrament.

Those universalist assumptions also allowed the morality of the Drug War to escape its original religious frameworks, practiced by people who did not share in the eschatological rationales. Wiley stands out as the most obvious example. He maintained those religious morals after he abandoned Christian belief, ritual, and church membership. He participated in and encouraged others to participate in a Christian project using those exact same Christian morals. Unless one insists that "religion" requires sincere and devout belief in order to count as "religion" (a position I reject), then Wiley was still practicing a kind of Christianity even if he had rejected it confessionally. Similarly, Aimee Semple McPherson and John Harvey Kellogg were premillennialists who were not expecting the world to gradually grow better until human goodness ushered in the Kingdom. Both participated alongside the postmillennialists of their day and supported reform movements initially founded as American contributions to the millennium. Whose religiosity is best for understanding McPherson's participation at Hobson's rally: her own, or that of Hobson, who orchestrated the event and invited her to belong to it? Was the rally postmillennialist or not? What about Kellogg? In working to "better" whiteness through eugenic breeding and substance prohibition, he embraced a progress goal antithetical to the decline narrative intrinsic to American premillennialism. Where, then, does postmillennialism begin and end as a cultural ethic? There isn't an easy answer and it may be that binaries like "secular" and "religious" don't always work out tidily.

We could keep advancing these questions over and over. If one says that Wiley was indeed still practicing Protestant morality even though he no longer believed in Christianity (which seems reasonable to me), what we are saying is that *his behavior and moral orientation* were Protestant. A logical extension, then, would be that anyone who practices such moralities would in some sense be practicing Protestantism, regardless of what ultimate truth they might subscribe to. The "once religious, always religious" problem admittedly still lurks here unresolved, and the problem of setting boundaries on what counts as "Protestant morality" lingers too. Much comes down to the interpretive and definitional choices that we make as scholars, but even with its attendant interpretive challenges, I continue to argue that the transdenominational Protestantism that launched the Drug War continued to direct it long after people stopped regularly using religious language to describe it. The antidrug cultures that Christian Temperance crafted have marched on into the present day.

Continued Legacy

Many scholars of the Drug War point to the legislative behemoth that has emerged over the last century, or they point to the increased militarization, or they point to the continued racism embedded within it. Those are all good things to consider, yet, as noted at the beginning of this book, scholars have often elided religion. At the turn of the century, London and Amsterdam would have been happier to continue selling opium in China and Java. Drug dealing is profitable and the proposition that "good people don't sell narcotics" was at that time still relatively new. Missionaries forced their hand, though, working hard to level public opinion against such practices. Bishop Brent's colonial mission to the Philippines unexpectedly led to The Hague Treaty, the bedrock upon which modern drug laws were built. Many of the other early laws in this period (local drug laws, the Pure Food and Drug Act of 1906, the Marihuana Tax Act of 1937) have also been important, lasting into the contemporary era either intact or as the precursors to laws that have since replaced them.

The Drug War's militarization also warrants attention. The DEA is essentially a special police force for drug control with a current annual budget that surpasses $3 billion. It began as the Federal Bureau of Narcotics in 1930, an underfunded side project of Treasury's management of Prohibition. Today the DEA operates domestically but also has a foreign presence from Santiago to Kabul, and, in their own language, regularly "disrupts" and "dismantles" drug production sites overseas. (These are euphemisms for shadow wars.) Few areas of US foreign policy extend as far into other nations' sovereignty as that of the Drug War. Oftentimes these interventions come with financial support for nations ready to cooperate with US drug policy. Disobedience can also produce economic sanctions that affect a nation's citizens; sociologist Daniel Patten has gone so far as to compare this approach to nations metaphorically being "incarcerated" for failure to cooperate with American drug policy.[9] In recent decades, the global War on Drugs has also at times blended into the War on Terror, with the "narcoterrorist" emerging as a new enemy. We also ought not consign the military side of the War on Drugs solely to foreign operations. When armed DEA agents storm household cannabis "farms" in San Bernardino or destroy cannabis crops on Wisconsin Indian reservations, this is a military action. It may not be classic, Battle-of-the-Somme-style war, but it relies on weaponized force in service to sovereign drug policy.

Race continues to be a central feature of the Drug War as well. The very first drug laws in the United States were specifically racial in nature, targeting alcohol consumption for American Indians and then opium smoking for Chinese immigrants in the West. Since then the racial interpretation of drug use has shifted, with African Americans and Latinx communities today receiving more drug policing, surveillance, and penalties than others.[10] Racial interpretations of substance use in the late nineteenth and early twentieth centuries led to the idea that some races were more prone to substance use and addiction, which led to police cultures that treated substance use differently for certain demographics. Early Drug War discourse made this explicit. Today this is still sometimes explicit, but it is more common to confessionally reject racialized drug expectations even as American legal systems continue to punish drug use differently along racial lines.

Systemic racism doesn't require confessional racism in order to exist. In other words, it's possible for institutional structures or social norms relating to race to discriminate against particular groups without any participant ever consciously agreeing that "some races are just better than others" as was common a century ago. The conflation of confessional racism and systemic racism is one reason so many white Americans today find the concept of systemic racism challenging to grasp; sometimes the expectation is that if all parties denounce racism doctrinally and if the law no longer explicitly enshrines racism, then racism shouldn't exist.[11] There's good evidence for systemic racism, though, and the Drug War is a greenhouse for it.

Black and Latinx folks are more likely to be arrested and sentenced for drug offenses today than members of other racial categories (six times more likely in the case of African Americans compared to white folks).[12] There are complex reasons for this, but much of it comes down to the invisible and often subconscious racism that's infused into surveillance, policing, and sentencing. Even when states make intentional efforts to reduce racial sentencing disparities (as Virginia did), aggregated data still show that African Americans—and Black men especially—receive stricter penalties.[13] There's also still explicit racism to be grappled with, such as emphases on Latin Americans as potential drug dealers or members of the "MS-13" gang. Although there is "no empirical support for the criminal immigrant narrative," as one study put it, this discourse has translated into new regulatory laws and sharper policing of Latinx communities.[14]

Drug offenses are financially costly for those caught in them. Some of this cost is direct, such as court costs, fines, prison deposit accounts (used for purchasing "extras" like the sneakers required to use a prison gym), or even the costs of phone calls, which can be predatorily priced. There are also indirect costs. Colin Dayan notes that "legal culture has carved up human differences into hierarchies capacious enough to accommodate subordination," suggesting that felons endure a kind of civil death.[15] I take her to mean that legally speaking, felons are permanently designated as lesser beings under the law. "Felon" is also a moral category, a scarlet letter to be forever worn to job interviews and on housing applications. Felonies do not necessarily bar someone from employment, but job applications demand that applicants explain themselves. In other words, felons (as well as lesser criminals) must account to others for what they have done, often futilely. Post-prison employment proves to be among the hardest challenges for those with criminal records; employers neither trust nor want them, often refusing to even consider applicants with convictions.[16] Over the last 20 years some states have also begun experimenting with "drug offender registries," public lists of drug offenders modeled after sex offender registries. The systemic racism embedded in the Drug War augments this approach, too—people of color are the ones most affected by such civil death and social blacklisting. These social consequences for substance use add up when compiled together. Those convicted of drug crimes are marked by it, forever relegated to a sociolegal taxon that often consigns them to fast food jobs and housing insecurity.

In today's culture addicts are still considered unfit, immoral, and a threat to whiteness. Understanding the earliest years of the Drug War can help us make sense of this phenomenon. Laws matter, international treaties matter, DEA militarization matters, and so on, but the only reason any of those have survived is that hegemonic moral expectations have supported their raisons d'être. Contemporary moral norms about substance use evolved over time from the earlier ones, which developed out of Protestant ideas about eschatology, subjectivity, race, and responsibility. While laws and regulatory institutions are objectively important, they're sustained by moral outcry. Those same moralities also shape individuals' experience of addiction. Morality is not just an abstract set of values or an assent to some idealized "good," it is a lived experience of the self.

Shame and Silence

Postcolonial theorist Gayatri Chakravorty Spivak noted the absence of subaltern voices in historiography, arguing that subalterns had been replaced by people speaking *about* them as a kind of academic ventriloquism. In addressing this problem Spivak conceded that sometimes voices may be irrecoverable and asked that in such cases scholars "measure silences."[17] There is a silence in this book. De Quincey may have been able to confess his opium addiction in 1821, but this was unusual even then. There are very, very few addicts who left firsthand accounts for us to read. Those who did usually considered themselves recovered and had specific ideological goals for sharing their story. Even most nineteenth-century addicts hid themselves.[18] Addicts are "known" in this book almost exclusively through the mediation of doctors, ideologues, clergy, and jurists, and that mediated knowledge was often coerced from addicts. According to the police and doctors monitoring substance use a century ago, "secrecy" represented an important symptom in addiction's etiology. They were probably right about this. Addicts understood their cultures, they recognized the moral landscape of substance use. Like all societies, America wasn't monolithic: Some people smoked cannabis in jazz clubs and some novelists romanticized cocaine. F. Scott Fitzgerald and Louis Armstrong were a little subversive. Many addicts were not interested in challenging normative morality, though, and indeed, many were themselves products of it. To confess and be known as an addict was not liberation, it was exposure.

Addicts' fears were justified and religion had a lot to do with how this circumstance developed. The demarcation between immorality and insanity was vague at best. Biomoralists' mapping of morality onto neurobiology contributed to this development, offering models wherein brain damage wrecked one's moral capacity. The notion that normal people usually try to (and indeed should *want* to) fit assimilationist norms also contributed. Medical experts were correct to think that substance use has cognitive effects, but it is the Protestant moral model of sober-rationality-as-virtue that truly marked non-normative cognition as bad. The discourses of the civilizing mission, of postmillennial progress, and of Protestantism more generally emphasized a particular style of cognition that privileged rationality and reason as ethical norms. (Religious approaches like Roman Catholicism don't disparage rationality, they just don't usually identify private human knowledge as the exclusive site for salvation.) Such schema rendered substance use an immoral and antisocial act.

Nobody can credibly challenge that alcohol or opium alters cognitive performance. What is less clear is that cognitive alterity is automatically bad. Christian Temperance activists observed that some alcoholics find themselves in destructive behavior patterns: addiction eats their money, harms their families, and can, in some cases, lead to serious psychological disturbance. That pattern certainly unfolded for some alcoholics, both historically and today. The jump happens when one asserts that because these destructive patterns happened for *some* people, alcohol is intrinsically bad for everyone. One might point to alcohol's positive role in joyful socializations, celebrations, or release from work stress as a counterexample. It can make first dates easier. Alcohol can indeed be destructive, but it can be constructive as well. The notion that substance use is an exclusively immoral act emerged from Christian Temperance efforts to normalize prohibitionist approaches as part of a wide-reaching, postmillennialist reform movement. While alcohol has since lost some of that totalizing approbation, the early Drug War's delegitimizing of anything found in the flexible category of "drugs" has survived quite intact.

Medical discourse alone cannot explain the moral reaction against substance use. There is no doubt that medicine identified certain kinds of substance use as deleterious. That's significant, but it doesn't explain how addicts came to be seen as bad people.[19] There's some evidence today that carbon monoxide emissions lead to dementia, and loads of evidence that it damages lungs and health more generally. Anyone who lives in a major city gets exposed to higher concentrations of carbon monoxide because of vehicular exhaust. Los Angelinos don't face special moral approbation for their exhaust exposure, though, and we don't generally treat those who make, repair, or sell cars as uniquely broken. The fact that medical discourse identifies some pollutants as harmful isn't enough to explain a moral backlash.

Medical discourse has a different value in a social world where one is responsible to the nation for their health, wealth, and productivity, and indeed, where a shared mission of "progress" relies on improvements to collective well-being. "Civilization" and "progress" were moral frameworks for American Protestants. They had their own attendant duties for which people were accountable to one another. Whether they were Protestant or not, everyone had a responsibility to their neighbors to contribute to that shared social well-being. Addicts were understood to refuse that duty—or perhaps to even be wholly incapable of it. The moral panic around drugs also meant that many people imagined addicts were working to deliberately undermine civilization. It's only vis-à-vis that Christian/secular postmillennialism that the addict emerged as an antisocial demonic figure, hell-bent on undermining America and its colonial wards.

It is also in this earlier era that the category of "drugs" coalesced. Cocaine, caffeine, cannabis, kava, and Coors don't do the same things physiologically. Cocaine and morphine addicts arguably have different problems. Turn-of-the-century discourse approached many of these substances as interchangeable though. Some of this approbation didn't stick, which is why today anyone can buy a scalding cup of coffee at any airport Starbucks. But the category of "drugs" began to emerge in this early era as a dumping ground for any "bad" substance whose consumption places the user into a deviant category. As time passed, that category expanded; one now finds methamphetamines, steroids, MDMA, and *salvia divinorum* as heroin's bedfellows—physiologically alien to opiates yet categorically allied. "Drugs" isn't defined by the consistent physiological effects of its substances, nor even really addiction, but rather by who uses those substances and why.

Religious interpretations of race, nation, medicine, morality, and progress are what made American Protestants really care about drugs. The threats of race suicide or degeneracy, of the Kingdom deferred, of moral rupture in the national covenant—these are what led to drug use being understood the way that it was. It is this confluence that turned addicts into monsters. If Americans were concerned about drug addiction in 1850, they were repulsed by it in 1930.

Early twentieth-century addicts had the weight of eugenics ideals against them, the disapproval of the church, the threat of incarceration, the gaze of an increasingly surveillance-oriented state, and the urgency of progress as their national moral imperative. Is it any wonder they were secretive? The religious framings that naturalized reactions of disgust to addicts have since largely muted or transmuted into other things. Postmillennialism is no longer the dominant eschatology for American Christians, confessional racism as authoritative science is a dead letter, and eugenics is largely in hibernation. Most American Protestants today expect that Jesus will return to build the Kingdom himself and do not see themselves as morally obligated to institute it through endless progress and social programs. Yet the moral repulsion to drug users persists independent of the structures that birthed it.

Final Thoughts

It is this banal, quotidian moral disgust that has been the Drug War's most enduring feature. From D.A.R.E. to *Star Trek: Voyager*, the depiction of substance users as immoral and antisocial continues to dominate public narratives about them. The list of which substances count as "drugs" changes. Attitudes toward cannabis use have shifted over the last 50 years to the point that today someone can openly smoke a joint in an Oregon park with little concern of public backlash. Other substances still engender shock or revulsion when used. The ways that disgust, shame, or reprobation manifest may look culturally different than they did a century ago, and addicts may interpret or internalize them differently, but they are assuredly still there. Despite its self-evident relevance to treatment, four-fifths of addicts in recovery programs are unwilling to divulge their addiction status to their primary care physicians.[20]

It is only through unpacking the origins and conceptual evolution of this moral landscape that we gain the option to decide for ourselves how we want to engage it. Some today may reckon with this moralization and still decide that cannabis use is a sin deserving reprimand. Certainly most of us (including myself) will continue to think that some substance use is physiologically harmful. Medically speaking quite a lot can go awry during cocaine consumption. I also do not mean to dismiss the experiences of those who have been hurt by others' substance use—that happens, too. Yet do we wish to remain shackled to the uninterrogated religious moralities of our forebears? Is it necessary to revile all substance users as antisocial, barely human people? Ethicist Jarrett Zigon has eloquently reframed the War on Drugs as "A War on People."[21] Matthew Pembleton similarly notes that "drugs don't make very good enemies by themselves."[22] They're right. Drugs are abstractions. There is no genuine possibility of war with them. The casualties of the Drug War are always and only ever human.

I did not initially set out to write a book about hegemonic morality. In trying to answer the "so what?" question about religion and the War on Drugs, though, I have kept coming back to this as the most significant answer. The moralities we have inherited are such that some addicts feel they are forever undeserving of children. Drug War practices have contributed to the over-policing and institutionalized wealth extraction of Black and Latinx communities. I do not agree with the late philosopher Dallas Willard about very much, and in fact I find most of his claims to be extraordinarily problematic. However, he noted in *The Disappearance of Moral Knowledge* that people practice and teach morality all the time without self-awareness of it. Morality is communicated through body language and tones of voice, the way we react when someone mentions a certain topic, what norms we automatically assume that other people accept when we discuss this or that particular matter.[23] On this one specific point Willard is right. There's good reason why we should discourage the use of some substances as medically risky, but our moral communications about who uses drugs and what kinds of people they are is one of the most important factors—perhaps even *the* most important factor—for how the Drug War will continue to unfold.

If there is one thing that I would encourage readers to take away from this book, it is this: The moral norms about substance use came from explicitly white supremacist forms of Protestantism, which have evolved and been rebranded at various points in the last century with new language and institutional structures. We ourselves didn't create those, we only inherited them. Today, the explanatory frameworks of the civilizing mission and postmillennialism aren't usually part of the picture, but the gestures, the emotional withdrawals, the body language, the tones of voice, and the other learned cultural expressions of moral signaling remain with us, and on the whole they remain condemnatory. Collectively we are still teaching addicts they should despise themselves. What we choose to communicate about people who use substances in our moral significations, or perhaps through our indifference, could permit the Drug War's casualties to continue piling up, or it could help shift the collective attitudes we hold. Addiction is hard and it can be a miserable problem for those caught in it. Maybe revulsion doesn't help.

ACKNOWLEDGMENTS

No one achieves anything alone.
—Leslie Knope, multiple occasions

This is my first book and at the end of this project I find myself deeply indebted to the work and support that others have offered me—this book could not have happened without them. Obviously my parents, Gene and Sherri Monteith, make the top of the list. Thank you mom and dad for your continued support after I tossed the dice on religious studies graduate programs, possibly one of the riskiest financial decisions anyone can make.

There were also folks who offered me spare rooms to crash in when I visited archives in DC and Seattle, for whom I remain grateful to this day. Thank you Sean Maloney, Jeff Morrison, Matt Swartzwelder and Matt Reitz, Joe Marino and Noelle Zalac, and Alexis Stern and Nathan Martina. (Alexis and Nathan, I apologize again for screaming at your cat after it hid in my room and jumped on me when I was sleeping.)

The very earliest parts of this research were funded while I was still a graduate student, meaning that I paid for part of it from a GoFundMe page. Special thanks go to friends and family who donated money so I could poke through dead people's mail: Adrienne Lee, Sean Forsythe, Rachel Getzinger, Barbara and Mike Moon, Mark and Dawn Burrell, Anna Collet, Cheryl Thomas, Michael Collins, Francois Goudrault, and Lindsay Moore. Additional thanks go to Elon University, who offered generous funding that supported the Geneva and Denver parts of this research, along with one final sweep through the federal records in DC.

Even more thanks go to those who either read parts of this book, discussed its content with me, or helped me think more clearly about these subjects. Thank you Candy Gunther Brown, Stephen Selka, M. Cooper Harriss, Patrick Michelson, Michael Grossberg, Amy Allocco, Brian Pennington, Geoffrey Claussen, Lauren Guilmette, Winnifred Sullivan, and Sarah Imhoff. Kerry Frey was also a supportive friend through this project, start to finish. Thank you to Jennifer Hammer at New York University Press for seeing potential in this book and offering helpful feedback on how to make it better.

Finally, librarians make a lot more happen than many people realize. Thank you to Elon University Libraries, but especially Patrick Rudd and Lynn Melchor. (I am pretty sure Lynn put 50,000 books in the interoffice mail for me.) There was also an archivist in Geneva whose name I didn't catch, but who helped me enormously when navigating an unfamiliar filing system, and who also permitted me to open up a 100-year-old tin of cocaine-based herpes cream that some long-dead bureaucrat left in the records. Thank you, librarians and archivists!

ARCHIVAL ABBREVIATIONS

Georgetown University Library Booth Family Center for Special Collections, Washington, DC
GU: Martin J. Griffin Papers

Library of Congress, Manuscript Division, Washington, DC
LOC-BRE: Papers of Charles H. Brent
LOC-BRI: Mark L. Bristol Papers
LOC-BRY: William Jennings Bryan Papers
LOC-HOB: Richmond P. Hobson Papers
LOC-PER: John J. Pershing Papers
LOC-WIL: Papers of Harvey W. Wiley

National Archives and Records Administration, College Park, Maryland
NARACP-DEA: Records of the Drug Enforcement Agency (RG170)
NARACP-DOS-1910: General Records of the Department of State (RG59), 1910–1929 Central Decimal File
NARACP-DOS-1930: General Records of the Department of State (RG59), 1930–39 Central Decimal File
NARACP-ICR: Records of International Conferences, Commissions, and Expositions (RG43): International Conference Records US Delegations to the International Opium Commission and Conferences NARACP-INS: Bureau of Insular Affairs (RG350): General Classified Files, 1898–1945
NARACP-OTCF: Office of Territories (RG126): Classified Files, 1907–1951

National Archives and Records Administration, Denver, Colorado
NARAD-BIA-LIQ: Records of the Bureau of Indian Affairs (RG75), Numerical Correspondence File, 1907–1939: Liquor Traffic
NARAD-BIA-CRO: Records of the Bureau of Indian Affairs (RG75), Numerical Correspondence File, 1914–1927: Crow Indian Agency

NARAD-BIA-PUE: Records of the Bureau of Indian Affairs (RG 5), Numerical Correspondence File, 1914–1927: Northern Pueblos Agency

National Archives and Records Administration, Washington, DC
NARAW-BIA-LIQ: Records of the Bureau of Indian Affairs (RG 75), Numerical Correspondence File, 1907–1939: Liquor Traffic
NARAW-BIA-CRO: Records of the Bureau of Indian Affairs (RG 75), Numerical Correspondence File, 1914–1927: Crow Indian Agency
NARAW-BIA-ROS: Records of the Bureau of Indian Affairs (RG 75), Numerical Correspondence File, 1914–1927: Rosebud
NARAW-BIA-YUM: Records of the Bureau of Indian Affairs (RG 75), Numerical Correspondence File, 1914–1927: Fort Yuma

Ohio History Center, Columbus, Ohio
OHC: Ohio History Connection Archives

Pennsylvania State University Special Collections Library, College Park, Pennsylvania
PSU: H. J. Anslinger Papers

Stanford University Archives, Palo Alto, California
SU: Jordan (David Starr) Papers (SC 058)

United Nations Archives, Geneva, Switzerland
LON: League of Nations—Archives 1919–1927

University of Washington Libraries' Special Collections, Seattle, Washington
UW-JON: Wesley L. Jones papers
UW-MIL: John F. Miller Papers

NOTES

INTRODUCTION

1 "Narcotic War Is Organized," *Los Angeles Times*, July 22, 1923: 1.

2 "Crusaders in Anti-Narcotic Parade," *The Bridal Call*, Vol. 7 (Aug. 1923): 16.

3 Linda M. Ambrose, "Aimee Semple McPherson," 143.

4 Ambrose, "Aimee Semple McPherson," 143; "Downtown Parade for Drug Drive: Thousands Join Line of March as Campaign on Narcotics Opens," *The Los Angeles Times*, July 22, 1923: I2; "To Celebrate Drug Drive: Parade and Program Planned for 21st Inst., with Great Public Meeting at Coliseum," *The Los Angeles Times*, July 12, 1923: 1.

5 "To Celebrate Drug Drive".

6 K. Healan Gaston, *Imagining Judeo-Christian America*, 46.

7 Anslinger is often quoted as using incredibly racist phrases, such as "reefer makes darkies think they are as good as white men." Although Anslinger was unquestionably racist, original sources for some of these quotes seem impossible to find. Citation trails eventually dead end in not fully credible secondary sources. As Peter Shrag observes in his endnotes, while Anslinger trafficked in racist explanations quite comfortably, some of the more damning statements attributed to him may be apocryphal. Peter Shrag, *Not Fit for our Society*, 135, 254n66.

8 See Laura Briggs, *Reproducing Empire*, 198; Sophia A. McClennen and Joseph R. Slaughter, "Introducing Human Rights and Literary Forms," 3–4; and Lila Abu-Lughod, *Do Muslim Women Need Saving?*

9 Margaret Urban Walker, *Moral Understandings*, 10.

10 Walker, *Moral Understandings*, 71–72, 79–81.

11 Judith Butler, *Giving an Account of Oneself*, 7, 19.

12 Butler, *Giving an Account of Oneself*, 22.

13 Joseph F. Spillane, *Cocaine*, 4.

14 Elisha Bartlett, *The "Laws of Sobriety,"* 3, 7.

15 Bartlett, *The "Laws of Sobriety,"* 5.

16 Jarrett Zigon, *A War on People*, 6.

17 Michel Foucault, *The History of Sexuality, Volume 1*, 89–97; Michel Foucault, *Discipline and Punish*, 26.

18 Spillane, *Cocaine*, 2.

19 Tracy Fessenden, *Culture and Redemption*; Sarah Barringer Gordon, *The Mormon Question*, 21, 85, 202–203; Tisa Wenger, *Religious Freedom*, 11–12.

20 Anthony M. Petro, *After The Wrath of God*, 5.

21 Fessenden, *Culture and Redemption*, 7, 92.

22 Jennifer Graber, *The Gods of Indian Country*, xxi, 9; Webb Keane, *Christian Moderns*, 6–7; Tomoko Masuzawa, *The Invention of World Religions*, 47, 57–58.

23 William James, *The Varieties of Religious Experience*, 31.

24 Sarah Imhoff, *The Lives of Jessie Sampter*, 33–35, 63.

25 For "fullness," see Charles Taylor, *A Secular Age*, 5.

26 Catharine L. Albanese, *America: Religions & Religion*, 279.

27 Wenger, *Religious Freedom*, 20.

28 George M. Marsden, *Fundamentalism and American Culture*, 49.

29 Albanese, *America*, 284; James H. Moorhead, *World Without End*, 6.

30 "Missionary Possibilities," *The Spirit of Missions*, Vol. 44, no. 12 (Dec. 1899): 650–651.

31 Christopher H. Evans, *The Social Gospel in American Religion*, 2–8.

32 David Morgan, *Protestants & Pictures*, 14; Jon Butler, *Awash in a Sea of Faith*, 217.

33 Blum notes that providentialism and trust in the millennium also shifted as time passed. Postmillennialism didn't disappear though, it only lost a bit of its near monopoly. It continued to be central to American culture and to shape American optimism in the state's power to advance moral reform. Edward J. Blum, "'To Doubt This Would Be to Doubt God,'" 217, 220–222; Mark A. Noll, *The Civil War as Theological Crisis*, 75–77.

34 Gaines M. Foster, *Moral Reconstruction*, 42, 57, 153–159, 176.

35 Sylvester A. Johnson, *African American Religions, 1500–2000*, 255–256, 270–273.

36 Kathleen Flake, "An Enduring Contest," 501; Gaston, *Imagining Judeo-Christian America*, 21–22, 41, 46–49, 52–56.

37 Graber, *The Gods of Indian Country*, xxi, 9; Keane, *Christian Moderns*, 6–7; Masuzawa, *The Invention of World Religions*, 47, 57–58; John Lardas Modern, *Secularism in Antebellum America*, 19–21; Winnifred Fallers Sullivan, *The Impossibility of Religious Freedom*, 7–8; Wenger, *Religious Freedom*, 26.

38 Wenger, *Religious Freedom*, 18–25.

39 Gale Kenny and Tisa Wenger, "Church, State, and 'Native Liberty' in the Belgian Congo," 161; Emily Conroy-Krutz, *Christian Imperialism*, 7.

40 Damien Tricoire, "The Enlightenment and the Politics of Civilization," 26–27, 33–35.

41 Julian Go, *American Empire and the Politics of Meaning*.

42 Sylvester Johnson, "Religion and American Empire in Mississippi, 1790–1833," 39–47; Conroy-Krutz, *Christian Imperialism*, 29.

43 Frances Power Cobbe, "The Evolution of Morals and Religion," 392–394.

44 Wenger, *Religious Freedom*, 3–5; Conroy-Krutz, *Christian Imperialism*, 14, 50.

45 Jonathan Z. Smith, "The Devil in Mr. Jones," 110.

46 Michel Foucault, *Power / Knowledge*, 131; Michel Foucault, *Psychiatric Power*, 362.

47 Terence Keel, *Divine Variations*.

48 Reginald Horsman, *Race and Manifest Destiny*; Matthew Frye Jacobson, *Whiteness of a Different Color*, 30–33; Tunde Adeleke, *UnAfrican Americans*, 80–82; Matthew McCullough, *The Cross of War*, 83–97.

49 Harriet Deacon, "Racial Categories and Psychiatry in Africa," 101–104.

50 Graham Richards, *Race, Racism, and Psychology*, 16; Collette Guillaumin, *Race, Sexism, Power, and Ideology*, 62–64; Jennifer Terry, *An American Obsession*, 31–34; Walter Demel, "How the 'Mongoloid Race' Came into Being," 84.

51 Go, *American Empire and the Politics of Meaning*, 28–32.

52 Arthur de Gobineau, *The Inequality of Human Races*, 3, 154–155.

53 Modern, *Secularism in Antebellum America*, 19–22.

54 Keane, *Christian Moderns*, 111.

55 Kathryn Gin Lum, *Damned Nation*, 117.

56 Kathleen L. Lodwick, *Crusaders Against Opium*, 181.

57 William Storrs Fry, *The Opium Trade with China*, 59.

58 Bertha K. Olgers, "What the Reformed Church Is Doing to Bring the Spirit of Christ in Race Relations," *The Presbyterian Survey: Official Magazine of the Presbyterian Church in the United States* (Nov. 1925), 668.

59 Stuart Hall et al., *Policing the Crisis*, 16.

CHAPTER 1. CHRISTIAN TEMPERANCE, MILLENNIAL PROGRESS, AND THE IMMORALITY OF ADDICTION

1 "Cincinnati Ladies Arrested," *Tiffin Tribune*, May 21, 1874, 2; Frances Elizabeth Willard, *Woman and Temperance*, 91–93.

2 Timothy A. Hickman, "Mania Americana," 1274.

3 Erika Rappaport, "Sacred and Useful Pleasures," 990–1016.

4 George M. Marsden, *Fundamentalism and American Culture*, 66–67.

5 For the sake of clear chronology, it is worth noting that although Prohibition did not become a serious contender on the national stage until the later parts of the nineteenth century, some states did experiment with prohibitory laws earlier than that. "The Maine Law" (as it was known) passed the Maine legislature in 1851, largely through the efforts of Neal Dow. Other states followed suit. However, these laws were all quickly repealed for various reasons, not the least of which was that they were hard to enforce. W. J. Rorabaugh, "Alcohol in America," 18; Sabine N. Meyer, *We Are What We Drink*, 21–23, 31–32.

6 E. Nelson, *The Use of Ardent Spirits in a Professing Christian A Great Sin*, 2–3.

7 Nelson, *The Use of Ardent Spirits*, 6, 7, 9.

8 Nelson, *The Use of Ardent Spirits*, 12.

9 Marsden, *Fundamentalism and American Culture*, 49.

10 Edward Hitchcock, *An Argument for Early Temperance*, 8.

11 Hitchcock, *An Argument for Early Temperance*, 59–62.

12 Hitchcock, *An Argument for Early Temperance*, 60, 63–65.

13 Hitchcock, *An Argument for Early Temperance*, 62, 65–66.

14 Hitchcock, *An Argument for Early Temperance*, 89.

15 Caroline Clark, "Contrasting Medical Models of Alcohol Problems in Victoria around 1900," 1756–1757.

16 Joe L. Coker, *Liquor in the Land of the Lost Cause*, 2, 26.

17 Elaine Frantz Parsons, *Manhood Lost*, 21.

18 Mark A. Noll, *The Civil War as a Theological Crisis*, 83–84.

19 Willard, *Woman and Temperance*, 95–98.

20 It is worth noting here that Tobey understood slavery to operate through two means: One is the process that we would today call addiction (this is what he means when he refers to indulging the appetite), and the second is drink slavery imposed by social power brokers—what we might today call "peer pressure." C. H. Taylor, *Proceedings of the Temperance Convention*, 12.

21 Bryan S. Katcher, "Public Health Then and Now," 275; Matthew Warner Osborn, *Rum Maniacs*, 28; William L. White, *Slaying the Dragon*, 3.

22 This is from Lyman Beecher's "The Signs of Intemperance," which was reprinted in a later anthology. William Haven Daniels, *The Temperance Reform and Its Great Reformers*, 74–75.

23 Eli F. Brown, *The House I Live In*, 79–82.

24 J. H. Kellogg, *Second Book in Physiology and Hygiene*, 235.

25 George Tugwell, *Temperance and Total Abstinence*, 4–5.

26 Charles L. Dana, "Alcoholism as a Cause of Insanity," 81.

27 R. J. Kinkead, "Alcoholic Insanity and Responsibility for Crime," *The British Medical Journal*, Vol. 1, no. 1464 (January 19, 1889): 197.

28 Michel Foucault, *Madness and Civilization*, 257.

29 Jonathan Zimmerman, "When the Doctors Disagree," 172.

30 Johan Edman, "Temperance and Modernity," 37–38.

31 Protestants frequently debated whether the wine at the Last Supper was actually alcoholic in any significant way, and if so, whether drinking was a historical reality of biblical times that no longer applied in the present day. Some argued that modern wine was far more alcoholic than biblical wine, and that the Last Supper had no leaven in the bread so perhaps there was also no leaven in the grapes. As for the latter argument, Temperance Christians pointed out that the Bible also depicted slavery, plural marriage, and divorce, but that did not mean God thought it was good and that it should continue for all time—alcohol was backwards, and progress demanded that it end. See John L. Merrill, "The Bible and the American Temperance Movement," 146, 149–150; Henry Colman, "Prohibition and Public Morals," *The North American Review*, Vol. 189, no. 640 (Mar. 1909): 410–411.

32 Woman's Christian Temperance Union, *The Pathfinder*, 3–7.

33 David Starr Jordan, "Scientific Temperance," in *Popular Science Monthly* (Jan. 1896): 344.

34 Jordan, "Scientific Temperance," 345.

35 Eugene S. Talbot, *Degeneracy*, 16, 57, 107–108, 318.

36 William Sadler, *Race Decadence*, 20.

37 Max Weber, *The Protestant Ethic and the Spirit of Capitalism*, 157–163.

38 Charles M. Shelton, "What Would Jesus Teach About Social Hygiene," *Liberty*, Vol. 14, no. 19 (May 8, 1937): 8.

39 For a good summary of Muscular Christian masculinity in relationship to labor and strength, see footnote 25 in Jonathan Ebel, "The Great War, Religious Authority, and the American Fighting Man," 110.

40 Lisa McGirr, *The War on Alcohol*, 20.

41 Douglas W. Carlson, "Drinks to His Own Undoing," 675.

42 Carlson, "Drinks to His Own Undoing," 675–676.

43 This book remained an important Protestant text for anti-alcohol sentiments for decades after its original publication. Arthur, *Ten Nights in a Bar-Room*, 11, 21, 28–29, 62, 86.

44 The *Advocate of Peace* was a transdenominational Protestant magazine dedicated to pacifism. "An Angel in a Saloon. A True Incident." *Advocate of Peace*, Vol. 5, no. 6 (June 1874): 3.

45 Neal Dow, "Results of Prohibitory Legislation," *North American Review*, Vol. 134, no. 304 (Mar. 1882): 316.

46 "Gain of Temperance Reform: Great Change Which Has Taken Place in Railroad and Newspaper Offices," *Chicago Daily Tribune* (Mar. 27, 1898): 31.

47 Christabel Osborn, "Economic Aspects of the Liquor Problem," 575.

48 George S. White, *Memoir of Samuel Slater*, 225.

49 Dow, "Results of Prohibitory Legislation," 315.

50 Richmond P. Hobson, untitled article for *The New York American*, March 2, 1915, Box 33, Folder 7, LOC-HOB.

51 Caroline Benedict Burrell and William Byron Forbush, *The Mother's Book*, 216.

52 For a good discussion of early American criticisms of alcohol-induced poverty, see Osborn, *Rum Maniacs*, 79–89.

53 Hitchcock, *An Argument for Early Temperance*, 58–61.

54 "Temperance. Forty-three Crusaders Arrested. Prayer Meeting in a Station House. A Copy of the State—the Mayor Interviewed—Another Proclamation—Immense Mass Meeting at St. Paul M.E. Church—Some Strong Talk," *Cincinnati Daily Gazette*, May 16, 1874.

55 "Temperance. Forty-three Crusaders Arrested."

56 "Temperance. Forty-three Crusaders Arrested."

57 McGirr, *The War on Alcohol*, 9; Norman H. Clark, *Deliver Us from Evil*, 94.

58 Quoted in Anna A. Gordon, *The Beautiful Life of Frances E. Willard*, 226.

59 Suzanne M. Marilley, "Frances Willard and the Feminism of Fear," 126, 132

60 "Morals and Politics," in *The American Issue*, Vol. 19, no. 1 (Jan. 1911): 1.

61 Barton E. Price, "Religion, Reform, and Patriotism in Southern Illinois," 172.

62 Charles Henry Brent, *European Nations and Christian Statesmanship*, undated manuscript, 5–6, Box 34, "European Nations and Christian Statesmanship" folder, LOC-BRE.

63 Charles Henry Brent, "Law and Order," manuscript [1921?], 4, Box 34, "articles" folder, LOC-BRE.

64 Crafts was referencing the 1887 *Mugler v. Kansas* case, which upheld state dry laws as constitutional. Wilbur F. Crafts, "What Business Has Church or State with Ethics?" in *The Union Signal*, Vol. 30, no. 22 (Sept 15, 1904): 3.

65 Richmond P. Hobson, *Personal and Confidential—Tentative Program—In the interest of National Prohibition Resolution in 63rd Cong.*, Box 33, Folder 8, LOC-HOB.

66 Zimmerman, "When the Doctors Disagree," 175–176.

67 Letter from United Brethren Church and Sunday School of Philomath, Oregon to Senator Wesley L. Jones, Feb. 24, 1918, Box 270, Folder 2, UW-JON.

68 Letter from First Baptist Church of Wentachee, Washington to Senator Wesley L. Jones, Apr. 11, 1918, Box 270, Folder 2, UW-JON.

69 Although the boundaries of "the great white race" and who counted as part of it were still unstable in 1911, it is clear that for Hobson whiteness was coterminous with American identity. *Congressional Record: Containing the Proceedings and Debates of the Sixty-First U.S. Congress, Third Session, Vol. XLVI* (Washington, DC: Government Printing Office, 1911), 1871; for the boundaries of whiteness and Irish/Italian/etc. as outsiders, see Matthew Frye Jacobson, *Whiteness of a Different Color*, 2–4, 31, 68, 241.

70 Elizabeth Tilton, "The Battle for Race-Survival": 16–17.

71 Marni Davis, "No Whisky Amazons in the Tents of Israel," 143–144.

72 Stephen S. Wise, "A Jewish View of Prohibition," *Scientific Temperance Journal*, Vol. 30, no. 3 (Aug. 1921): 148.

73 John F. Quinn, *Father Mathew's Crusade*, 2–3, 154–157.

74 Letter from Ferdinand Kittell to Martin Griffin, Nov. 6, 1897, Box 2, Folder 11, GU.

75 Judith Butler, "Is Judaism Zionism?," 71.

CHAPTER 2. SIN, ADDICTION, AND BIOMORALITY

1 *State v. Fong Loon*, 29 Idaho 248, 158 P. 258–259 (1916).

2 Howard Padwa, *Social Poison*, 34–35.

3 Thomas De Quincey, *Confessions of an English Opium-Eater*, 3, 41.

4 Padwa, *Social Poison*, 24–25.

5 Jacques-Joseph Moreau, *Hashish and Mental Illness*, 18.

6 Bicêtre names a Parisian asylum. Moreau, *Hashish and Mental Illness*, 7–9.

7 Moreau, *Hashish and Mental Illness*, 8.

8 Matthew Warner Osborn, *Rum Maniacs*, 192.

9 T. D. Crothers, *The Disease of Inebriety from Alcohol, Opium, and Other Narcotic Drugs*, 323–325.

10 Robert E. Corradini, *Narcotics and Youth Today*.

11 Berry et al., "Substances of Abuse and Their Clinical Implications," 112–116; Sharma et al., "Opium Withdrawal Delirium," 48–51.

12 Zhen-Yu Ren et al., "Abnormal Pain Response in Pain-Sensitive Opiate Addicts After Prolonged Abstinence Predicts Increased Drug Craving"; Sarah M. Sweitzer

et al., "Mechanical Allodynia and Thermal Hyperalgesia Upon Acute Opioid Withdrawal in the Neonatal Rat."

13 J. B. Mattison, *The Treatment of Opium Addiction*, 30–31; William Stewart, "A Remarkable Case of Morphine Addiction," *The British Medical Journal*, Vol. 1, no. 1084 (11 May 1889): 1051–1052; Alfred C. Prentice, "The Problem of the Narcotic Drug Addict," *Journal of the American Medical Association*, Vol. 76, no. 3 (4 June 1921): 1553; George Pettey, *The Narcotic Drug Diseases and Allied Ailments*, 13.

14 Nicole Rafter et al., *The Criminal Brain*, 46; Stephen Tomlinson, *Head Masters*, 68.

15 Tomlinson, *Head Masters*, 73.

16 Malcolm Macmillan, *An Odd Kind of Fame*, 23; Rafter et al., *The Criminal Brain*, 58.

17 Daniel Patrick Thurs, *Science Talk*, 23.

18 Tomlinson, *Head Masters*, 85, 89–90.

19 Heather H. Vacek, *Madness*, 41.

20 Vacek, *Madness*, 77.

21 John Gach, "Biological Psychiatry in the Nineteenth and Twentieth Centuries," 386.

22 David Stack, "William Lovett and the National Association for the Political and Social Improvement of the People," 1041.

23 Richmond P. Hobson, "War on the Liquor Traffic: Address by Captain Richmond Pearson Hobson, M.C., at a Reformer's Conclave of Thirty One National Organizations Devoted to Social and Moral Uplift. Washington D.C." (Washington, DC: International Reform Bureau, n.d.), 3. Box 37, Folder 1, LOC-HOB.

24 Richmond P. Hobson, mass-mailed circular letter, undated [1915?], Box 37, Folder 3, LOC-HOB.

25 International Narcotic Education Association, "Identical Plank Suggested for Consideration of Resolutions Committees of Both National Parties / Resume of Narcotic Facts," undated [1924], Box 56, Folder 4, LOC-HOB.

26 Richmond P. Hobson, "Extract from Address Delivered by Captain Richmond P. Hobson Before the Phi Delta Kappa of New York University, New York, April 9, 1932 on the Subject The History of Narcotic Drug Exploitation and the Philosophy of Narcotic Drug Control," p. 3, Box 69, Folder 14, LOC-HOB.

27 J. H. Kellogg, *Second Book in Physiology and Hygiene*, 239.

28 George E. Dawson, "Psychic Rudiments and Morality," 217.

29 Originally from 1899, *JAMA* reprinted the article in 1999. T. D. Crothers, "Criminal Morphomania," ed. Jennifer Relling, in *Journal of the American Medical Association*, Vol. 282, no. 6 (Aug. 11, 1999): 590.

30 The author proposed that some addicts became addicts through legitimate medical use, but that some addicts were immoral and became addicts by temptation and contact with those who were already habitués. George M. Kober, "The Progress and Achievements of Hygiene," in *Science*, Vol. 6, no. 152 (Nov. 26, 1897): 798.

31 It is noteworthy that Dr. Stein premised his larger argument upon Ecclesiastes and Proverbs, claiming that modern psychiatric therapies were really just "a repeti-

tion of ancient truths." Calvert Stein, "The Role of Mental Hygiene in General Practice," *The New England Journal of Medicine*, Vol. 214, no. 14 (Apr. 2, 1936): 671.

32 Anthony M. Petro, *After The Wrath of God*, 5.

33 H. Wayne Morgan, *Drugs in America*, 6.

34 The humoral approach appears not to have maintained a prominent place in the later addiction theories of my sources, but according to Salem it was important for the development of alcoholism theories in the earlier era. Elizabeth Ann Salem, "Gendered Bodies, Nervous Minds," 31–32, 39.

35 Salem, "Gendered Bodies, Nervous Minds," 140–142.

36 Morgan, *Drugs in America*, 27.

37 See for instance *JAMA*'s criticism of the British Opium Commission, in which they denounce the Commission's claims that opium addiction in Indian children is a harmless phenomenon; *JAMA* suggests they have only reached such an absurd conclusion because the commissioners are unscientific. "Opium Habit in Children," *Journal of the American Medical Association*, Vol. 29, no. 11 (Sept. 11, 1897): 544–545. The dating of anti-quackery comes from the AMA's website. Although we should not ignore the fact that medicine is its own regime of truth and that some authorities may wish to guard their influence (including the AMA), it is also true that unregulated medical practice permitted a wide assortment of absurd and/or dangerous remedies and treatments. American Medical Association, https://www.ama-assn.org/ (accessed May 12, 2021).

38 "Drug Habits," *Journal of the American Medical Association*, Vol. 41, no. 16 (Oct. 17, 1903): 969.

39 The language at times comes quite close to Hobson's word choices, suggesting that he may have been familiar with the contents. Albrecht Erlenmeyer, *On the Treatment of the Morphine Habit*, ix–xi.

40 Frederick Heman Hubbard, *The Opium Habit and Alcoholism*, 1–2.

41 "Drug Habits," in *Maryland Medical Journal*, Vol. 32 (Jan. 26, 1895): 273.

42 William L. White, *Slaying the Dragon*, 120–121.

43 Charles K. Mills, *First Lessons in Physiology and Hygiene*, 231.

44 Pettey, *The Narcotic Drug Diseases and Allied Ailments*, 303.

45 Pettey, *The Narcotic Drug Diseases and Allied Ailments*, 305.

46 Ernest S. Bishop, *The Narcotic Drug Problem*, 36.

47 Arthur W. Booth et al., "The Narcotic Drug Problem," *New York State Journal of Medicine*, Vol. 23, no. 5 (May 1923): 222.

48 Rafter et al., *The Criminal Brain*.

49 Thomas Sweeting to Dr. Joseph L. Stephenson, letter, Mar. 21, 1887, Collection Catalog Number: VFM 1355, OHC.

50 Robert A. Buerki, "Medical Views on Narcotics and Their Effects in the Mid-1890s," 6.

51 William S. Birch, "A New Treatment for Morphine Addiction," in *Boston Medical and Surgical Journal*, Vol. 150, no. 15 (Apr. 14, 1904): 401–403.

52 Louis Casamajor, "The Treatment of the Toxemias of Dangerous Trades and of Drugs," 691.

53 White, *Slaying the Dragon*, 136–138.

54 White, *Slaying the Dragon*, 37–40, 87.

55 White, *Slaying the Dragon*, 67–75.

56 Carl Scheffel, "Nursing Care of Alcoholic and Drug Addictions," *The American Journal of Nursing*, Vol. 19, no. 2 (Nov. 1918): 106.

57 John M. O'Connor, "The 'Cure' for Drug Addiction," *Narcotic Education*, Vol. 1, no. 1 (July 1927): 10.

58 "Liquor and Drug Advertisements," *The New England Journal of Medicine*, Vol. 201, no. 7 (Aug. 15, 1929): 338.

59 White, *Slaying the Dragon*, 152–153.

60 The list of symptoms is much longer in the original article. "Departments: Medicine: Analysis of Narcotic Drug Addiction," in *The Lancet*, Vol. 113, no. 10 (Mar. 6, 1915): 274.

61 "Talmadge and Tobacco: The First of Ten Sermons on the Ten Modern Plagues: A Sweeping Condemnation of All Narcotics, and Especially of Nicotine—The Reverend Pastor Speaks from His Own Experience," in *The Washington Post* (Nov. 14, 1881): 2.

62 Bunting traced his spiritual awakening to Dwight Moody, a popular premillennialist evangelist at the turn of the century, and his Christian maturation to Rev. Stephen H. Tyng and the Church of the Holy Trinity (Episcopalian). Charles A. Bunting, *Hope for the Victims*, 5, 7, 14.

63 Bunting, *Hope for the Victims*, 17.

64 Bunting, *Hope for the Victims*, 18–19.

65 Bunting, *Hope for the Victims*, 17.

66 J. G. Kerr, "Opium in China," 71.

67 Kerr, "Opium in China,"

68 This was a British periodical, but the principle outlined above was a transatlantic one. "Repentance and Faith: Their Order and Connection," *The Christian* (Aug. 17, 1871): 3.

69 A. M. Watt, "Delivered from the Morphine-Habit," *The Gospel Trumpet*, Vol. 34, no. 30 (July 30, 1914): 473.

70 John L. Nevius, *Demon Possession and Allied Themes*, 423–426.

71 Leslie E. Keeley, *The Morphine Eater*, 20.

72 Keeley, *The Morphine Eater*, 22.

73 Bartlett B. James, "Prevention of Addiction," *Narcotic Education*, Vol. 1, no. 2 (Oct. 1927): 25.

74 Charles F. Stokes, "The Military, Industrial and Public Health Features of Narcotic Addiction," *Journal of the American Medical Association*, Vol. 70, no. 11 (Mar. 16, 1918): 766–768.

75 Charles Reasons, "The Politics of Drugs," 389.

CHAPTER 3. DEGENERACY, EUGENICS, AND THE GREAT
AMERICAN RACE

1   Kathleen W. Jones, *Taming the Troublesome Child*, 38. 172

2   William Healy, *The Individual Delinquent*, 34–35; William Healy, "Present Day
    Aims and Methods in Studying the Offender."

3   Barry C. Feld, "Criminalizing the Juvenile Court," 203.

4   Mabel Carter Rhoades, "A Case Study of Delinquent Boys in the Juvenile Court of
    Chicago," 58–59; "Ruin of Eleven Girls Caused by Low Wages and Love of Finery,"
    The Day Book, Vol. 5, no. 290 (Sept. 6, 1916): 1–2; "White Slavers Lure Girl in Loop
    Store," *The Day Book*, Vol. 5, no. 118 (Feb. 15, 1916): 1–2.

5   Rhoades, "A Case Study of Delinquent Boys in the Juvenile Court of Chicago," 61.

6   This comes from a private letter to his patron, quoted in Graham Parker, "The
    Juvenile Court Movement," 285.

7   See footnote 18 in John Chynoweth Burnham, "Psychology, Psychiatry, and the
    Progressive Movement," 462; Albert R. Roberts and Patricia Brownell, "A Century
    of Forensic Social Work," 363.

8   Hull House's leadership came largely from Protestant backgrounds but did not
    consider the institution to be explicitly linked to any particular style. Addams
    herself deviated in significant ways from what was Progressive Era normative
    Christianity, such as foregoing Christ as a mediator and relating to God as a
    Goddess. James B. Hunt, "Jane Addams: The Presbyterian Connection," 232–235;
    Camilla Stivers, "Unfreezing the Progressive Era," 540–541.

9   Joseph F. Spillane, *Cocaine*, 96, 110.

10 Sarah Imhoff, *The Lives of Jessie Sampter*, 41.

11 Jane Addams, *A New Conscience and an Ancient Evil*, 120, 125.

12 Victoria Gettis is accurate in her quotes, but I find Healy more ambivalent in
    his approach than she presents him. Gettis is right that Healy argues biologi-
    cal determinists such as Lombroso and Talbot go too far and that degenerate
    stigmata aren't enough to predict criminality. At the same time, Healy explicitly
    identifies degenerative stigmata as morally significant in his case studies—he
    wants it both ways. See also Nackenoff and Sullivan for Lathrop/Hull House
    connection. Victoria Gettis, *The Juvenile Court and the Progressives*, 70; Carol
    Nackenoff and Kathleen S. Sullivan, "The House that Julia (and Friends) Built,"
    172, 175, 189.

13 Healy, *The Individual Delinquent*, 29–30, 57–58, 64, 305, 786.

14 Healy, *The Individual Delinquent*, 259–260, 276–277.

15 W. Grant Hague, *The Eugenic Mother and Baby*, 3.

16 Francis Galton, *Inquiries into Human Faculty and Its Development*, 24–25.

17 B. A. Morel, *Traité des Dégénérescences Physiques*, viii–ix, 407.

18 Howard Padwa, *Social Poison*, 46–47; Nicole Rafter et al., *The Criminal Brain*,
    106–110; William L. White, *Slaying the Dragon*, 120.

19 Eugene S. Talbot, *Degeneracy*, 104.

20 This conflicts with some other theorists, who thought opium use led to sterility. Talbot, *Degeneracy*, 110–111.

21 For another example, see St. Louis doctor Charles Hughes's article from the same year, which closes with a list of more than 200 people—mostly disabled children—who he thought the world would be better off were they dead. C. H. Hughes, "The Neurotic Salvage of Suicide," *Alienist and Neurologist*, Vol. 19, no. 1 (1898): 104–115.

22 This notion was related to Lamarckian approaches to heredity; those traits that parents acquired would be passed down to children. Elof Axel Carlson, "The Hoosier Connection," 12.

23 Spillane, *Cocaine*, 96, 110–113, 143–144.

24 Harry Bruinuis, *Better for All the World*, 56; J. Duncan MacNair, "Colony Life of an Epileptic, Social and Religious," 67–72; William Pryor Letchworth, *Care and Treatment of Epileptics*, 87; Michigan, *Twenty-Third Biennial Report of the Michigan State Board of Corrections and Charities, 1915–1916*, 115–116.

25 White, *Slaying the Dragon*, 31–33, 108–109, 120–121.

26 White, *Slaying the Dragon*, 220–222.

27 He specifies alcohol here, but it is clear from his book as a whole that he considers other substance use a cognate problem. White, *Slaying the Dragon*, 272–273.

28 William Healy, *Personality in Formation and Action*, 26.

29 Matthew Frye Jacobson, *Whiteness of a Different Color*, 2–4, 40, 207.

30 Theodore Roosevelt, *A Compilation of the Messages and Speeches of Theodore Roosevelt, 1901–1905*, 576–577, 579.

31 Matthew Frye Jacobson, *Whiteness of a Different Color*, 80–81.

32 Josiah Strong, *Our Country*, 160.

33 Strong, *Our Country*, 40, 59, 69, 73, 160, 217–222.

34 Strong, *Our Country*, 175.

35 This book is not eugenicist per se, but it did make eugenic assumptions such as the one quoted. *The Standard History of the World by Great Historians*, 1989.

36 Harvey Washington Wiley, "The Rights of the Unborn," 136–142.

37 Ellsworth Huntington, *Tomorrow's Children*, vii, 23, 31–32.

38 W. D. Weatherford, *Present Forces in Negro Progress*, 21.

39 "The Chinese and America," *The Chautauquan*, Vol. 1, no. 8 (May 1881): 366–367.

40 Joshua Paddison, *American Heathens*, 19, 106, 120–121.

41 B. A. Owens-Adair, *Human Sterilization*, 10, 136, 139–140; William S. Sadler, *Race Decadence*, 5–6, 156, 249, 306, 351–352, 354.

42 William J. Robinson, *Eugenics, Marriage and Birth Control*, 191–192.

43 The language of degeneracy was beginning to enter textbooks by at least the 1880s if not earlier. (The historical record has not been kind to textbook preservation; surveying the entire textbook landscape is impossible.) It is unclear to what extent 1880s textbooks intended to link degeneracy with substance use.

44 Sarah F. Buckelew and Margaret Wiseham Lewis, *Practical Work in the School Room, Part 1*, 140, 156.

45 E. Franklin Smith, *Text-Book of Anatomy, Physiology, and Hygiene*, 124.

46 Robert E. Corradini, *Narcotics and Youth Today*, 101–102.

47 Corradini, *Narcotics and Youth Today*, 85, 103.

48 "Chapter 187: Prevention of the Procreation of Habitual Criminals, Idiots, Feeble-Minded, Insane and Diseased and Degenerate Persons," available at https://www.legis.iowa.gov/docs/publications/iactc/35.1/CH0187.pdf (accessed June 5, 2021).

49 Harry H. Laughlin, "Eugenics Record Office: Bulletin no 10B" (Cold Spring Harbor, NY: Eugenics Record Office, 1914), 18.

50 "Van Epps' Plain Talk," *The Evening Times-Republican*, Nov. 21, 1912, 2.

51 "Ask Wedding Rule," *The Greene Recorder*, June 5, 1912, 8.

52 Christine Rosen, *Preaching Eugenics*, 16–18, 139–140; Melissa J. Wilde, *Birth Control Battles*, 77–82.

53 Paddison, *American Heathens*, 9; Kelly J. Baker, *Gospel According to the Klan*.

54 Sadler would also go on to start a new religious movement known as "Urantia," which was itself informed by Ellen White's version of Seventh-Day Adventism. Sadler was related to Kellogg—see Bull and Lockhart for this. Malcolm Bull and Keith Lockhart, *Seeking a Sanctuary*, 73; Sadler, *Race Decadence*, vi, 5–6, 156, 190, 249, 253, 306, 351–352, 354.

55 Brian C. Wilson, *Dr. John Harvey Kellogg and the Religion of Biologic Living*, 22, 26–27, 31.

56 Alexandra Minna Stern, *Eugenic Nation*, 51.

57 Jonathan Peter Spiro, *Defending the Master Race*, 251.

58 Spiro, *Defending the Master Race*, 53.

59 Rosen, *Preaching Eugenics*, 90.

60 Wilson, *Dr. John Harvey Kellogg and the Religion of Biologic Living*, 142–147, 153–154.

61 John Harvey Kellogg, *Man the Masterpiece*, vii–viii.

62 Kellogg, *Man the Masterpiece*, 485–486, 502–503.

63 Kellogg, *Man the Masterpiece*, 637–639.

64 Richmond P. Hobson to John D. Rockefeller, Jr., letter, June 18, 1914, Box 35, Folder 4, LOC-HOB.

65 Original reads "centures if." "Centuries of" is the only plausible revision for the typo. Richmond P. Hobson, "For New York American March 2, 1915," Box 33, Folder 7, LOC-HOB.

66 Richmond Pearson Hobson, *Alcohol and the Human Race*, 110, 165–166, 178–183.

67 Another term in vogue at the time was "the laws of health." The basic premise was that God designed bodies to function in particular ways and set up rules for how to maintain them in good health; to violate those laws is to impose upon God's goodwill. The phrase itself strips religion from the language.

68 Thomas W. Shannon, *Single Standard Eugenics*, ix, 31.

69 Shannon, *Single Standard Eugenics*, 75–78, 142.

70 Shannon, *Single Standard Eugenics*, 19, 80–82.

71 Rosen, *Preaching Eugenics*, 53–54; Wilde, *Birth Control Battles*, 83; Dennis Durst, "Evangelical Engagements with Eugenics, 1900–1940," 45–47.

72 I interpret them as speaking metaphorically but it's also possible Robinson and Fisher meant "millennium" literally. See for instance La Reine Helen Baker, *Race Improvement or Eugenics*, 116; Irving Fisher, "What the Health Movement Means," *Good Health*, Vol. 44, no. 10 (Oct. 1909): 770; Robinson, *Eugenics and Marriage*, 88.

73 Ruth Clifford Engs, *The Progressive Era's Health Reform Movement*, 358; *Proceedings of the First National Conference on Race Betterment*, xii; "The Third Race Betterment Conference," *Science*, Vol. 66, no. 1719 (Dec. 9, 1927): 554–555.

74 Phillip J. Hilts, *Protecting America's Health*, 13; James Harvey Young, "Two Hoosiers and the Two Food Laws of 1906," 305.

75 Harvey W. Wiley, *An Autobiography*, 31, 40; Harvey W. Wiley, "Not Safe to Follow Paul's Advice," *Good Housekeeping*, Vol. 66, no. 3 (Mar. 1918): 82.

76 Wiley closed his speech with the following: "I would fain return to the faith of my father and contemplate with him a world of hopeful saints, a heaven of redeemed souls. But to my mind the difficulties in the way of this belief are greater than those which beset the doctrine formulated by Darwin. But way down deep in my heart I have still a hope that after all these storms and strifes there may come good, a reunion with those who love us and whom we love. This is heredity. It comes from a long ancestry of believers. Perhaps it may prove true. I, for one, shall be glad." Harvey Washington Wiley, "Evolution" (1892), Box 187, Folder "Articles, Addresses + Writings / 1892–94," LOC-WIL.

77 The document does not specify which university chapel, but given the date (Nov. 1, 1869), it was likely read at Hanover College in Indiana. Harvey Washington Wiley, "What the Age Will Demand of the Coming Man," unpublished sermon, 1869, pp. 2–3, Box 185, Folder "Articles, Addresses + Writings / 1869," LOC-WIL.

78 Wiley, "What the Age Will Demand of the Coming Man," 3.

79 Wilson, *Dr. John Harvey Kellogg and the Religion of Biologic Living*, 16–17.

80 Wilson, *Dr. John Harvey Kellogg and the Religion of Biologic Living*, 7.

81 Wilson, *Dr. John Harvey Kellogg and the Religion of Biologic Living*, 17.

82 Charles Taylor, *A Secular Age*, 2.

83 It is worth mentioning that Michael Barkun uses the phrase "secular millennialism" in very similar ways to my own and is noting many of the same features of nineteenth- and early twentieth-century political culture. Michael Barkun, *A Culture of Conspiracy: Apocalyptic Visions in Contemporary America*, 2nd edition (Berkeley: University of California Press, 2013), 31–34.

84 This is not to say that Wiley did not continue to write about God and Christianity nominally. It is clear that Wiley abandoned the "religious fervor" of his youth, but he was not interested in converting other Americans to agnosticism/atheism, and he continued to make passing references to God/Christianity in his later years when it suited his argument.

85 Harvey W. Wiley, "Making the New American," *Good Housekeeping*, Vol. 69, no. 3 (Sept. 1919): 68.

86 Wiley, "Making the New American," 68, 164–167.

87 Carlson, "The Hoosier Connection," 28.

88 Harvey Washington Wiley, "Habit Forming Drugs," Box 190, Folder "Articles, Addresses + Writings / 1906," LOC-WIL.

89 Wiley, "Habit Forming Drugs."

90 Hilts, *Protecting America's Health*, 42–44, 46–47, 52–54.

91 Richard Davenport-Hines, *The Pursuit of Oblivion*, 212.

92 Harvey W. Wiley, *Not by Bread Alone*, 307–308.

93 William Atherton de Puy, "The Guardian of Ninety-Million Stomachs: Dr. Harvey W. Wiley at the Bureau of Chemistry," *Scientific American* (July 29, 1911): 95.

94 Early trial decisions about the Pure Food and Drug Act suggest that courts had an extremely high bar for how serious a violation needed to be for them to enforce it. In *United States v. Johnson*, for instance, Dr. Ora Alexander Johnson was charged with violating the Act because his patent medicine was labeled and sold as a cure for cancer. (Johnson's drug did not cure cancer.) The Supreme Court of the United States found in favor of Dr. Johnson, arguing that "the statements in question did not fit within the Act but that they were mere expressions of opinion." In other words, SCOTUS held that it was fine for Johnson to market his patent medicine as a cure for cancer and that the Act was about ingredients rather than medical efficacy. *United States v. 40 Barrels & 10 Kegs of Coca-Cola*, 191 F. 431 (D. Tenn. April 6, 1911); *United States v. Johnson*, 221 U.S. 488 (U.S. May 29, 1911).

95 William N. Bullard, "Chronic Tea Poisoning," *The Boston Medical and Surgical Journal*, Vol. 114, no. 14 (Apr. 8, 1886): 314–318.

96 "The Evils of Tea-Drinking," *Journal of the American Medical Association*, Vol. 29, no. 19 (Nov. 6, 1897): 971.

97 The author also targets coffee for the same reasons. "The Evils of Tea-Drinking," 971–972.

98 J. H. Kellogg, *Life*, 525–526.

99 E. Sherman Clouting, "Case of Temporary Insanity Following The Ingestion of Large Quantities of Whisky and Caffein," *Journal of the American Medical Association*, Vol. 50, no. 8 (Feb. 22, 1908): 604–605.

100 H. W. Wiley, "Danger to the Public from Praise of Caffein," *Journal of the American Medical Association*, Vol. 58, no. 10 (May 11, 1912): 1463.

101 See for instance Harvey W. Wiley, "Antikamnia Scattered Broadcast," *Good Housekeeping*, Vol. 56, no. 4 (Apr. 1913): 544–545; Harvey W. Wiley, "Soft Drinks," in *Good Housekeeping*, Vol. 69, no. 4 (Oct. 1919): 194.

102 Harvey W. Wiley, "The Drugging of Children," pamphlet, Box 200, Folder "Bureau of Chemistry, 1905–1912, LOC-WIL."

103 Martha M. Allen, "Dangerous 'Soft' Drinks," *The Union Signal*, Vol. 35, no. 21 (May 27, 1909): 5.

104 "The Coffee Debate," *The Union Signal*, Vol. 32, no. 13 (Mar. 29, 1906): 15.

105 Peter N. Stearns, *Shame*, 99.

106 Noel Glover, "Citizenship at Odds," 152; Imhoff, *The Lives of Jessie Sampter*, 75, 87–88.

107 Sharon L. Snyder and David T. Mitchell, *Cultural Locations of Disability*, 125.

108 Padwa, *Social Poison*, 52; Spillane, *Cocaine*, 5.

109 Arthur Woods, *Dangerous Drugs*, 48.

110 Woods, *Dangerous Drugs*, 37.

111 Wiley, *Not by Bread Alone*, 251.

112 John A. Hawkins, *Opium and Opium Addicts*, 52, 61, 76, 79–81, 109–110.

CHAPTER 4. US COLONIALISM AND SUBSTANCE USE PROHIBITION

1 Ahahui Puuhonua O Na Hawaii, "Memorial and Resolution," Box 643, Folder "Hawaii. Liquor Traffic (Part 1)," NARACP-OTCF.

2 Ahahui Puuhonua O Na Hawaii to Secretary of Interior Franklin Lane, petition, Apr. 2, 1918, Box 643, Folder "Hawaii. Liquor Traffic (Part 1)," NARACP-OTCF.

3 Robert A. Williams, Jr., *The American Indian in Western Legal Thought*, 76, 79–80.

4 Brian W. Dippie, *The Vanishing American*, 32–36.

5 Noenoe K. Silva, *Aloha Betrayed*, 46, 51–53, 58.

6 Silva, *Aloha Betrayed*, 144.

7 Noelani Arista, *The Kingdom and the Republic*, 61–66.

8 Julian Go, *American Empire and the Politics of Meaning*, 5.

9 In 1910, Native Hawaiians accounted for roughly 10,000 members of Hawaii's voting class, with white settlers representing only around 4,000. John S. Whitehead, "Western Progressives, Old South Planters, or Colonial Oppressors," 302–303.

10 See U.S. Congress, House, *Joint Resolution Providing for a Special Election in the Territory of Hawaii*, 61st Congress, 2d sess., 1910, S.J. Res. 80, Rep 61–771; Secretary of the Navy Josephus Daniels to Secretary of the Interior Franklin Lane, letter, Jan. 24, 1918, Box 643, Folder "Hawaii. Liquor Traffic (Part 1)," NARACP-OTCF; "Memorandum for the Secretary of War: Prohibition in Hawaii," May 14, 1917, Box 643, Folder "Hawaii. Liquor Traffic (Part 1)," NARACP-OTCF.

11 Lila Abu-Lughod, *Do Muslim Women Need Saving?*, 39, 43.

12 Executive Order 2815 of March 2, 1918, untitled. [This predates the *Federal Register*.] Found in Box 643, Folder "Hawaii. Liquor Traffic (Part 1)," NARACP-OTCF.

13 Sarah Dees, "An Equation of Language and Spirit," 196, 204.

14 Emily Conroy-Krutz, *Christian Imperialism*, 14, 50.

15 J. W. Powell, "From Barbarism to Civilization," *The American Anthropologist*, Vol. 1, no. 2 (Apr. 1888): 98, 100.

16 Powell, "From Barbarism to Civilization," 101–102.

17 Jonathan Z. Smith, "What a Difference a Difference Makes," 252.

18 Peter Silver, *Our Savage Neighbors*, 161, 228–229, 257–258.

19 Philip J. Deloria, *Indians in Unexpected Places*, 16.

20 Sylvester Johnson, "Religion and Empire in Mississippi, 1790–1833," 38–42.

21 Johnson, "Religion and Empire in Mississippi, 1790–1833," 47.

22 Donald L. Fixico, *Bureau of Indian Affairs*, 12–15.

23 Fixico, *Bureau of Indian Affairs*, 9, 17.

24 Stuart Banner, *How the Indians Lost Their Land*, 228, 230–231, 233, 240.

25 Jennifer Graber, *The Gods of Indian Country*, 29, 86, 118; Tisa Wenger, *Religious Freedom*, 104–106.

26 Jacqueline Fear-Segal and Susan D. Rose, *Carlisle Industrial School*, 12–14, 18, 21–22.

27 Jill E. Martin, "The Greatest Evil," 37–42.

28 Gilbert Quintero, "Making the Indian," 58.

29 Peter C. Mancall, "I Was Addicted to Drinking Rum," 100.

30 "Editorial Comment: No Short Cuts Will Solve the Indian Problem," *The Red Man*, Vol. 5, no. 7 (March 1913): 303.

31 "Editorial Comment: No Short Cuts Will Solve the Indian Problem," 304.

32 Rev. Sherman Coolidge, "American Indians for the Honor of Their Race," *The Red Man*, Vol. 6, no. 7 (Mar. 1914): 252.

33 Coolidge, "American Indians," 255.

34 Judith E. Tintinalli et al., *Tintinalli's Emergency Medicine*, ebook without page numbers.

35 J. Bryan Page and Merrill Singer, *Comprehending Drug Use*, 25; Thomas C. Maroukis, *The Peyote Road*, 14.

36 Alexander Dawson, *The Peyote Effect*, 7.

37 Dees, "An Equation of Language and Spirit," 196.

38 Omer C. Stewart, *Peyote Religion*, 58–62, 69.

39 Stewart, *Peyote Religion*, 65–66, 69.

40 Supt. Ret Millard to Commissioner of Indian Affairs Francis E. Leupp, letter, Dec. 24, 1908. Box 2, folder 2489–08, NARAW-BIA-LIQ; Nellie Bad Boy to Commissioner of Indian Affairs Cato Sells, letter, Apr. 30, 1919, Box 22, folder 122–2, NARAD-BIA-CRO.

41 Supt. Charles E. Shell to Chief Special Officer William E. Johnson, letter, Sept. 27, 1909, Box 3, folder 2989–08 NARAW-BIA-LIQ.

42 Joseph D. Calabrese, *A Different Medicine*, 19.

43 Chief of Police Sam W. Tulk to Supt. J. George Wright, letter, Dec. 16, 1923, Box 4, Folder 2989–08, NARAW-BIA-LIQ.

44 Stewart, *Peyote Religion*, 128–129.

45 Havelock Ellis, "Mescal: A New Artificial Paradise," *The Contemporary Review*, Vol. 73 (Jan. 1898): 140–141.

46 Rev. Walter C. Roe to Rev. Wilbur F. Crafts, letter, Nov. 21, 1908, Box 2, Folder 2989–08, NARAW-BIA-LIQ.

47 "Hearing of the delegation of Omaha Indians, consisting of Daniel Webster, Harry Lyon and Parrish Sansouci, before Assistant Commissioner Abbott, in regard to the use of mescal," transcript, Mar. 25, 1912, Box 3, Folder 2989–08, NARAW-BIA-LIQ.

48 "Mescal Buttons," report, Jan. 28, 1910, Box 3, Folder 2989–08, NARAW-BIA-LIQ.

49 The article survives in a clipping at the National Archives; it is, however, un-labeled. Likely originated in New York. "Opens War on Mescal Bean," Box 3, Folder 2989–08, NARAW-BIA-LIQ; Chief Special Officer William E. Johnson to Joseph Bondy's Sons, letter, May 7, 1909, Box 3, Folder 2989–08, NARAW-BIA-LIQ.

50 Herman Harms to John K. Hardy, Esq., letter, Mar. 10, 1916, Box 2, Folder 2989–08, NARAW-BIA-LIQ.

51 John Semans, State of Nebraska, County of Thurston affidavit, Oct. 11, 1911, Box 3, Folder 2989–08, NARAW-BIA-LIQ.

52 Walter C. Roe, "Mescal Peyote or Anhalonium Lewisii," report, undated, Box 3, Folder 2989–08, NARAW-BIA-LIQ; R. D. Hall to Asst. Commissioner of Indian Affairs F. H. Abbott, letter, Jan. 30, 1912, Box 3, folder 2989–08, NARAW-BIA-LIQ.

53 Chief Special Officer William E. Johnson to Charles S. Dalrymple, letter, Feb. 28, 1910, Box 3, Folder 2989–08, NARAW-BIA-LIQ.

54 "Extract from letter to The Honorable Harvey W. Wiley, Washington, D.C. Dec. 14th, 1908," unpublished manuscript, Box 2, Folder 2989–08, NARAW-BIA-LIQ.

55 Rev. Walter C. Roe to Rev. Wilbur F. Crafts, letter, Nov. 21, 1908, Box 2, Folder 2989–08, NARAW-BIA-LIQ.

56 Walter C. Roe, "Mescal Peyote or Anhalonium Lewisii," Box 3, Folder 2989–08, NARAW-BIA-LIQ.

57 Roe, "Mescal Peyote or Anhalonium Lewisii."

58 Roe, "Mescal Peyote or Anhalonium Lewisii."

59 Rev. Henry W. Vruwink, "Peyote or Mescal," manuscript, no date [1915?], Box 3, folder 2989–08, NARAW-BIA-LIQ.

60 Vruwink, "Peyote or Mescal."

61 Rev. Henry Vruwink, About Indians (New York: Women's Board of Domestic Missions Reformed Church in America, undated), 6. Found in Box 3, folder 2989–08, NARAW-BIA-LIQ.

62 Vruwink, About Indians, 7–8.

63 Tisa Wenger, We Have a Religion, 138.

64 Wilfred T. Grenfell wrote the book's introduction. F.A. McKenzie, "Pussyfoot" Johnson, 6.

65 McKenzie, "Pussyfoot" Johnson, 18–19.

66 McKenzie, "Pussyfoot" Johnson, 35.

67 McKenzie, "Pussyfoot" Johnson, 60–61.

68 W. P. Marshall to Supt. C. H. Asbury, letter, Jul. 12, 1920, Box 22, Folder 122, NARAD-BIA-CRO; Asst. Commissioner of Indian Affairs E. B. Meritt to Spt. Byron A. Sharp, letter, Apr. 24, 1926, Box 4, folder 14727–26, NARAW-BIA-YUM.

69 Special Officer Jesse E. Flanders to Commissioner of Indian Affairs Francis E. Leupp, letter, Jul. 15, 1908, Box 1, folder 49346–08, NARAW-BIA-LIQ.

70 Chief Special Officer William E. Johnson to Commissioner of Indian Affairs Francis E. Leupp, letter, Feb. 4, 1909, Box 1, folder 49346–08, NARAW-BIA-LIQ.

71 Stewart, Peyote Religion, 134.

72 Johnson repeatedly cited this law as "Act of Congress approved Jan. 30, 1897 (29 Stat. L. 506)." Chief Special Officer William E. Johnson to G. A. Taft, letter, Apr. 28, 1909, Box 3, Folder 2989–08, NARAW-BIA-LIQ; Chief Special Officer William E. Johnson to J.W. Rogers, letter, May 13, 1909, Box 3, folder 2989–08, NARAW-BIA-LIQ.

73 William E. Johnson to Commissioner of Indian Affairs Francis E. Leupp, letter, Apr. 17, 1909, Box 3, Folder 2989–08, NARAW-BIA-LIQ.

74 William E. Johnson to Commissioner of Indian Affairs Francis E. Leupp, telegram, Apr. 23, 1909, Box 3, folder 2989–08, NARAW-BIA-LIQ.

75 Chief Special Officer William E. Johnson to Earnest Stecker, letter, May 4, 1910, Box 3, Folder 2989–08 NARAW-BIA-LIQ; Chief Special Officer William E. Johnson to C. C. Brannon, letter, Feb. 18, 1910, Box 3, folder 2989–08, NARAW-BIA-LIQ.

76 Chief Special Officer William E. Johnson to Supt. Charles E. Shell, letter, Oct. 25, 1909, Box 3, Folder 2989–08, NARAW-BIA-LIQ.

77 Acting Commissioner of Indian Affairs F. Abbott to Wormser Bros, letter, Oct. 13, 1909, Box 3, Folder 2989–08, NARAW-BIA-LIQ.

78 Chief Special Officer William E. Johnson to Wormser Bros., letter, May 14, 1909, Box 3, folder 2989–08, NARAW-BIA-LIQ.

79 Chief Special Officer William E. Johnson to G. A. Taft, letter, Apr. 28, 1909, Box 3, Folder 2989–08, NARAW-BIA-LIQ.

80 Chief Special Officer William E. Johnson to J. W. Rogers, letter, May 13, 1909, Box 3, Folder 2989–08, NARAW-BIA-LIQ.

81 Havelock Ellis, "Mescal: A Study of a Divine Plant," *Popular Science Monthly* (May 1902): 71.

82 The shipment went through an intermediary named Peck and Velsor. Peck and Velsor to William E. Johnson, letter, Aug. 23, 1910; and Chief Special Officer William E. Johnson to Peck and Velsor, letter, Aug. 31, 1910, Box 3, folder 2989–08, NARAW-BIA-LIQ.

83 L. A. Slane to L. Villegas, letter, Sept. 3, 1909, Box 3, folder 2989–08, NARAW-BIA-LIQ.

84 *United States of America v. Harry Black Bear*, Sept. 8, 1916. Found in Box 3, Folder 2989–08, NARAW-BIA-LIQ.

85 *S.B. no. 9, An Act to Amend Section 8 of Chapter 66, Laws of Utah, 1915, Relating to the Sale of Narcotic Drugs; Providing that the Same may not be Sold Except Upon Prescription; Providing for the Registry of Such Sales and Providing That Preparations Containing Any of Said Drugs may be Sold only by a Registered Pharmacist.* Found along with BIA documentation identifying that the bill passed. Chief Special Officer Henry A. Larson to Commissioner of Indian Affairs Cato Sells, letter, Mar. 7, 1917, Box 3, Folder 2989–08, NARAW-BIA-LIQ.

86 Rennard Strickland, "The Tribal Struggle for Indian Sovereignty," 75.

87 Supt. Charles H. Asbury to Supt. O. M. Boggess, letter, Mar. 16, 1923, Box 22, Folder 122–2, NARAD-BIA-CRO.

88 Supt. O. M. Boggess to Supt. C. H. Asbury, letter, Mar. 20, 1923, Box 22, Folder 122–2, NARAD-BIA-CRO.

89 Supt. Charles H. Asbury to Commissioner of Indian Affairs Charles H. Burke, letter, May 16, 1923, Box 22, Folder 122–2, NARAD-BIA-CRO.

90 Presumably Asbury, but letter unsigned. Supt. [of Crow Agency] to Commissioner of Indian Affairs Charles H. Burke, letter, May 9, 1922, Box 22, folder 122–2, NARAD-BIA-CRO.

91 Supt. Charles H. Asbury to Hon. Harry L. Gandy, letter, June 30, 1920, Box 22, Folder 122–2, NARAD-BIA-CRO.

92 It is unclear whether or not this policy went into effect. There appears to have been hesitancy on the part of one Crow elder that may have undercut its passage. "Peyote. Regulations relating to the introduction, use and possession of Peyote on Crow Reservation, Montana," undated [1922], Box 22, Folder 122–2, NARAD-BIA-CRO.

93 Acting Supt. J. A. Coe to Commissioner of Indian Affairs Charles H. Burke, letter, Mar. 22, 1922, and letter from Supt. [illegible signature; initials CVS] to Commissioner of Indian Affairs Charles H. Burke, letter, Apr. 7, 1922, Box 29, Folder 14560-1920, NARAW-BIA-ROS.

94 Department of the Interior—Office of Indian Affairs, "Circular No. 1522. Peyote," circular letter, Mar. 28, 1919, Box 2, Folder 2989–08, NARAW-BIA-LIQ.

95 Special Officer William R. [Nourson?] to Asst. Commissioner E. B. Meritt, letter, Apr. 11, 1919, Box 2, Folder 2989–08, NARAW-BIA-LIQ.

96 Special Officer G.[N?] O'Neill to Commissioner of Indian Affairs Cato Sells, letter, Apr. 14, 1919, Box 2, folder 2989–08, NARAW-BIA-LIQ.

97 S. A. Vennick to unknown recipient, draft of letter, undated, Box 22, Folder 122–2, NARAD-BIA-CRO.

98 Robert E. L. Newberne, *Peyote: An Abridged Compilation from the Files of the Bureau of Indian Affairs* (Washington, DC: Government Printing Office, 1922), 32. Found in Box 22, Folder 122–2, NARAD-BIA-CRO.

99 Maroukis, *The Peyote Road*, 50–51.

100 Rev. R. D. Hall to Asst. Commissioner F. H. Abbott, letter, Jan. 30, 1912, Box 3, folder 2989–08, NARAW-BIA-LIQ.

101 U.S. Congress, Senate, Committee on Indian Affairs, *Indian Appropriation Bill, 1919: Hearings before the Committee on Indian Affairs*, 65th Cong., 2nd sess., 1918, 29–31.

102 Stewart, *Peyote Religion*, 203.

103 Supt. [initials AWL] to Commissioner of Indian Affairs Charles H. Burke, letter, May 27, 1922, Box 3, folder 126, NARAD-BIA-PUE.

104 Walter L. Bolander to Supt. A. W. Leech, letter, May 3, 1922, Box 3, Folder 126, NARAD-BIA-PUE.

105 Stewart, *Peyote Religion*, 207.

106 Supt. C. J. Crandall to Commissioner of Indian Affairs Charles H. Burke, letter, Jan. 12, 1924, Box 3, Folder 126, NARAD-BIA-PUE.

107 "Remarks of Committee of Indians with Reference to the Use of Peyote. Henry Standing Bear, Interpreter," transcript, undated [probably Feb. 1937], Box 4, Folder 2989–08, NARAW-BIA-LIQ.

108 "Remarks of Committee of Indians with Reference to the Use of Peyote."

109 Rosebud Sioux Tribal Council, "Regulating Use of Peyote," proposed ordinance, undated [perhaps July 1937], Box 4, folder 2989–08, NARAW-BIA-LIQ.

110 Asst. Commissioner William Zimmerman Jr. to Supt. C. R. Whitlock, letter, Oct. 29, 1937, Box 4, folder 2989–08, NARAW-BIA-LIQ.

111 Henry Franklin York, affidavit—State of Nebraska, County [blank], Oct. 13, 1911, Box 3, folder 2989–08, NARAW-BIA-LIQ.

112 Wenger, *Religious Freedom*.

CHAPTER 5. PROTESTANTS, COLONIALISM, AND INTERNATIONAL DRUG REFORM

1 Letter written by a staffer on Crowdy's behalf. Author unknown, letter to Dr. Warnshuis, 21 April 1922, Box R707, Folder 20278, LON.

2 League of Nations Opium Advisory Committee, "Item No. 12 of Agenda. Statement to the Advisory Committee on Traffic in Opium, Appointed by the League of Nations from the International Missionary Council, May 4th, 1923," unpublished document, 8 May 1923, Box R707, Folder 20278, LON.

3 Elizabeth Kelly Gray, "The Trade-Off," 220, 227.

4 Matthew McCullough, *The Cross of War*, 4.

5 McCullough, *The Cross of War*, 15, 19, 21, 38, 41, 83, 86–87.

6 Paul A. Kramer, *The Blood of Government*, 1, 5, 11, 117; Natalia Molina, *How Race Is Made in America*, 68–69; Nicole Trajano Molnar, *American Mestizos, the Philippines, and the Malleability of Race*, 48; Jerome Dowd, *The Negro Races*, 292; Victor S. Clark, "Labor Conditions in Java," 923–924.

7 Susan A. Brewer, *Why America Fights*, 17, 45.

8 Julian Go, *American Empire and the Politics of Meaning*, 6.

9 Go, *American Empire and the Politics of Meaning*, 30, 40.

10 This account was published after McKinley's death. Rusling recounts a conversation involving himself, the late president, and several other Methodists, but some details of the exchange make one suspicious about accuracy. President McKinley's audience keeps trying to leave before he has finished speaking (unusual for presidents), and his points about the Philippines are very thorough and orderly for a casual conversation. The most likely scenario is that some sort of conversation about the Philippines occurred and Rusling later cleaned it up for publication. It is also possible, however, that what he attributes to McKinley was actually based on an 1898 speech by Albert Beveridge, which Rusling's article follows quite closely (see Jones for quote). James F. Rusling, "Interview with President McKinley," *Christian Advocate*, Vol. 78, no. 4 (22 Jan. 1903): 137; Gregg Jones, *Honor in the Dust*, 95.

11 Charles Henry Brent, entries for October 8 and 9, 1901, Box 1, 1901 Diary, LOC-BRE.

12 Charles Henry Brent, "Address to the Quill Club, Manila—June 22, 1908," Box 34, Folder "Speeches," LOC-BRE.

13 Letter from Charles Henry Brent to Bishop Hall, 5 May 1904, Box 6, Folder "Jan.–June 1904," LOC-BRE.

14 It is unclear what this manuscript was intended for. It appears to be a book chapter for an unlocatable title. Charles Henry Brent, "European Nations and Christian Statesmanship," [undated—sometime 1920–1924], 2, Box 34, folder "European Nations and Christian Statesmanship," LOC-BRE.

15 Brent, "European Nations and Christian Statesmanship," 3, 5–7.

16 Brent, "European Nations and Christian Statesmanship," 8–9.

17 Letter from Charles Henry Brent to William Howard Taft, 4 Nov. 1908, Box 8, Folder "Nov. 1908," LOC-BRE.

18 Officially, this fact-finding mission was called "the Opium Commission." The specific instructions in Brent's letter advised the committee "to visit Japan, Formosa, Upper Burmah and Java, and such other countries as the Civil Governor may designate, for the purpose of investigating the use of opium and the traffic therein, and the rules, ordinances and laws regulating such use and traffic." Signature illegible. "A. M. Fergusson?" [Executive Secretary for the Government of the Philippine Islands Executive Bureau] to Charles Henry Brent, letter, 31 July 1903, Box 6, Folder "Jan.–Dec. 1903," LOC-BRE.

19 Arnold H. Taylor, "American Confrontation with Opium Traffic in the Philippines," 311–316.

20 David T. Courtwright, *Forces of Habit*, 153–154; Daniel J. P. Wertz, "Idealism, Imperialism, and Internationalism," 468.

21 Taylor, "American Confrontation with Opium Traffic in the Philippines," 309.

22 John V. Crangle, "Joseph Whitwell Pease and the Quaker Role in the Campaign to Suppress the Opium Trade in the British Empire," 63.

23 Famed reformer Lord Shaftesbury called British opium policy "destructive" and "inconsistent with the honor and duties of a Christian kingdom," and Cardinal Manning called it "high treason against man himself." The Archbishop of Canterbury also disapproved of the opium trade. Crangle, "Joseph Whitwell Pease and the Quaker Role in the Campaign to Suppress the Opium Trade in the British Empire," 64–65.

24 Rev. A. E. Moule, *The Use of Opium and Its Bearing on the Spread of Christianity in China*, 1–2.

25 Rev. W. M. Young's testimony can be found in Wilbur F. Crafts et al., *Protection of Native Races Against Intoxicants & Opium*, 95–97.

26 Kathleen L. Lodwick, *Crusaders Against Opium*, 29.

27 Lodwick, *Crusaders Against Opium*, 31–32.

28 Lodwick, *Crusaders Against Opium*, 40.

29 Elizabeth Andrew and Katherine Bushnell, *Opium and Vice*. Found in Collection CLC RM41 titled "Drugs" at the Library of Congress.

30 Crafts et al., *Protection of Native Races Against Intoxicants & Opium*; J. B. Brown, "Politics of the Poppy," 102.

31 Charles H. Brent to President Theodore Roosevelt, letter, July 24, 1906, Box 6, Folder "Jan.–Dec. 1906," LOC-BRE; President Theodore Roosevelt to Charles H. Brent, letter, 28 Aug. 1906, Box 6, Folder "Jan.–Dec. 1906," LOC-BRE.

32 Anne L. Foster, "Medicine to Drug," 114.

33 Helena Barop, "Building the 'Opium Evil' Consensus," 133–134.

34 International Opium Commission, *Report of the Proceedings, February 1 to February 26, 1909*, 50. Copy found in File 511.4 A1, Box 5397, NARACP-DOS-1910.

35 Ian Tyrell, *Reforming the World*, 153.

36 Gaines M. Foster, *Moral Reconstruction*, 110.

37 Wilbur F. Crafts, "What Business has Church or State with Ethics?" *The Union Signal*, Vol. 30, no. 22 (15 Sept. 1904): 3.

38 Crafts, "What Business has Church or State with Ethics?," 13.

39 Wilbur Fisk Crafts et al., *Intoxicating Drinks & Drugs in All Lands and Times*, 14.

40 By "consequential" I mean that the Harrison Narcotic Tax Act of 1914 was designed to prohibit non-medical substance use as well as to end self-medication. The 1906 Pure Food and Drug Act preceded the Harrison Act, but its purview pertained to product labeling.

41 Hamilton Wright, "The International Opium Conference," 114.

42 The Bureau of Insular Affairs initially planned to conduct opium revenues into public education for Filipinos (and education of course represented one of the major concerns of the civilizing mission). Ian Tyrrell suggests that it was evangelical pushback via petitionary letters that resulted in prohibitory policies instead. Tyrrell, *Reforming the World*, 147, 150–152.

43 Foster, *Moral Reconstruction*, 115.

44 Charles A. Blanchard to President William H. Taft, petition, 9 Jan. 1911, File 511.4 A1/957, Box 5399, NARACP-DOS-1910.

45 Foster, *Moral Reconstruction*, 29, 97–99.

46 "The W.C.T.U. Petition for the Brussels Treaty," *The Literary Digest* Vol. 4, no. 4 (Nov. 29, 1891): 25.

47 "Against the Canteen," *The National Advocate*, Vol. 33, no. 8 (1898): 128.

48 A letter to Hamilton Wright from a British lawyer working with an Anti-Opium Society uses the language of "our mutual friend" in reference to Crafts, then discusses the positive report he has of Wright in the information that Crafts has been channeling to him on Wright's behalf. It is unclear from context exactly how close Crafts and Wright were. Crafts wrote a strongly worded letter to Secretary of State William Jennings Bryan in 1914 demanding better treatment of Wright. J. G. Alexander to Hamilton Wright, letter, Oct. 8, 1913, File 511.4 A1/1468, Box 5402, NARACP-DOS-1910; Wilbur F. Crafts to Secretary of State William Jennings Bryan, letter, June 12, 1914, File 511.4 A1/1478, Box 5402, NARACP-DOS-1910; Tyrrell, *Reforming the World*, 163.

49 Cara Lea Burnidge, *A Peaceful Conquest*, 3, 18, 24.

50 Burnidge, *A Peaceful Conquest*, 1, 3.

51 Burnidge, *A Peaceful Conquest*, 78.

52 President-Elect Woodrow Wilson to William Jennings Bryan, letter, 21 Feb. 1913, Box 29, Folder "1913 Jan.–Mar.," LOC-BRY.

53 The pharmaceutical lobby also had a hand in shaping the bill. Harrison directed, introduced, and guided the bill, but he left much of the craftwork to Wright. Indeed, a few months after the bill's passage, Harrison (who by then was Governor General of the Philippines) wrote Wright to congratulate him for its success. David F. Musto, *The American Disease*, 54–57, 61; Francis Burton Harrison to Hamilton Wright, letter, 9 Mar. 1915, Box 1, Folder "Official and Private Correspondence / 1914," NARACP-ICR.

54 Redford and Benjamin Powell, "Dynamics of Intervention in the War on Drugs," 524–526.

55 The assessment of China's bargaining strength is my own interpretation. The credit to China for instigating this treaty clause derives from State Department communiques. See Telegram from "L.W.R." to Secretary of State [Robert Lansing], 18 Mar. 1919, File 511.4 A1/1544, Box 5403, NARACP-DOS-1910.

56 Wright, "The International Opium Conference," 129–131.

57 E. N. van Kleffens, untitled internal report, 22 May 1920, Box R706, Folder 4524, LON.

58 Quincy Wright, "The Opium Question," 285–286.

59 Michael D. Callahan, *Mandates and Empire*, 3, 6.

60 Specific names vary for these groups. Some are "Committees," some "Associations," some "Societies," but they were connected.

61 Arthur Sowerby to Sir Eric Drummond, letter, 17 Sept. 1920, Box R706, Folder 7859, LON.

62 Secretary of the Advisory Committee on Traffic in Opium to Sir Malcolm Delevingne, letter, 19 April 1923, Box R706, Folder 3442, LON.

63 The IAOAP was distinct and separate from the National Anti-Opium Association, which reflected a larger Chinese constituency. "A Record of Work Done," *Bulletin of the International Anti-Opium Association Peking*, Vol. 1, no. 5 (Nov. 30, 1919): 10. Found in Box R706, Folder 2990, LON.

64 E. N. van Kleffens, internal memo, 26 July 1920, Box R706, Folder 5603, LON.

65 Susan Pedersen, *The Guardians*, 29; Denys P. Myers, "The Mandate System of the League of Nations," 75–76.

66 "Extracts from Report on British Cameroons, for the year 1922," internal report, Box R787, Folder 35941, LON.

67 "Extracts from Report on Tanganyika Territory, for the year 1922," internal report, Box R787, folder 35941, LON.

68 "Extracts from The Second Report on Western Samoa for the year ended the 31st March, 1922. Pages 12, 18, 19, 29," internal report, box R787, folder 35941, LON.

69 M. Gilchrist, untitled internal report, 16 June 1926, Box R787, Folder 51459, LON; "Advisory Committee on Traffic in Opium: The Drug Question in Mandated

Territories: Item 9 of the Agenda: Summary prepared by the Secretariat," internal report, 12 May 1926, Box R787, Folder 51459, LON.

70 See Box R35, Folder 34160 and Folder 37475, LON.

71 Native Races and the Liquor Traffic United Committee to Prime Minister J. Ramsay Macdonald, "Memorial of the Native Races and the Liquor Traffic United Committee," petition, 31 Mar. 1924, Box R35, Folder 37475, LON.

72 Dr. Charles F. Harford, "The Great Powers and the Liquor Traffic among the Native Races," *Proceedings of the International Conference against Alcoholism at Geneva, 1st–3rd September 1925*, ed. R. Hercod (Lausanne, Switzerland: International Bureau Against Alcoholism, 1925), 15, found in Box R35, Folder 51952, LON.

73 Tyrrell, *Reforming the World*, 82, 131–133, 164.

74 E. N. van Kleffens, internal memo, 4 May 1920, Box R706, Folder 4173, LON.

75 I. Nitobe to Dr. van Hamel, internal memo, 2 Sept. 1920, Box R706, Folder 6526, LON; John Loudon to Sir Eric Drummond, letter, 24 April 1920, Box R706, Folder 4173, LON.

76 E. N. van Kleffens, internal memo, 4 May 1920; Box R706, Folder 4173, LON; "At its forthcoming meeting on April 17th the Council of the League will take up the question of the reappointment or replacement of the three assessors to the opium committee, one of whom is Mrs. Hamilton Wright. According to certain opinions in Geneva Mrs. Wright's work has not been regarded as particularly helpful as it is said that her attitude has been critical rather than constructive. I am informed however that in all probability she will be reappointed. There is no desire to drop her unless some more competent American expert can be found." Grew to Secretary of State Charles Evans Hughes, telegram, 12 Apr. 1923, File 511.4 A1/1753, Box 5405, NARACP-DOS-1910.

77 Elizabeth Washburn Wright to Mr. [William] Phillips, letter, 24 July 1922. File 511.4 A1/1660, Box 5404, NARACP-DOS-1910.

78 Elizabeth Washburn Wright to Admiral Mark Bristol, letter, 2 Apr. 1930, Box 80, Folder "Mrs. Hamilton Wright," LOC-BRI.

79 This citation is correct. For unclear reasons, Bristol's records include correspondence between Wright and people other than Bristol. Charles H. Brent to Elizabeth Washburn Wright, 18 Mar. 1929, Box 80, Folder "Mrs. Hamilton Wright," LOC-BRI.

80 Constance Drexel, "Are We Our Brothers' Keepers? How Our Country Is Fighting the Drug Evil," *Harper's Monthly Magazine* (Nov. 1924): 736.

81 Charles Henry Brent, "The Moral Side of the Opium Question," *The Christian Work* (22 Mar. 1924): 367.

82 "Gin Lane" was an eighteenth-century print depicting drunken, debauched people sinning in London. Harry d'Erlanger, *The Last Plague of Egypt*, 13.

83 League of Nations, "Advisory Committee on Traffic in Opium and Other Dangerous Drugs. Use of tea as a stimulant or narcotic. Note by Dr. Askren of the American Mission, Fayoum, submitted by the representative of Egypt." Found in Box 16:

Subject Files of the Bureau of Narcotics and Dangerous Drugs, 1916–1970, Folder "Egypt #1," NARACP-DEA.

84 Hugh Byas, "Japanese Seize Mukden in Battle with the Chinese; Rush More Troops to City," *New York Times*, Sept. 19, 1931: 1; Louise Young, *Japan's Total Empire*, 3.

85 Japan and Persia were both credited with contributing to illicit substance use in Harbin. Norman Smith, *Intoxicating Manchuria*, 29.

86 John M. Jennings, "The Forgotten Plague," 805–808.

87 On December 25, 1906, the American governor in Cuba alerted Washington about Japanese agents they had captured spying on American military installations. Cable from Governor [Charles] Magoon, 25 Dec. 1906, Box 36, in Subsection 1898–1913, NARACP-INS.

88 Speaking to Congress in 1911, he predicted that a Japanese attack was imminent in the next two years. He advised fortifying the Panama Canal, transferring most of the American fleet to the Pacific, and argued Pearl Harbor was the only suitable place for a standoff. He spoke of Japanese aggression elsewhere, too. "Naval Appropriation Bill," 20 Feb. 1911, in 61st Cong., 3rd Sess., *Congressional Record* 46, pt. 3: 2990–2991.

89 Sao-Ke Alfred Sze, "China Talks Back," *Liberty Magazine*, no. 32 (11 Aug. 1934): 20; "Drug Control: Summary of *Foreign Policy Report*: Threat of Oriental Opium," *Washington Post*, (1 Mar. 1937): 9.

90 This group was unconnected with the British ones. The National Anti-Opium Association, *China in the Grip of Japanese Drug Traffickers: Memorandum Presented to the Commission of Inquiry of The League of Nations* (Shanghai: National Anti-Opium Association, 1932). Found in Collection CLC RM41 titled "Drugs" at the Library of Congress.

91 Richmond P. Hobson to F. P. Keppel, letter, 11 Aug. 1934, Box 69, Folder 12, LOC-HOB.

92 Harry Anslinger, "Outline of Speech Before the International Association of Chiefs of Police at St. Petersburg, Florida, October 13, 1931," Microfilm Reel 1, PSU.

93 "Congressman John Miller! Hard Worker! Result Getter!" (pamphlet), 1930, Box 1, Folder 21, UW-MIL.

94 See Kramer's statement on June 4, 1934. 73 Cong. Rec. 10424 (1934).

95 *Deportation of Alien Criminals, Gunmen, Narcotic Dealers, Defectives, Etc.: Hearings Before The Committee on Immigration and Naturalization, House of Representatives, Sixty-Ninth Congress, First Session* (Washington, DC: Government Printing Office, 1926), 13.

96 *Deportation of Alien Criminals, Gunmen, Narcotic Dealers, Defectives, Etc.*, 19.

97 *Deportation of Alien Criminals, Gunmen, Narcotic Dealers, Defectives, Etc.*, 59.

98 Ervin Hacker, "Criminality and Immigration," *Journal of the American Institute of Criminal Law and Criminology*, Vol. 20, no. 3 (Nov. 1929): 431.

99 Wenger, *Religious Freedom*, 56.

CHAPTER 6. THE PRODUCTS OF A MORAL PANIC

1 Hobson delivered this same address to the National Conference of the Daughters of the American Revolution, which took place in Constitution Hall on April 24, 1931 (Box 69, Folder 14, LOC-HOB). Richmond Pearson Hobson, "World War Upon the Dope Ring," radio script for National Broadcast Company's "Red Network," 22 Feb. 1931, Box 67, Folder 3, LOC-HOB.

2 Jordan identifies this proposed alcohol professorship in letters to Hobson and Caleb Saleeby. David Starr Jordan to Richmond P. Hobson, letter, 29 June 1922, and David Starr Jordan to Dr. Caleb W. Saleeby, letter, 29 June 1922, Box 105, Folder 914, SU; David Starr Jordan to Richmond P. Hobson, letter, 12 Aug. 1922, Box 105, Folder 916, SU.

3 Richmond Pearson Hobson, "World War Upon the Dope Ring," radio script for National Broadcast Company's "Red Network," 22 Feb. 1931, Box 67, Folder 3, LOC-HOB.

4 Matthew R. Pembleton, *Containing Addiction*, 37.

5 Stuart Hall et al., *Policing the Crisis*, 16.

6 Erich Goode and Nachman Ben-Yehuda, *Moral Panics*, 62–63.

7 Katherine A. Chavigny, "Reforming Drunkards in Nineteenth-Century America," 109–113.

8 Gaines M. Foster, *Moral Reconstruction*, 37–39.

9 See Stephen K. Green, *The Bible, the School, and the Constitution*, 11–14; Tracy Fessenden, *Culture and Redemption*, 66–83.

10 Jonathan Zimmerman, *Innocents Abroad*, 10.

11 Horace Mann, *Lectures on Education*, 165–166, 169, 172, 174, 207–210.

12 Jonathan Zimmerman, "When the Doctors Disagree," 172–175; Jonathan Zimmerman, *Distilling Democracy*, 2.

13 Mary H. Hunt, *A History of the First Decade of the Department of Scientific Temperance Instruction*, 6.

14 Hunt, *A History of the First Decade of the Department of Scientific Temperance Instruction*, v.

15 Norton Mezivinsky, "Scientific Temperance in the Schools," 48; Zimmerman, *Distilling Democracy*, 75.

16 Constitutionally this is the most that Congress could regulate when it came to public education since state schools were under state jurisdiction. Senate Committee on Labor and Education, 2355 S. rp 85, 8 Feb. 1886; 24 Stat. 69, 49 Cong. Ch. 362.

17 David Tyack et al., *Law and the Shaping of Public Education, 1785–1954*, 157–158.

18 Mary Hunt, *The Child's Health Primer for Primary Classes*.

19 Chilion B. Allen and Mary A. Allen, *The Man Wonderful in the House Beautiful*, 9–10.

20 Allen and Allen, *The Man Wonderful in the House Beautiful*, 242–245, 252, 257, 302–305, 308–313.

21 Albert F. Blaisdell, *How to Keep Well*, iii, 62–63, 66, 159–165.

22 Eli F. Brown, *The House I Live In*, 5–6, 26–27, 49, 79–82.

23 William B. Warner, "Truth and Trust and the Eighteenth-Century Anglophone Newspaper," 32–33.

24 Goode and Ben-Yehuda, *Moral Panics*, 90.

25 Joshua Paddison, *American Heathens*, 90, 123, 139–154; Lon Kurashige, *Two Faces of Exclusion*.

26 "The Devil's Heaven," in *Milwaukee Daily Sentinel*, June 27, 1877, 2.

27 "A Chinaman's Lonely Death," in *St. Louis Globe-Democrat*, Mar. 15, 1877, 2; "Opium Smuggling," [*San Francisco*] *Daily Evening Bulletin*, June 21, 1876, 3; "Opium Smokers: A Walk Through the Chinese Quarter," *New York Times*, Mar. 22, 1880, 2; "Clubs of Opium Smokers: Where Victims of a Deadly Drug Indulge Their Appetites," *Chicago Tribune*, Mar. 17, 1889, 26.

28 Untitled, *Boston Daily Advertiser*, July 10, 1877, 1.

29 Paul Gootenberg, *Cocaine*, 2.

30 Joseph F. Spillane, *Cocaine*, 91–96.

31 "Baltimore Negroes in the Thrall of Cocaine: Amazing and Dangerous Growth of a Habit Unknown a Decade Ago," *Baltimore Sun*, Dec. 16, 1906, 15.

32 "Negro, Cocaine Crazed, Kills Three With Gun," *Harrisburg Telegraph*, July 16, 1910, 1.

33 "Negro Cocaine Fiend Kills Police Chief; Lynching Threatened," *Austin American*, June 20, 1914, 2.

34 "Woman Leaps Through Window in Raid; Escapes," *St. Louis Post-Dispatch*, Sept. 14, 1907, 1.

35 Khalil Gibran Muhammad, *The Condemnation of Blackness*, 5, 51–52, 56.

36 Muhammad, *The Condemnation of Blackness*, 39–41.

37 "Men and Religion Conservation Congress: Seven Months of Campaigning has Come to a Close," *New York Observer*, Vol. 90, no. 17 (April 25, 1912): 519.

38 This was a YMCA publication. Richmond P. Hobson, "The Church in Relation to Temperance," 156.

39 Hobson, "The Church in Relation to Temperance," 157–160.

40 Richmond P. Hobson, "Speech of Capt. Richmond P. Hobson Delivered at Tuscaloosa, Alabama, March 21, 1914," 4–5, Box 30, Folder 8, LOC-HOB.

41 Malcolm Delevigne to Dame Rachel Crowdy, letter, 14 April 1926, Box R775, Folder 26835, LON.

42 David Starr Jordan to Richmond P. Hobson, letter, 6 Dec. 1923, Box 110, Folder 946, SU; David Starr Jordan to Richmond P. Hobson, letter, 18 June 1924, Box 113, Folder 962, SU; Olin West to David Starr Jordan, letter, 15 Aug. 1924 and David Starr Jordan to Richmond P. Hobson, letter, Aug. 27, 1924, Box 113, Folder 965, SU.

43 Pershing appears to have been hesitant to participate in the organization in the first place, and to have disagreed with some of the WCNE's goals. In December H.S. Middlemiss wrote Pershing informing him that Hobson had not paid her $1250 per their contract and that he was being cagey about it. She planned to sue.

Pershing resigned very soon after the letter. John J. Pershing to Walter Lineberger, letter, 6 Jan. 1926; H. S. Middlemiss to John J. Pershing, letter, 8 Dec. 1926; Richmond P. Hobson to John J. Pershing, telegram, 29 Dec. 1926; John J. Pershing to Richmond P. Hobson, telegram, 6 Jan. 1927; all in Box 216, Folder 6, LOC-PER.

44 "Pastors Laud War on Drugs: Indorse Work of Citizens' Committee of 100," *Los Angeles Times*, June 26, 1923, II3.

45 "Snatched by Dealers in Human Souls!," *Washington Post*, June 22, 1924, SM1.

46 "N.T.J." of Department of State, "Education against the Use of Narcotics," internal memo, undated [probably May 1929], File 800.114 N 16 INTERNATIONAL NARCOTIC EDUCATION ASSOCIATION/29, Box 4539, NARACP-DOS-1930.

47 Charles E. Terry and Mildred Pellens, *The Opium Problem*, xiii, 1.

48 Susan L. Speaker, "Demons for the Twentieth Century," 212, 222–229.

49 Jim Baumohl, "Maintaining Orthodoxy," 226–227.

50 Mark A. R. Kleiman and James E. Hawdon, *Encyclopedia of Drug Policy*, 546.

51 Richard Davenport-Hines, *The Pursuit of Oblivion*, 231.

52 David F. Musto, *The American Disease*, 200–202

53 *Deportation of Alien Criminals, Gunmen, Narcotic Dealers, Defectives, Etc.: Hearings Before The Committee on Immigration and Naturalization, House of Representatives, Sixty-Ninth Congress, First Session* (Washington, DC: Government Printing Office, 1926), 13, 19.

54 "Congressman John Miller! Hard Worker! Result Getter!" (pamphlet), 1930, Box 1, Folder 21, UW-MIL.

55 World Conference for Narcotic Education to Gen. John J. Pershing, letter, 9 Oct. 1925, Box 216, Folder 6, LOC-PER.

56 Richmond P. Hobson, "Extracts from the Address of Admiral Richmond P. Hobson at the Massing of the Colors, St. Thomas Church, New York, November 8th, 1937," Box 77, Folder 10, LOC-HOB.

57 Richmond P. Hobson to John D. Rockefeller, letter, 23 Apr. 1928, Box 56, Folder 2, LOC-HOB.

58 Narcotic Education Week mostly ended when Hobson died in 1937, but some places continued to observe it after this. N.E.W. may have been celebrated first in Los Angeles in 1923, since Hobson made a passing reference to it in 1926. World Conference for Narcotic Education to Gen. John J. Pershing, letter, 8 Sept. 1926, Box 216, Folder 6, LOC-PER.

59 "Temperance Education Week" involved not only organized school programming around temperance and introducing temperance topics to children, but also engaging the community, media, and churches to support anti-alcohol goals; "White Ribbon Day" was sometimes used to celebrate WCTU victories, and sometimes to campaign for new reforms. It was unrelated to the contemporary White Ribbon Day, which is about opposing male violence against women. WCTU *Report of the Seventh Convention*, 120; Louise C. Purington, "Temperance and Missions— World White Ribbon Day," *The Union Signal*, Vol. 30, no. 15 (28 July 1904): 3; "'Drys' May Mass in Washington: Anti-Liquor People Planning 'White Ribbon'

Day During Next Session of Congress," *Detroit Free Press* (19 Apr. 1915): 3; "Program for Anti-Cigaret Day, May 20, 1906," *The Union Signal*, Vol. 32, no. 16 (19 Apr. 1906): 11.

60 Harold G. Hoffman, "Proclamation," 31 Jan. 1936, Box 67, Folder 5, LOC-HOB.

61 "Narcotic Education Week Observed," *The Hearne Democrat*, Feb. 20, 1931: 8.

62 F. Harris Leavitt to World Narcotic Defense Association, letter, 31 Jan. 1936, Box 67, Folder 5, LOC-HOB.

63 Patrick T. Campbell to Richmond Pearson Hobson, letter, 22 Jan. 1936, Box 67, Folder 5, LOC-HOB.

64 J. W. Septon to WNDA, letter, 31 Jan. 1936, Box 67, Folder 5, LOC-HOB.

65 William McGinley to Richmond Pearson Hobson, letter, 28 Jan. 1936 and Helen L. Byrnes to WNDA, letter, 23 Jan. 1936, Box 67, Folder 5, LOC-HOB.

66 James De Wolf Perry to Richmond Pearson Hobson, letter, 24 Jan. 1936, Box 67, Folder 5, LOC-HOB.

67 C. B. Jordan to E. C. Elliott, letter, 1 Feb. 1936, Box 67, Folder 5, LOC-HOB.

68 International Narcotic Education Association, "Marihuana or Indian Hemp and its Preparations," Box 46: Subject Files of the Bureau of Narcotics and Dangerous Drugs, 1916–1970, Folder 1 of World Narcotic Defense Association, 1931–1937, NARACP-DEA.

69 Milton R. Palmer to G. S. Brewster, letter, 5 Mar. 1929, Box 67, Folder 1, LOC-HOB.

70 Howard W. Dickey to Richmond Pearson Hobson, letter, 10 May 1933, Box 64, Folder 2, LOC-HOB.

71 Gazi Mustafa Kemal to Captain Richmond P. Hobson, letter, 20 June 1934, Box 67, Folder 4, LOC-HOB.

72 World Narcotic Defense Association, *Sixth Annual Narcotic Education Week: February 21 to 28, 1932: A Rally Call!* Box 67, Folder 3, LOC-HOB.

73 *Union Signal*, Vol. 62, no. 4 (25 Jan. 1936).

74 L. S. Adams, "The World Narcotic Drug Situation," radio address, WABC / National Hook-up, 27 Feb. 1932, Box 67, Folder 3, LOC-HOB.

75 Ida B. Wise Smith, "Narcotic Education," radio address, CBS's Chicago studio, 21 Feb. 1935, Box 67, Folder 3, LOC-HOB.

76 Wise Smith, "Narcotic Education," 6–7.

77 H. R. Laslett and Charles Dalton, *Hygiene*, 8–10, 37–39.

78 [West Virginia] State Department of Education, *A Guide for Teachers Concerning Alcoholic Drinks and Narcotics*, 4, 78, 82–83.

79 Musto, *The American Disease*, 7.

80 See Zimmerman for end date. Zimmerman, *Distilling Democracy*, 115.

81 Andrew Monteith, "The Words of McKenna," 1086–1087.

CONCLUSION

1 CNN, "Program Offers $300 to Sterilize Women," 23 Apr. 2010, https://www.youtube.com/watch?v=eRxo66SzGUU (accessed June 10, 2021).

2   Project Prevention, http://www.projectprevention.org/ (accessed June 10, 2021).

3   Project Prevention.

4   Project Prevention.

5   Erika Dergas, "The Organization Formally Known as CRACK," 190.

6   Christine Rosen, *Preaching Eugenics*, 186; Alexandra Minna Stern, *Eugenic Nation*, 238–239.

7   Iris Lopez, *Matters of Choice*, 7–8.

8   Cara Lea Burnidge, *A Peaceful Conquest*, 3, 59; Christopher H. Evans, *The Social Gospel in American Religion*, 3, 9; Kathleen Flake, "An Enduring Contest," 498–499; Megan Goodwin, *Abusing Religion*, 7, 9–10; Tisa Wenger, *Religious Freedom*, 3, 11, 20.

9   Daniel Patten, "The Mass Incarceration of Nations and the Global War on Drugs," 89–90.

10 Imani Perry, *More Beautiful and More Terrible*, 102–105; Marisol LeBrón, *Policing Life and Death*, 53–55, 64–70; Michael Tonry, *Punishing Race*, 53–76.

11 Imani Perry, *More Beautiful and More Terrible*, 5–7, 15–22, 33–44. See also João H. Costa Vargas, *The Denial of Antiblackness*, 1–4.

12 Miriam Boeri, *Hurt*, 100–101.

13 Lori Ellis, "Examining Sentencing Disparity in Virginia," 117–119, 122–128.

14 Philip M. Pendergast et al., "The Criminal Immigrant Narrative, 1800–2015," 68–71, 74–75.

15 Colin Dayan, *The Law Is a White Dog*, 40.

16 Elizabeth Westrope, "Employment Discrimination on the Basis of Criminal History," 369–370.

17 Gayatri Chakravorty Spivak, "Can the Subaltern Speak?," 48.

18 William L. White, *Slaying the Dragon*, 149.

19 See Spillane for a concurrent opinion. Joseph F. Spillane, *Cocaine*, 161.

20 Linda Richter and Susan E. Foster, "Effectively Addressing Addiction Requires Changing the Language of Addiction," 62–63.

21 Jarrett Zigon, *A War on People*.

22 Matthew Pembleton, *Containing Addiction*, 314.

23 Dallas Willard, *The Disappearance of Moral Knowledge*, 35–40.

Abu-Lughod, Lila. *Do Muslim Women Need Saving?* Cambridge, MA: Harvard University Press, 2013.

Addams, Jane. *A New Conscience and an Ancient Evil.* New York: MacMillan, 1912.

Adeleke, Tunde. *UnAfrican Americans: Nineteenth-Century Black Nationalists and the Civilizing Mission* Lexington: University of Kentucky Press, 1998.

Albanese, Catharine L. *America: Religions & Religion*, 5th ed. Boston: Wadsworth, 2013.

Allen, Chilion B. and Mary A. Allen. *The Man Wonderful in the House Beautiful: An Allegory. Teaching the Principles of Physiology and Hygiene, and the Effects of Stimulants and Narcotics.* New York: Fowler and Wells, 1883.

Ambrose, Linda M. "Aimee Semple McPherson." *Handbook of Pentecostal Identity.* Editor Adam Stewart. DeKalb: Northern Illinois University Press, 2012, 142–146.

Andrew, Elizabeth and Katherine Bushnell. *Opium and Vice: Recent Personal Investigations.* London: Dyer Brothers, 1894.

Arista, Noelani. *The Kingdom and the Republic: Sovereign Hawai'i and the Early United States.* Philadelphia: University of Pennsylvania Press, 2019.

Arthur, T. S. *Ten Nights in a Bar-Room and What I Saw There.* Chicago: David C. Cook Publishing Co., 1854.

Baker, Kelly J. *Gospel According to the Klan: The KKK's Appeal to Protestant America, 1915–1930.* Lawrence: University of Kansas Press, 2011.

Baker, La Reine Helen. *Race Improvement or Eugenics: A Little Book on a Great Subject.* New York: Dodd, Mead and Co., 1912.

Banner, Stuart. *How the Indians Lost Their Land: Law and Power on the Frontier.* Cambridge, MA: Harvard University Press, 2005.

Barop, Helena. "Building the 'Opium Evil' Consensus—The International Opium Commission of Shanghai." *The Journal of Modern European History*, Vol. 13, no. 1 (2015): 115–137.

Bartlett, Elisha. *The "Laws of Sobriety" and "The Temperance Reform": An Address Delivered before the Young Men's Temperance Society in Lowell, March 6, 1836.* Lowell, MA: Dearborn and Bellows, 1836.

Baumohl, Jim. "Maintaining Orthodoxy: The Depression-Era Struggle over Morphine Maintenance in California." *Altering American Consciousness: The History of Alcohol and Drug Use in the United States, 1800–2000.* Editors Sarah W. Tracy and Caroline Jean Acker. Amhurst: University of Massachusetts Press, 2004, 225–266.

Berry, James H., Carl R. Sullivan, Julie Kmiec, and Antoine Douaihy. "Substances of Abuse and Their Clinical Implications." *Substance Use Disorders*. Editors Antoine B. Douaihy and Dennis C. Daley. Oxford: Oxford University Press, 2014, 93–136.

Bishop, Ernest S. *The Narcotic Drug Problem*. New York: MacMillan Co., 1920.

Blaisdell, Albert F. *How to Keep Well: A Text-Book of Health For Use in the Lower Grade of Schools with Special Reference to the Effects of Stimulants and Narcotics on the Bodily Life*. Boston: Lee and Shepard Publishers, 1885.

Blum, Edward J. "'To Doubt This Would Be to Doubt God': Reconstruction and the Decline of Providential Confidence." *Apocalypse and the Millennium in the American Civil War Era*. Editors Ben Wright and Zachary W. Dresser. Baton Rouge: Louisiana State University Press, 2013, 210–252.

Boeri, Miriam. *Hurt: Chronicles of the Drug War Generation*. Berkeley: University of California Press, 2018.

Brewer, Susan A. *Why America Fights: Patriotism and War Propaganda from the Philippines to Iraq*. New York: Oxford University Press, 2009.

Briggs, Laura. *Reproducing Empire: Race, Sex, Science, and US Imperialism in Puerto Rico*. Berkeley: University of California Press, 2002.

Brown, Eli F. *The House I Live In: An Elementary Physiology for Children in the Public Schools*. Cincinnati, OH: Van Antwerp, Bragg, and Co., 1887.

Brown, J. B. "Politics of the Poppy: The Society for the Suppression of the Opium Trade." *Journal of Contemporary History*, Vol. 8, no. 3 (July 1973): 97–111.

Bruinius, Harry. *Better for All the World: The Secret History of Forced Sterilization and America's Quest for Racial Purity*. New York: Alfred A. Knopf, 2006.

Buckelew, Sarah F. and Margaret Wiseham Lewis. *Practical Work in the School Room, Part 1: A Transcript of the Object Lessons of the Human Body*. New York: A. Lovell and Company, 1884.

Buerki, Robert A. "Medical Views on Narcotics and Their Effects in the Mid-1890s." *Pharmacy in History*, Vol. 17, no. 1 (1975): 3–12.

Bull, Malcolm and Keith Lockhart. *Seeking a Sanctuary: Seventh-Day Adventism and the American Dream*, 2nd ed. Bloomington: Indiana University Press, 2007.

Bunting, Charles A. *Hope for the Victims of Alcohol, Opium, Morphine, Cocaine, and Other Vices: A Narration of Successful Efforts During Ten Years of Personal Labor, Devoted as Christ's Instrument to Redeem the Slaves of Such Habits, in the New York Christian Home for Intemperate Men*. New York: Christian Home Building, 1888.

Burnam, John Chynoweth. "Psychology, Psychiatry, and the Progressive Movement." *American Quarterly*, Vol. 12, no. 4 (Winter 1960): 457–465.

Burnidge, Cara Lea. *A Peaceful Conquest: Woodrow Wilson, Religion, and the New World Order*. Chicago: University of Chicago Press, 2016.

Burrell, Caroline Benedict and William Byron Forbush. *The Mother's Book: A Handbook for the Physical, Mental, and Moral Training of Children*. New York: The University Society, 1919.

Butler, Jon. *Awash in a Sea of Faith: Christianizing the American People*. Cambridge, MA: Harvard University Press, 1990.

Butler, Judith. "Is Judaism Zionism?" *The Power of Religion in the Public Sphere*. Editors Eduardo Mendieta and Jonathan Vanantwerpen. New York: Columbia University Press, 2012.

———. *Giving an Account of Oneself*. New York: Fordham University Press, 2005.

Calabrese, Joseph D. *A Different Medicine: Postcolonial Healing in the Native American Church*. New York: Oxford University Press, 2013.

Callahan, Michael D. *Mandates and Empire: The League of Nations and Africa, 1914–1931*. Brighton, UK: Sussex Academic Press, 1999.

Carlson, Douglas W. "'Drinks to His Own Undoing': Temperance Ideology in the Deep South." *Journal of the Early Republic*, Vol. 18, no. 4 (Winter 1998): 659–691.

Carlson, Elof Axel. "The Hoosier Connection: Compulsory Sterilization as Moral Hygiene." *A Century of Eugenics in America: From the Indiana Experiment to the Human Genome Era*. Editor Paul A. Lombardo. Bloomington: Indiana University Press, 2011, 11–25.

Casamajor, Louis. "The Treatment of the Toxemias of Dangerous Trades and of Drugs." *The Modern Treatment of Nervous and Mental Diseases by American and British Authors, Volume II*. Editors William A. White and Smith Ely Jelliffe. Philadelphia: Lea & Febiger, 1913, 672–695.

Chavigny, Katherine A. "Reforming Drunkards in Nineteenth-Century America: Religion, Medicine, Therapy." *Altering American Consciousness: The History of Alcohol and Drug Use in the United States, 1800–2000*. Editors Sarah W. Tracy and Caroline Jean Acker. Amhurst: University of Massachusetts Press, 2004, 108–123.

Clark, Caroline. "Contrasting Medical Models of Alcohol Problems in Victoria around 1900." *Addiction*, Vol. 107, no. 10 (October 2012): 1756–1764.

Clark, Norman H. Deliver Us From Evil: An Interpretation of American Prohibition. (New York: W. W. Norton & Co., 1976.

Clark, Victor S. "Labor Conditions in Java." *Bulletin of the Bureau of Labor*, no. 58 (May 1905): 906–954.

Cobbe, Frances Power. "The Evolution of Morals and Religion." *Darwinism in Morals, and Other Essays*. Edinburgh: Williams and Norgate, 1872.

Cohen, Michael M. "Jim Crow's Drug War: Race, Coca Cola, and the Southern Origins of Drug Prohibition." *Southern Culture*, Vol. 12, no. 6 (Fall 2006): 55–79.

Coker, Joe L. *Liquor in the Land of the Lost Cause: Southern White Evangelicals and the Prohibition Movement*. Lexington: University of Kentucky Press, 2007.

Conroy-Krutz, Emily. *Christian Imperialism: Converting the World in the Early American Republic*. Ithaca, NY: Cornell University Press, 2015.

Corradini, Robert E. *Narcotics and Youth Today*. New York: Foundation for Narcotics Research and Information, 1934.

Courtright, David T. *Forces of Habit: Drugs and the Making of the Modern World*. Cambridge, MA: Harvard University Press, 2001.

Crafts, Wilbur Fisk Crafts et al. *Intoxicating Drinks & Drugs in All Lands and Times: A Twentieth Century Survey of Intemperance, Based on a Symposium of Testimony*

From One Hundred Missionaries and Travelers, 10th ed. Washington, DC: International Reform Bureau, 1909.

———. *Protection of Native Races Against Intoxicants & Opium: Based on Testimony from One Hundred Missionaries and Travelers*. Chicago: Fleming H. Revell Co., 1900.

Crangle, John V. "Joseph Whitwell Pease and the Quaker Role in the Campaign to Suppress the Opium Trade in the British Empire." *Quaker History*, Vol. 68, no. 2 (Autumn 1979): 63–74.

Crothers, T. D. *The Disease of Inebriety from Alcohol, Opium, and Other Narcotic Drugs:, its Etiology, Pathology, Treatment and Medico-Legal Relations*. New York: E.B. Treat, 1893.

Dana, Charles L. "Alcoholism as a Cause of Insanity." *The Annals of the American Academy of Political and Social Science*, Vol. 34, no. 1 (July 1909): 81–84.

Daniels, William Haven. *The Temperance Reform and Its Great Reformers*. New York: Nelson & Phillips, 1878.

Davenport-Hines, Richard. *The Pursuit of Oblivion: A Global History of Narcotics*. New York: W.W. Norton & Co., 2002.

Davis, Marni. "'No Whisky Amazons in the Tents of Israel': American Jews and the Gilded Age Temperance Movement." *American Jewish History*, Vol. 94, no. 3 (Sept. 2008): 143–173.

Dawson, Alexander. *The Peyote Effect: From the Inquisition to the War on Drugs*. Oakland: University of California Press, 2018.

Dawson, George E. "Psychic Rudiments and Morality." *The American Journal of Psychology*, Vol. 11, no. 2 (Jan. 1900): 217.

Dayan, Colin. *The Law Is a White Dog: How Legal Rituals Make and Unmake Persons*. Princeton, NJ: Princeton University Press, 2011.

Deacon, Harriet. "Racial Categories and Psychiatry in Africa: The Asylum on Robbin Island in the Nineteenth Century." *Race, Science and Medicine, 1700–1960*. Editors Waltraud Ernst and Bernard Harris. London: Routledge, 1999, 101–122.

Dees, Sarah. "An Equation of Language and Spirit: Comparative Philology in the Study of American Indian Religions." *Method & Theory in the Study of Religion*, Vol. 27, no. 3 (2015): 195–219.

Dergas, Erika. "The Organization Formally Known as CRACK: Project Prevention and the Privatized Assault on Reproductive Wellbeing." *Race, Gender, and Class*, Vol. 19, no. 3 (2012): 179–195.

D'Erlanger, Harry. *The Last Plague of Egypt*. London: Lovat Dickson & Thompson Ltd, 1936.

de Gobineau, Arthur. *The Inequality of Human Races*. Translator Adrian Collins. New York: G.P. Putnam's Sons, 1915.

Deloria, Philip J. *Indians in Unexpected Places*. Lawrence: University Press of Kansas, 2004.

Demel, Walter. "How the 'Mongoloid Race' Came into Being: Late Eighteenth-Century Constructions of East Asians in Europe." *Race and Racism in Modern East Asia:*

Western and Eastern Constructions. Editors Rotem Kowner and Walter Demel. Leiden: Brill, 2012, 59–86.

De Quincey, Thomas. *Confessions of an English Opium-Eater*, 5th ed. London: Bradbury & Evans, 1847.

Dippie, Brian W. *The Vanishing American: White Attitudes and US Indian Policy*. Middletown, CT: Wesleyan University Press, 1982.

Dowd, Jerome. *The Negro Races: A Sociological Study, Vol. II*. New York: Neale Publishing Co. 1914.

Durst, Dennis. "Evangelical Engagements with Eugenics, 1900–1940." *Ethics & Medicine*, Vol. 18, no. 2 (Summer 2002): 45–53.

Ebel, Jonathan. "The Great War, Religious Authority, and the American Fighting Man." *Church History*, Vol. 78, no. 1 (March 2009): 99–133.

Edman, Johan. "Temperance and Modernity: Alcohol Consumption as a Collective Problem, 1885–1913." *Journal of Social History*, Vol. 49, no. 1 (Fall 2015): 20–52.

Ellis, Lori. "Examining Sentencing Disparity in Virginia: The Impact of Race and Sex on Mitigating Departures for Drug Offenders." *Race, Ethnicity and Law*. Editor Mathieu Deflem. Bingley, UK: Emerald, 2017.

Engs, Ruth Clifford. *The Progressive Era's Health Reform Movement: A Historical Dictionary* Westport, CT: Praeger, 2003.

Erlenmeyer, Albrecht. *On the Treatment of the Morphine Habit*. Detroit: George S. Davis, 1889.

Evans, Christopher H. *The Social Gospel in American Religion: A History*. New York: New York University Press, 2017.

Fear-Segal, Jacqueline and Susan D. Rose. *Carlisle Industrial School: Indigenous Histories, Memories, and Reclamations*. Lincoln: Nebraska University Press, 2016.

Feld, Barry C. "Criminalizing the Juvenile Court." *Crime and Justice*, vol. 17, no. 3 (1993): 197–280.

Fessenden, Tracy. *Culture and Redemption: Religion, the Secular, and American Literature*. Princeton, NJ: Princeton University Press, 2007.

Fixico, Donald L. *Bureau of Indian Affairs*. Santa Barbara, CA: Greenwood, 2012.

Flake, Kathleen. "An Enduring Contest: American Christianities and the State." *American Christianities: A History of Dominance and Diversity*. Editors Catherine A. Brekus and W. Clark Gilpin. Chapel Hill: University of North Carolina Press, 2011, 491–508.

Foster, Anne L. "Medicine to Drug: Opium's Transimperial Journey." *Crossing Empires: Taking US History into Transimperial Terrain*. Editors Kristin L. Hoganson and Jay Sexton. Durham, NC: Duke University Press, 2020, 112–132.

Foster, Gaines M. *Moral Reconstruction: Christian Lobbyists and the Federal Legislation of Morality, 1865–1920*. Chapel Hill: University of North Carolina Press, 2002.

Foucault, Michel. *Psychiatric Power: Lectures at the Collège de France, 1973–1974*. Editor Jacques Lagrange, translator Graham Burchell. New York: Picador, 2003.

———. *Discipline and Punish: The Birth of the Prison*. Translator Alan Sheridan. New York: Vintage Press, 1995.

———. *The History of Sexuality, Volume 1: An Introduction.* Translator Robert Hurley. New York: Vintage Books, 1990.

———. *Madness and Civilization: A History of Insanity in the Age of Reason.* Translator Richard Howard. New York: Vintage Books, 1988.

———. *Power / Knowledge: Selected Interviews and other Writings, 1972–1977.* Editor Colin Gordon, translator Colin Gordon et al. New York: Pantheon Books, 1980.

Fry, William Storrs. *The Opium Trade with China.* London: Pelham Richardson, 1840.

Gach, John. "Biological Psychiatry in the Nineteenth and Twentieth Centuries," *History of Psychiatry and Medical Psychology: With an Epilogue on Psychiatry and the Mind-Body Relation.* Editors Edwin R. Wallace IV and John Gach. New York: Springer, 2008, 381–418.

Galton, Francis. *Inquiries into Human Faculty and Its Development.* London: MacMillan, 1883.

Gaston, K. Healan. *Imagining Judeo-Christian America: Religion, Secularism, and the Redefinition of Democracy.* Chicago: University of Chicago Press, 2019.

Gettis, Victoria. *The Juvenile Court and the Progressives.* Urbana: University of Illinois Press, 2000.

Glover, Noel. "Citizenship at Odds: Disability, Liberalism, and the Shame of Interdependence." *American Shame: Stigma and the Body Politic.* Editor Myra Mendible. Bloomington: Indiana University Press, 2016, 145–163.

Go, Julian. *American Empire and the Politics of Meaning: Elite Political Cultures in the Philippines and Puerto Rico during US Colonialism.* Durham, NC: Duke University Press, 2008.

Goode, Erich and Nachman Ben-Yehuda. *Moral Panics: The Social Construction of Deviance.* Second edition. Chichester, UK: Wiley-Blackwell, 2009.

Goodwin, Megan. *Abusing Religion: Literary Persecution, Sex Scandals, and American Minority Religions.* New Brunswick, NJ: Rutgers University Press, 2020.

Gootenberg, Paul. *Cocaine: Global Histories.* New York: Routledge, 1999.

Gordon, Anna A. *The Beautiful Life of Frances E. Willard: A Memorial Volume.* Chicago: Woman's Temperance Publishing Association, 1898.

Gordon, Sarah Barringer. *The Mormon Question: Polygamy and Constitutional Conflict in Nineteenth-Century America.* Chapel Hill: University of North Carolina Press, 2002.

Graber, Jennifer. *The Gods of Indian Country: Religion and the Struggle for the American West.* New York: Oxford University Press, 2018.

Gray, Elizabeth Kelly. "The Trade-Off: Chinese Opium Traders and Antebellum Reform in the United States, 1815–1860." *Drugs and Empires: Essays in Modern Imperialism and Intoxication, 1500–1930.* Editors James H. Mills and Patricia Barton. Basingstroke, UK: Palgrave Macmillan, 2007, 220–242.

Green, Stephen K. *Inventing a Christian America: The Myth of the Religious Founding.* New York: Oxford University Press, 2015.

———. *The Bible, the School, and the Constitution: The Clash that Shaped Modern Church-State Doctrine.* New York: Oxford University Press, 2012.

Grenfell, Wilfred T. in F. A. McKenzie. *"Pussyfoot" Johnson: Crusader—Reformer—A Man Among Men*. New York: Fleming H. Revell Co., 1920.

Guillaumin, Collette. *Race, Sexism, Power, and Ideology*. London: Routledge, 1995.

Hague, W. Grant. *The Eugenic Mother and Baby: A Complete Home Guide*. New York: Hague Publishing Co., 1913.

Hall, Stuart et al. *Policing the Crisis: Mugging, The State, and Law and Order*. London: Macmillan Press, 1978.

Hawkins, John A. *Opium and Opium Addicts*. Boston: Bruce Humphries Inc, 1937.

Healy, William. *Personality in Formation and Action*. New York: W.W. Norton & Co, 1938.

———. *The Individual Delinquent: A Text-Book of Diagnosis and Prognosis For All Concerned in Understanding Offenders*. Boston: Little, Brown & Co., 1920.

———. "Present Day Aims and Methods in Studying the Offender." *Journal of the American Institute of Criminal Law and Criminology*, Vol. 4, no. 2 (July 1913): 204–211.

Hickman, Timothy A. "Mania Americana: Narcotic Addiction and Modernity in the United States, 1870–1920." *The Journal of American History*, Vol. 90, no. 4 (March 2004): 1269–1294.

Hilts, Phillip J. *Protecting America's Health: The FDA, Business, and One Hundred Years of Regulation*. New York: Alfred A. Knopf, 2003.

Hitchcock, Edward. *An Argument for Early Temperance; Addressed to the Youth of the United States*. Whipple and Damrell: Boston, 1837.

Hobson, Richmond P. *Alcohol and the Human Race*. New York: Fleming H. Revell Co., 1919.

———. "The Church in Relation to Temperance." *Messages of the Men and Religion Forward Movement: Vol. I: Congress Addresses*. New York: Association Press, 1912, 152–164.

Horsman, Reginald. *Race and Manifest Destiny: The Origins of American Racial Anglo-Saxonism* Cambridge, MA: Harvard University Press, 1981.

Hubbard, Frederick Heman. *The Opium Habit and Alcoholism: A Treatise on The Habits of Opium and its Compounds; Alcohol; Chloral-Hydrate; Chloroform; Bromide Potassium; and Cannabis Indica: Including Their Therapeutical Indications: With Suggestions for Treating Various Painful Complications*. New York: A. S. Barnes & Co., 1881.

Hunt, James B. "Jane Addams: The Presbyterian Connection." *American Presbyterians*, Vol. 68, no. 4 (Winter 1990): 231–244.

Hunt, Mary H. *A History of the First Decade of the Department of Scientific Temperance Instruction in Schools and Colleges, of the Woman's Christian Temperance Union in Three Parts*, 3rd ed. Boston: Washington Press, 1892.

———. *The Child's Health Primer for Primary Classes: With Special Reference to the Effects of Alcoholic Drinks, Stimulants, and Narcotics Upon the Human System*. New York: A.S. Barnes & Co., 1884.

Huntington, Ellsworth. *Tomorrow's Children: The Goal of Eugenics*. New York: John Wiley and Sons, 1935.

Imhoff, Sarah. *The Lives of Jessie Sampter: Queer, Disabled, Zionist*. Durham, NC: Duke University Press, 2022.

Jacobson, Matthew Frye. *Whiteness of a Different Color: European Immigrants and the Alchemy of Race*. Cambridge, MA: Harvard University Press, 1998.

James, William. *The Varieties of Religious Experience*. New York: Penguin Books, 1982.

Jennings, John M. "The Forgotten Plague: Opium and Narcotics in Korea under Japanese Rule, 1910–1945." *Modern Asian Studies*, Vol. 29, no. 4 (October 1995): 795–815.

Johnson, Sylvester A. *African American Religions, 1500–2000: Colonialism, Democracy, and Freedom*. New York: Cambridge University Press, 2015.

———. "Religion and American Empire in Mississippi, 1790–1833." *Gods of the Mississippi*. Editor Michael Pasquier. Bloomington: Indiana University Press, 2013, 36–55.

Jones, Gregg. *Honor in the Dust: Theodore Roosevelt, War in the Philippines, and the Rise and Fall of America's Imperial Dream*. New York: New American Library, 2012.

Jones, Kathleen W. *Taming the Troublesome Child: American Families, Child Guidance, and the Limits of Psychiatric Authority*. Cambridge, MA: Harvard University Press, 1992.

Katcher, Bryan S. "Public Health Then and Now: Benjamin Rush's Educational Campaign against Hard Drinking." *American Journal of Public Health*, Vol. 83, no. 2 (February 1993): 273–282.

Keane, Webb. *Christian Moderns: Freedom and Fetish in the Mission Encounter*. Berkeley: University of California Press, 2007.

Keel, Terence. *Divine Variations: How Christian Thought Became Racial Science*. Stanford, CA: Stanford University Press, 2018.

Keeley, Leslie E. *The Morphine Eater: From Bondage to Freedom*. Dwight, IL: C.L. Palmer & Co., 1881.

Kellogg, John Harvey. *Life: Its Mysteries and Miracles*. Battle Creek, MI: Modern Medicine Publishing Co., 1910.

———. *Man the Masterpiece or Plain Truths Plainly Told about Boyhood, Youth, and Manhood*. Battle Creek, MI: Modern Medicine Publishing Co., 1909.

———. *Second Book in Physiology and Hygiene*. New York: American Book Company, 1894.

Kenny, Gale and Tisa Wenger,. "Church, State, and 'Native Liberty' in the Belgian Congo." *Comparative Studies in Society and History*, Vol. 62, no. 1 (2020): 156–185.

Kerr, J. G. "Opium in China." *Opinions of Over 100 Physicians on the Use of Opium in China*. Editor William Hector Park. Shanghai: American Presbyterian Mission Press, 1899, 69–72.

Kleiman, Mark A. R. and James E Hawdon. *Encyclopedia of Drug Policy, Vol 2*. Thousand Oaks, CA: SAGE, 2011.

Kramer, Paul A. *The Blood of Government: Race, Empire, the United States, & The Philippines*. Chapel Hill: University of North Carolina Press, 2006.

Kurashige, Lon. *Two Faces of Exclusion: The Untold History of Anti-Asian Racism in the United States*. Chapel Hill: University of North Carolina Press, 2016.

Laslett, H. R. and Charles Dalton. *Hygiene: A Way to Happiness*. Editor Forrest D. Mc-Crae. Crawfordsville, IN: R.R. Alexander & Sons, 1936.

LeBrón, Marisol. *Policing Life and Death: Race, Violence, and Resistance in Puerto Rico*. Berkeley: University of California Press, 2019.

Letchworth, William Pryor. *Care and Treatment of Epileptics*. New York: G.P. Putnam's Sons. 1900.

Lodwick, Kathleen L. *Crusaders Against Opium: Protestant Missionaries in China, 1874–1917*. Lexington: University Press of Kentucky, 1995.

Lopez, Iris. *Matters of Choice: Puerto Rican Women's Struggle for Reproductive Freedom*. New Brunswick, NJ: Rutgers University Press, 2008.

Lum, Kathryn Gin. *Damned Nation: From the Revolution to Reconstruction*. New York: Oxford University Press, 2014.

MacDonald, Arthur. *Abnormal Man: Being Essays on Education and Crime and Related Subjects, with Digests of Literature and a Bibliography*. Washington, DC: Government Printing Office, 1893.

Macmillan, Malcolm. *An Odd Kind of Fame: Stories of Phineas Gage*. Cambridge, MA: MIT Press, 2002.

MacNair, J. Duncan. "Colony Life of an Epileptic, Social and Religious." *Transactions of the National Association for the Study of Epilepsy and the Care and Treatment of Epileptics, Seventh Annual Meeting, Richmond, VA., Oct. 24, 1907, Vol. V*. Editor William P. Spratling. Dansville, NY: F.A. Owen Co., 1907, 67–73.

Mancall, Peter C. "'I Was Addicted to Drinking Rum': Four Centuries of Alcohol Consumption in Indian Country." *Altering American Consciousness: The History of Alcohol and Drug Use in the United States, 1800–2000*. Editors Sarah W. Tracy and Caroline Jean Acker. Amhurst: University of Massachusetts Press, 2004, 91–107.

Mann, Horace. *Lectures on Education*. Boston: Ides & Dunn, 1855.

Marilley, Suzanne M. "Frances Willard and the Feminism of Fear." *Feminist Studies*, Vol. 19, no. 1 (Spring 1993): 123–146.

Maroukis, Thomas C. *The Peyote Road: Religious Freedom and the Native American Church*. Norman: University of Oklahoma Press, 2010.

Marsden, George M. *Fundamentalism and American Culture*, 2nd ed. New York: Oxford University Press, 2006.

Martin, Jill E. "'The Greatest Evil': Interpretations of Indian Prohibition Laws, 1832–1953." *Great Plains Quarterly*, Vol. 23, no. 1 (Winter 2003): 35–53.

Masuzawa, Tomoko. *The Invention of World Religions: Or, How European Universalism was Preserved in the Language of Pluralism*. Chicago: University of Chicago Press, 2005.

Mattison, J. B. *The Treatment of Opium Addiction*. New York: G.B. Putnam's Sons. 1885.

McClennen, Sophia A. and Joseph R. Slaughter. "Introducing Human Rights and Literary Forms; or, the Vehicles and Vocabularies of Human Rights." *Comparative Literature Studies*, Vol. 46, no. 1 (2009): 1–19.

McCullough, Matthew. *The Cross of War: Christian Nationalism and US Expansion in the Spanish-American War*. Madison: University of Wisconsin Press, 2014.

McGirr, Lisa. *The War on Alcohol: Prohibition and the Rise of the American State*. New York: W.W. Norton & Co., 2016.

Merrill, John L. "The Bible and the American Temperance Movement: Text, Context, and Pretext." *The Harvard Theological Review*, Vol. 81, no. 2 (April 1988): 145–170.

Meyer, Sabine N. *We Are What We Drink: The Temperance Battle in Minnesota*. Champaign: University of Illinois Press, 2015.

Mezivinsky, Norton. "Scientific Temperance in the Schools." *History of Education Quarterly*, Vol. 1, no. 1 (Mar. 1961): 48–56.

Michigan. *Twenty-Third Biennial Report of the Michigan State Board of Corrections and Charities, 1915–1916*. Lansing: Wynkoop Hallenbeck Crawford Co. 1916.

Modern, John Lardas. *Secularism in Antebellum America: With Reference to Ghosts, Protestant Subcultures . . .* Chicago: University of Chicago Press, 2013.

Molina, Natalia. *How Race Is Made in America: Immigration, Citizenship, and the Historical Power of Racial Scripts*. Berkeley: University of California Press, 2014.

Molnar, Nicole Trajano. *American Mestizos, the Philippines, and the Malleability of Race:1898–1961*. Columbia: University of Missouri Press, 2017.

Monteith, Andrew. "'The Words of McKenna': Healing, Political Critique, and the Evolution of Psychonaut Religion since the 1960s Counterculture." *Journal of the American Academy of Religion*, Vol. 84, no. 4 (Winter 2016): 1081–1109.

Moorhead, James H. *World Without End: Mainstream American Protestant Visions of the Last Things, 1880–1925*. Bloomington: Indiana University Press, 1999.

Moreau, Jacques-Joseph. *Hashish and Mental Illness*. Editors Hélène Peters and Gabriel G. Nahas, translator Gordon J. Barnett. New York: Raven Press, 1973.

Morel, B. A. *Traité des Dégénérescences Physiques, Intellectuelles et Morales de l'Espèce Humaine et des Causes qui Produisent ces Variétés Maladives*. Paris: J. B. Ballière, 1857.

Morgan, David. *Protestants & Pictures: Religion, Visual Culture and the Age of American Mass Production*. New York: Oxford University Press, 1999.

Morgan, H. Wayne. *Drugs in America: A Social History, 1800–1980*. Syracuse, NY: Syracuse University Press, 1981.

Moule, A. E. *The Use of Opium and Its Bearing on the Spread of Christianity in China: A Paper Read Before the Shanghai Missionary Conference, 19th May, 1877*. Shanghai: Church Missionary Society, 1877.

Muhammad, Khalil Gibran. *The Condemnation of Blackness: Race, Crime, and the Making of Modern Urban America*. Cambridge, MA: Harvard University Press, 2010.

Musto, David F. *The American Disease: Origins of Narcotic Control*, 3rd ed. New York: Oxford University Press, 1999.

Myers, Denys P. "The Mandate System of the League of Nations." *The Annals of the American Academy of Political and Social Science*, Vol. 96 (July 1921): 74–77.

Nackenoff, Carol and Kathleen S. Sullivan. "The House that Julia (and Friends) Built: Networking Chicago's Juvenile Court." *Statebuilding from the Margins: Between*

Reconstruction and the New Deal. Editors Carol Nackenoff and Julie Novkov. Philadelphia: University of Pennsylvania Press, 2014, 171–202.

Nelson, E. *The Use of Ardent Spirits in a Professing Christian A Great Sin: A Discourse, Delivered Before the Temperance Society in Woburn, December 14, 1829*. Boston: Peirce and Williams, 1830.

Nevius, John L. *Demon Possession and Allied Themes: Being an Inductive Study of Phenomena of our Own Times*. Chicago: Fleming H. Revell Co., 1894.

Noll, Mark A. *The Civil War as a Theological Crisis*. Chapel Hill: University of North Carolina Press, 2006.

———. *America's God: From Jonathan Edwards to Abraham Lincoln*. New York: Oxford University Press, 2002.

Osborn, Christabel. "Economic Aspects of the Liquor Problem." *The Economic Journal*, Vol. 8, no. 32 (December 1898): 572–577.

Osborn, Matthew Warner. *Rum Maniacs: Alcoholic Insanity in the Early American Republic*. Chicago: Chicago University Press, 2014.

Owens-Adair, B. A. *Human Sterilization: It's Social and Legislative Aspects* [sic]. No publisher information, 1922.

Paddison, Joshua. *American Heathens: Race, Religion, and Reconstruction in California*. Berkeley: University of California Press, 2012.

Padwa, Howard. *Social Poison: The Culture and Politics of Opiate Control in Britain and France, 1821–1926*. Baltimore, MD: Johns Hopkins University Press, 2012.

Page, J. Bryan and Merrill Singer. *Comprehending Drug Use: Ethnographic Research at the Social Margins*. New Brunswick, NJ: Rutgers University Press, 2010.

Parker, Graham. "The Juvenile Court Movement: The Illinois Experience." *The University of Toronto Law Journal*, Vol. 26, no. 3 (Summer 1976): 253–306.

Parsons, Elaine Frantz. *Manhood Lost: Fallen Drunkards and Redeeming Women in Nineteenth-Century United States*. Baltimore, MD: Johns Hopkins University Press, 2003.

Patten, Daniel. "The Mass Incarceration of Nations and the Global War on Drugs: Comparing the United States' Domestic and Foreign Policies." *Social Justice*, Vol. 43, no. 1 (2016): 85–105.

Pedersen, Susan. *The Guardians: The League of Nations and the Crisis of Empire*. New York: Oxford University Press, 2015.

Pembleton, Matthew R. *Containing Addiction: The Federal Bureau of Narcotics and the Origins of America's Global Drug War*. Amhurst: University of Massachusetts Press, 2017.

Pendergast, Philip M., Tim Wadsworth, and Joshua LaPress. "The Criminal Immigrant Narrative, 1800–2015." *The Handbook of Race, Ethnicity, Crime, and Justice*. Editors Ramiro Martinez, Jr., Megan E. Hollis, and Jacob I. Stowell. Hoboken, NJ: Wiley Blackwell, 2018.

Perry, Imani. *More Beautiful and More Terrible: The Embrace and Transcendence of Racial Inequality in the United States*. New York: New York University Press, 2011.

Petro, Anthony M. *After The Wrath of God: AIDS, Sexuality, and American Religion*. New York: Oxford University Press, 2015.

Pettey, George Eugene. *The Narcotic Drug Diseases and Allied Ailments: Pathology, Pathogenesis, and Treatment*. Philadelphia: F. A. Davis Company, 1913.

Price, Barton E. "Religion, Reform, and Patriotism in Southern Illinois: A Case Study, 1852–1900." *Journal of the Illinois State Historical Society*, Vol. 107, no. 2 (Summer 2014): 171–203.

Proceedings of the First National Conference on Race Betterment. Battle Creek, MI: Race Betterment Foundation, 1914.

Quinn, John F. *Father Mathew's Crusade: Temperance in Nineteenth-Century Ireland and Irish America*. Amhurst: University of Massachusetts Press, 2002.

Quintero, Gilbert. "Making the Indian: Colonial Knowledge, Alcohol, and Native Americans." *American Indian Culture and Research Journal*, Vol. 25, no. 4 (2001): 57–71.

Rafter, Nicole, Chad Posick, and Michael Roque. *The Criminal Brain: Understanding Theories of Crime*, 2nd ed. New York: New York University Press, 2016.

Rappaport, Erika. "Sacred and Useful Pleasures: The Temperance Tea Party and the Creation of a Sober Consumer Culture in Early Industrial Britain." *Journal of British Studies*, Vol. 52, no. 4 (October 2013): 990–1016.

Reasons, Charles. "The Politics of Drugs: An Inquiry into the Sociology of Social Problems." *The Sociological Quarterly*, Vol. 15, no. 3 (Summer 1974): 381–404.

Redford, Audrey and Benjamin Powell. "Dynamics of Intervention in the War on Drugs: The Buildup to the Harrison Narcotic Tax Act of 1914." *The Independent Review*, Vol. 20, no. 4 (Spring 2016): 509–530.

Ren, Zhen-Yu et al. "Abnormal Pain Response in Pain-Sensitive Opiate Addicts after Prolonged Abstinence Predicts Increased Drug Craving." *Psychopharmacology*, Vol. 204 (2009): 423–429.

Rhoades, Mabel Carter. "A Case Study of Delinquent Boys in the Juvenile Court of Chicago." *American Journal of Sociology*, Vol. 13, no. 1 (July 1907): 56–78.

Richards, Graham. *Race, Racism, and Psychology: Towards A Reflexive History*. London: Routledge, 1997.

Richter, Linda and Susan E. Foster. "Effectively Addressing Addiction Requires Changing the Language of Addiction." *Journal of Public Health Policy*, Vol. 35, no. 1 (2014): 60–64.

Roberts, Albert R. and Patricia Brownell. "A Century of Forensic Social Work: Building the Past to the Present." *Social Work*, Vol. 44, no. 4 (July 1999): 359–369.

Robinson, William J. *Eugenics, Marriage, and Birth Control: Practical Eugenics*. 2nd ed. New York: The Critic and Guide Co., 1922.

Roosevelt, Theodore. *A Compilation of the Messages and Speeches of Theodore Roosevelt, 1901–1905*. Editor Alfred Henry Lewis. New York: Bureau of National Literature and Art, 1906.

Rorabaugh, W. J. "Alcohol in America." *OAH Magazine of History*, Vol. 6, no. 2 (Fall 1991): 17–19.

Rosen, Christine. *Preaching Eugenics: Religious Leaders and the Eugenics Movement.* New York: Oxford University Press, 2004.

Sadler, William. *Race Decadence: An Examination of the Causes of Racial Degeneracy in the United States.* Chicago: McClurg & Co., 1922.

Salem, Elizabeth Ann. "Gendered Bodies, Nervous Minds: Creating Addiction in America, 1770–1910." PhD dissertation, Case Western Reserve University, 2016.

Shannon, Thomas W. *Single Standard Eugenics.* Marietta, OH: S.A. Mullikin Co., 1914.

Sharma, Ravi C., Ramesh Kumar, Dinesh Dutt Sharma, and Pankaj Kanwar. "Opium Withdrawal Delirium: Two Case Studies." *Psychopharmacological Bulletin*, Vol. 47, no. 1 (2017): 48–51.

Shrag, Peter. *Not Fit for our Society: Immigration and Nativism in America.* Berkeley: University of California Press, 2010.

Silva, Noenoe K. *Aloha Betrayed: Native Hawaiian Resistance to American Colonialism.* Durham, NC: Duke University Press, 2004.

Silver, Peter. *Our Savage Neighbors: How Indian War Transformed Early America.* New York: W.W. Norton, 2008.

Smith, E. Franklin. *Text-Book of Anatomy, Physiology, and Hygiene.* New York: William R. Jenkins, 1898.

Smith, Jonathan Z. "What a Difference a Difference Makes." *Relating Religion: Essays in the Study of Religion.* Chicago: University of Chicago Press, 2004, 251–302.

———. "The Devil in Mr. Jones." *Imagining Religion: From Babylon to Jonestown.* Chicago: University of Chicago Press, 1982, 102–120.

Smith, Norman. *Intoxicating Manchuria: Alcohol, Opium, and Culture in China's Northeast.* Vancouver: University of British Columbia Press, 2012.

Snyder, Sharon L. and David T. Mitchell. *Cultural Locations of Disability.* Chicago: University of Chicago Press, 2006.

Speaker, Susan L. "Demons for the Twentieth Century: The Rhetoric of Drug Reform, 1920–1940." *Altering American Consciousness: The History of Alcohol and Drug Use in the United States, 1800–2000.* Editors Sarah W. Tracy and Caroline Jean Acker. Amhurst: University of Massachusetts Press, 2004, 203–225.

———. "'The Struggle of Mankind Against Its Deadliest Foe': Themes of Counter-Subversion in Anti-Narcotic Campaigns, 1920–1940." *Journal of Social History*, Vol. 34, no. 3 (Spring 2001): 591–610.

Spillane, Joseph F. *Cocaine: From Medical Marvel to Modern Menace in the United States, 1884–1920.* Baltimore, MD: Johns Hopkins University Press, 2000.

Spiro, Jonathan Peter. *Defending the Master Race: Conservation, Eugenics, and the Legacy of Madison Grant.* Burlington: University of Vermont Press, 2009.

Spivak, Gayatri Chakravorty. "'Can the Subaltern Speak?' revised edition." *Can the Subaltern Speak?* Editor Rosalind C. Morris. New York: Columbia University Press, 2010, 21–80.

Stack, David. "William Lovett and the National Association for the Political and Social Improvement of the People." *The Historical Journal*, Vol. 42, no. 4 (December 1999): 1027–1050.

The Standard History of the World by Great Historians, Vol. IV. Editor John H. Clifford. New York: The University Society Inc., 1914.

Stearns, Peter N. *Shame: A Brief History*. Urbana: University of Illinois Press, 2007.

Stern, Alexandra Minna. *Eugenic Nation: Faults and Frontiers of Better Breeding in Modern America*. 2nd ed. Oakland: University of California Press, 2016.

Stewart, Omer C. *Peyote Religion: A History*. Norman: University of Oklahoma Press, 1987.

Stivers, Camilla. "Unfreezing the Progressive Era: The Story of Julia Lathrop." *Administrative Theory & Praxis*, Vol. 24, no. 3 (September 2002): 537–554.

Strickland, Rennard. "The Tribal Struggle for Indian Sovereignty: The Story of the Cherokee Cases." *Indian Law Stories*. Editors Carole Goldberg, Kevin K. Washburn, and Philip P. Frickey. New York: Foundation Press, 2011, 61–80.

Strong, Josiah. *Our Country: Its Possible Future and Its Present Crisis*. New York: American Home Missionary Society, 1885.

Sullivan, Winnifred Fallers. *The Impossibility of Religious Freedom*, 2nd ed. Princeton, NJ: Princeton University Press, 2018.

Sweitzer, Sarah M. et al. "Mechanical Allodynia and Thermal Hyperalgesia upon Acute Opioid Withdrawal in the Neonatal Rat." *Pain*, Vol. 110 (2004): 269–280.

Talbot, Eugene S. *Degeneracy: Its Causes, Signs, and Results*. London: Walter Scott Ltd., 1898.

Taylor, Arnold H. *American Diplomacy and the Narcotics Traffic, 1900–1939: A Study in International Humanitarian Reform*. Durham, NC: Duke University Press, 1969.

———. "American Confrontation with Opium Traffic in the Philippines." *Pacific Historical Review*, Vol. 36, no. 3 (August 1967): 307–324.

Taylor, C. H. *Proceedings of the Temperance Convention, Held in Tremont Temple, Boston, Wednesday February 22nd, 1871 For the Purpose of Organizing A New State Temperance Society*. Boston: Massachusetts Total Abstinence Society, 1871.

Taylor, Charles. *A Secular Age*. Cambridge, MA: Harvard University Press, 2007.

Terry, Charles E. and Mildred Pellens. *The Opium Problem*. New York: Haddon Craftsmen, 1928.

Terry, Jennifer. *An American Obsession: Science, Medicine, and Homosexuality in Modern Society*. Chicago: University of Chicago Press, 1999.

Thurs, Daniel Patrick. *Science Talk: Changing Notions of Science in American Culture*. New Brunswick, NJ: Rutgers University Press, 2007.

Tilton, Elizabeth. "The Battle for Race-Survival: Prohibition Will Help to Win It." *Save America: Allegiance to the Constitution: Observance of Law*. Editor Elizabeth Tilton. Boston: Woman's National Committee for Law Enforcement, 1924.

Tintinalli, Judith E. et al. *Tintinalli's Emergency Medicine: A Comprehensive Study Guide, 9th Edition*. Publisher location unknown: McGraw Hill, 2020.

Tomlinson, Stephen. *Head Masters: Phrenology, Secular Education, and Nineteenth-Century Social Thought*. Tuscaloosa: University of Alabama Press, 2005.

Tonry, Michael. *Punishing Race: A Continuing American Dilemma*. New York: Oxford University Press, 2011.

Tricoire, Damien. "The Enlightenment and the Politics of Civilization: Self-Colonization, Catholicism, and Assimilationism in Eighteenth-Century France." *Enlightened Colonialism: Civilization Narratives and Imperial Politics in the Age of Reason.* Editor Damien Tricoire. Cham, Switzerland: Palgrave MacMillan, 2017, 25–46.

Tyack, David, Thomas James, and Aaron Benevot. *Law and the Shaping of Public Education, 1785–1954.* Madison: University of Wisconsin Press, 1987.

Tyrell, Ian. *Reforming the World: The Creation of America's Moral Empire.* Princeton, NJ: Princeton University Press, 2010.

Vacek, Heather H. *Madness: American Protestant Responses to Mental Illness.* Waco, TX: Baylor University Press, 2015.

Vargas, João H. Costa. *The Denial of Antiblackness: Multiracial Redemption and Black Suffering.* Minneapolis: University of Minnesota Press, 2018.

Vice Commission of Chicago. *The Social Evil in Chicago: A Study of Existing Conditions with Recommendations by The Vice Commission of Chicago.* Chicago: The Vice Commission of Chicago, 1911.

Walker, Margaret Urban. *Moral Understandings: A Feminist Study in Ethics.* New York: Routledge, 1998.

Warner, William B. "Truth and Trust and the Eighteenth-Century Anglophone Newspaper." *Travelling Chronicles: News and Newspapers from the Early Modern Period to the Eighteenth Century Newspaper.* Editors Siv Gøril Brandtzæg, Paul Goring, and Christine Watson. Leiden: Brill, 2018, 27–48.

Weatherford, W. D. *Present Forces in Negro Progress.* New York: Association Press, 1912.

Weber, Max. *The Protestant Ethic and the Spirit of Capitalism.* Translator Talcott Parsons. London: Routledge, 1997.

Wenger, Tisa. *Religious Freedom: The Contested History of an American Ideal.* Chapel Hill: University of North Carolina Press, 2017.

——. *We Have a Religion: The 1920s Pueblo Dance Controversy and American Religious Freedom.* Chapel Hill: University of North Carolina Press, 2009.

Wertz, Daniel J. P. "Idealism, Imperialism, and Internationalism: Opium Politics in the Colonial Philippines, 1898–1925." *Modern Asian Studies,* Vol. 47, no. 2 (March 2013): 467–499.

Westrope, Elizabeth. "Employment Discrimination on the Basis of Criminal History: Why an Anti-Discrimination Statute is a Necessary Remedy." *Journal of Criminal Law and Criminology,* Vol. 108, no. 2 (2018): 367–398.

[West Virginia] State Board of Education–Division of Elementary Schools. *A Guide for Teachers Concerning Alcoholic Drinks and Narcotics: Elementary Schools.* Unknown location: unknown publisher, 1936.

White, George S. *Memoir of Samuel Slater: Father of American Manufacturers, with Remarks on the Moral Influence of Manufactories in the United States.* Philadelphia: publisher unidentified, 1835.

White, William L. *Slaying the Dragon: The History of Addiction Treatment and Recovery in America,* 2nd ed. Bloomington, IL: Chestnut Health Systems, 2014.

Whitehead, John S. "Western Progressives, Old South Planters, or Colonial Oppressors: The Enigma of Hawai'i's 'Big Five,' 1898–1940." *Western Historical Quarterly*, Vol. 30, no. 3 (Autumn 1999): 295–326.

Wilde, Melissa J. *Birth Control Battles: How Race and Class Divided American Religion.* Oakland University of California Press, 2020.

Wiley, Harvey W. *An Autobiography.* Indianapolis, IN: Bobbs-Merrill Co., 1930.

———. "The Rights of the Unborn." Reprinted in B. A. Owens-Adair, *Human Sterilization,* 1922, 136–142.

———. *Not by Bread Alone: The Principles of Human Nutrition.* New York: Hearst's International Library Co., 1915.

Willard, Dallas. *The Disappearance of Moral Knowledge.* Editors Steven L. Porter, Aaron Preston, and Gregg A. Ten Elshof. New York: Routledge, 2018.

Willard, Frances Elizabeth. *Woman and Temperance: Or, the Work and Workers of the Woman's Christian Temperance Union.* Hartford, CT: Park Publishing Co., 1883.

Williams, Robert A. Jr. *The American Indian in Western Legal Thought: The Discourses of Conquest.* New York: Oxford University Press, 1990.

Wilson, Brian C. *Dr. John Harvey Kellogg and the Religion of Biologic Living.* Bloomington: Indiana University Press, 2014.

Woman's Christian Temperance Union. *Report of the Seventh Convention of the World's Woman's Christian Temperance Union: Tremont Temple, Boston, Mass., United States of America October 17–23rd, 1906.* No publication place: no publisher named, no date [1907?]

———. *The Pathfinder; Or, National Plans for Securing Scientific Temperance Education in Schools and Colleges.* New York: A.S. Barnes & Co, 1885.

Woods, Arthur. *Dangerous Drugs: The World Fight Against Illicit Traffic in Narcotics.* New Haven, CT: Yale University Press, 1931.

Wright, Hamilton. "The International Opium Conference." *The American Journal of International Law,* Vol. 7, no. 1 (January 1913): 108–139.

Wright, Quincy. "The Opium Question." *The American Journal of International Law,* Vol. 18, no. 2 (April 1924): 281–295.

Young, James Harvey. "Two Hoosiers and the Two Food Laws of 1906." *Indiana Magazine of History,* Vol. 88, no. 4 (December 1992): 303–319.

Young, Louise. *Japan's Total Empire: Manchuria and the Culture of Wartime Imperialism.* Berkeley: University of California Press, 1998.

Zigon, Jarrett. *A War on People: Drug User Politics and a New Ethics of Community.* Oakland: University of California Press, 2019.

Zimmerman, Jonathan. *Innocents Abroad: American Teachers in the American Century.* Cambridge, MA: Harvard University Press, 2006.

———. *Distilling Democracy: Alcohol Education in America's Public Schools, 1880–1925.* Lawrence: University of Kansas Press, 1999.

———. "'When the Doctors Disagree': Scientific Temperance and Scientific Authority, 1891–1906." *Journal of the History of Medicine and Allied Sciences,* Vol. 48, no. 2 (April 1993): 171–197.

INDEX

abolitionism, 17, 25, 34, 36–38, 54

addiction (drug): causal relationship to immorality, crime, 12, 60–62, 69–73, 77–78, 83, 101, 117, 153, 189, 193, 200–201, 204, 208, 211–212, 222; as contagious, 2, 85, 172, 200, 247n30; as disability, 77, 90–91, 114, 200, 216; as hereditary, 62, 76, 90–91, 98, 114, 216–218, 223; as "living death," 180, 208; and madness, 61–65, 70, 79, 189, 213; medical addiction, 73, 75–76, 98, 115, 176; relationship to degeneracy, 6, 62, 72, 76, 88–91, 100–104, 114, 117–119, 222–223; as replacement for nervous deficiency, 75; as slavery, 17, 25, 84–85, 116, 137, 180, 193, 210–211, 221; as untreatable, incurable, 79–80; as voluntary or habit, 11, 62, 65, 74–78, 80–83, 98–99, 136; as weapon, 29, 173–175, 200. See also alcoholism; addicts; addiction theory; addiction treatment

addiction theory, 26–27, 60–62, 64–67, 71–80, 98, 185, 222, 248n34

addiction treatment, 78–80, 175–176, 215, 219, 234; abstinence only, 84, 201; maintenance treatment, 80, 165, 173, 201; miracles, Christian conversion, 82–84; rehabilitation centers, farms, hospitals, 78–79, 82, 94, 175–176

addicts (drug): blacklisted 229–230; as burden to society, 72–73, 99–101, 174, 216–217, 223, 225, 232; drug fiend, 12, 76, 86, 100, 137, 171, 193; drug offender registries, 230; as liars, 60, 71, 76, 83, 90, 98, 190; as objectionable, repulsive, or monstrous, 72, 76, 98, 114–116, 180, 215–220, 223, 230–235; as secretive, 115–116, 201; as threat to others, 1–2, 12, 42, 73, 77–78, 85, 100, 102, 118, 153, 174–175, 189–191, 193–195, 199–202, 208–212, 215–217, 224–225,

230, 232; recovered addicts, 114, 230. See also addiction; alcoholism; drugs

Africa, 163, 168–169

African Americans, 97, 102, 192–197, 210, 221, 228–229, 234

Ahahui Puuhonua O Na Hawaii (Hawaiian Protective Association), 120–121, 123

Alabama, 181, 197

Alaska, 142

alcohol: as anti-Christian, 2, 32–39, 44, 49–50, 52–54, 97, 196–197; as cause of crime, 35, 40–41, 47, 70; as cause of madness, 39–41, 62, 66, 69–70, 189–190, 197; as cause of other immorality, 34–35, 39–41, 45–47, 66, 69, 184, 189; as constructive, 232; immorality of drinking alcohol, 12, 34–35, 41; as inappropriate for communion table, 189, 244n31; and law, 40, 185–188, 209; as model for, interchangeable with other substances, 34–35, 57, 61–62, 65, 74, 76, 82, 131; as poison, toxin, 31, 33–34, 42, 55, 57, 83, 93, 197; relationship to degeneracy, 42, 54, 70, 98–99, 102–104, 184, 197; as sickening, 42, 190; as threat to the US, civilization, 44, 52, 53–56, 102–103, 175, 184, 197; as threat to indigenous populations, 120–121, 123, 128–130, 161, 163, 168–169, 197; as wasteful, 35, 43–44, 47, 53, 130. See also Christian temperance; drugs; prohibition

alcoholism, 36, 39, 62, 129, 133, 136, 148, 175, 184–185, 226, 231; alcoholics as burden to others, 37, 45–48, 99; alcoholics as dangerous to others, 51, 184, 189–190; blacklisting alcoholics, 46; as causing poverty, 37–38, 44–47, 189–190; as sin, heathenism, 31, 82–83, 185–186; as self-imposed, 38, 79–80; as slavery, 26, 36–38, 50–52, 58, 83–87, 185, 244n20. See also addiction theory; alcohol

ABOUT THE AUTHOR

ANDREW MONTEITH is Assistant Professor and the Distinguished Emerging Scholar of Religious Studies at Elon University in North Carolina.